... and External Readers	Staff & Research Students

ELEMENTS OF
TRANSPORTATION

KENNIKAT PRESS SCHOLARLY REPRINTS

Dr. Ralph Adams Brown, Senior Editor

Series on
MAN AND HIS ENVIRONMENT

Under the General Editorial Supervision of
Dr. Roger C. Heppell

Professor of Geography, State University of New York

ELEMENTS OF TRANSPORTATION

A DISCUSSION OF STEAM RAILROAD
ELECTRIC RAILWAY, AND OCEAN AND
INLAND WATER TRANSPORTATION

BY

EMORY R. JOHNSON, Ph.D.

KENNIKAT PRESS
Port Washington, N. Y./London

ELEMENTS OF TRANSPORTATION

First published in 1909
Reissued in 1970 by Kennikat Press
Library of Congress Catalog Card No: 70-113285
ISBN 0-8046-1321-4

Manufactured by Taylor Publishing Company   Dallas, Texas

KENNIKAT SERIES ON MAN AND HIS ENVIRONMENT

CONTENTS

PART I.—STEAM RAILWAY TRANSPORTATION

CHAPTER I

CHAPTER II

CHAPTER III

CHAPTER IV

CHAPTER V

CHAPTER VI

CHAPTER VII

CHAPTER XII

CHAPTER XIII

CHAPTER XIV

CHAPTER XV

PART II.—ELECTRIC RAILWAY TRANSPORTATION

PART IV.—INLAND WATERWAYS; RIVER, LAKE,
AND CANAL TRANSPORTATION

CHAPTER XXXVI

LIST OF ILLUSTRATIONS AND MAPS

ILLUSTRATIONS

PART I

STEAM RAILWAY TRANSPORTATION

CHAPTER I

TRANSPORTATION DEFINED

TRANSPORTATION, like farming or manufacturing, is one of the world's business activities. It is the business that has to do with travel, traffic, and communication, or with the movement of persons and things and with the mechanical transmission of ideas.

The System and Service Distinguished.—The transportation business may be thought of in either one of two ways: The first picture which the word transportation brings to the mind is the one of railroads, steamships, waterways, and highways—the mechanical means of travel and traffic. Taken as a whole, these agencies are called the transportation *system*. It is constructed and operated by engineers and other technical experts, and it is studied in all its parts in schools of civil and mechanical engineering. The other side of transportation is the *service* performed by the railways and the other parts of the system. It is the service that is mainly studied in this book.

It is, of course, impossible to separate the service from the agencies that perform the work of transportation; but we can and shall study railways, trains, vessels, and vehicles, not with reference to their construction and operation, but with regard to what they do. The steam railroad and electric railways, the ocean carriers, and the lake, river, and canal craft, will be described in order that we may know what our transportation system is, how it performs its work

3

and what changes and improvements are being made. It
will be understood, however, that the goal of our effort is
a knowledge of the transportation service.

Transportation is a Service of a Public Nature.—The more
we study the railway and other transportation services the
more fully we shall come to realize that they are unlike
those performed by merchants, manufacturers and other
men or companies engaged in trade and production. Society
could not exist without the services of public carriers.
Business, at least as we know it to-day, would be impossible. Neither could governments maintain order, enforce
laws, and provide, as they do in hundreds of ways, for the
common welfare if the transportation and communication
services were lacking. The fact that transportation makes
our social order possible, that it is necessary for carrying
on business, and that our political well-being depends upon
it, causes us to regard the services of a common carrier as
of a public nature.

In all countries, some of the transportation work, as,
for instance, providing highways, maintaining waterways,
and handling the mails, is done by government; and in
many countries even the railways are owned and run by
the state. The nature of the service, however, does not
depend upon whether it is performed by the public or for
the public. It is what is done, not who does it, that gives
the service its public nature. As our great Supreme Court
has said, in speaking of railroads, "Whether the use of a
railroad is a private one depends in no measure upon the
question who constructed it or who owns it. It has never
been considered a matter of any importance that the road
was built by the agency of a private corporation. No matter who is the agent, the function performed is that of the
state. Though the ownership is private the use is public."

Method and Scope of this Volume.—This fact suggests what should be the course and scope of our study. As each transportation agent is taken up in turn, it is briefly described; next its services are studied, then the relations of the carriers and of their services to the public are analyzed, and finally what regulation of these services by the Government is necessary or desirable. In the study of railway transportation, for example, the order of procedure is to ascertain what our railway system is, to understand what its freight, passenger, mail and express services are, what rates and fares are charged and how they are made, and what control over the railroad services and charges is exercised by the State Legislatures, by Congress, and by the Courts.

The services rendered by the steam and electric railways outrank in volume and public importance those of any other means of transportation; and, as yet, the steam railroads have much greater mileage and traffic than do the electric lines. This may be otherwise in the not distant future; but for the present it is wise to give the study of steam railroads somewhat more space than is devoted to other agencies in a volume on transportation. Two fifths of this book are devoted to steam railroads, while the remaining three fifths are given to transportation upon electric railways, upon the ocean, and upon inland waterways. The magnitude of ocean transportation and the high degree of its technical development and business organization make it desirable to give a relatively full account of the ocean carrier and its services.

Although the telegraph, the telephone, and the wireless telegraph are logically a part of the general transportation system, it has been deemed best to omit from this volume a discussion of the transmission services. Perhaps it is quite as well, in view of their technical difficulties, that these services should be considered in a more advanced treatise upon transportation.

Relation of Transportation to Economics and Civics.—The study of transportation derives added value and interest from the fact that it lightens the pathway to a knowledge of economics and government. To know transportation is to be acquainted with one of the largest and most focal of the subjects that economics—the science of business affairs —seeks to explain. Likewise, in studying the transportation services, all of which are of a public nature and many of which are performed by the state, important functions of Government are being investigated by the student who observes the Government in operation, either carrying on the transportation services, or requiring its agents, the railroad and other corporations, to perform their work as public carriers in accordance with the rules and regulations laid down by the state. Thus in this book may be found one of the gateways to the political and social sciences.

CHAPTER II

ORIGIN AND GROWTH OF THE AMERICAN RAILWAY

The First Railway in the United States.—The history of the American railway now covers a period of fourscore years. The pioneer line was the Baltimore & Ohio, and the first rail of this historic road was laid on July 4, 1828, by Charles Carroll, the only man then living who had signed the Declaration of Independence. Thus, as President Hadley of Yale University said in 1885, "One man's life formed the connecting link between the political revolution of the last century and the industrial revolution of the present."

The Baltimore & Ohio Railroad was the pioneer, in that it was the first road to be constructed for the general use of the public. Two years earlier a short tramway, operated by a stationary engine and by horses, had been built in Massachusetts from the Quincy quarries to the Neponset River to transport the stone used in building Bunker Hill Monument. This same year, 1826, a coal mining company began using a railroad over the mountains from Carbondale to Honesdale, Pa., and the following year another coal company put a similar road into service at Mauch Chunk, Pa. These mountain roads were built for private use, and the cars were operated by the force of gravity and by means of stationary engines. They were not railroads in the present meaning of the term.

Other Early Roads.—The construction of numerous lines followed close upon the beginning of work upon the Balti-

7

more & Ohio. The present great New York Central System originated in the charter granted in 1826 to the Mohawk & Hudson, seventeen miles of which, from Albany to Schenectady, were opened for traffic in 1831. Between 1830 and 1835, three lines were built out of Boston, one to Providence, another to Lowell, and a third to Worcester. The Worcester line was extended to Albany by 1841. The following year one could travel by rail from Boston to Buffalo. The germ of the Pennsylvania System was the Columbia Railroad, built by the State of Pennsylvania from Philadelphia to Columbia on the Susquehanna River. It was put into operation in 1834. Three years later, private corporations had built lines from Philadelphia to New York Bay and to Baltimore. The next year the Reading Railroad up the Schuylkill Valley was in operation. Railroad building in the South began in South Carolina with the line from Charleston to Hamburg on the Savannah River opposite Augusta. When this road, 137 miles in length, was opened in 1834, it had the distinction, for a short time, of being the longest railroad in the world.

Railway Construction Prior to 1850.—At the end of the first ten years of railroad building there were 2,800 miles in use, and a decade later, 1850, the mileage was 9,000. This rate of progress seems slow in comparison with what was done at a later time, especially after 1880, when the construction, during a single year, was often greater than the total for the first twenty years. It is, however, easy to understand why railroad extension was not rapid at the beginning. Capital was then not plentiful, as it is now; nor had the day of large corporations and great undertakings arrived. Moreover, it was uncertain at the start of railroad building, and for some time afterwards, whether

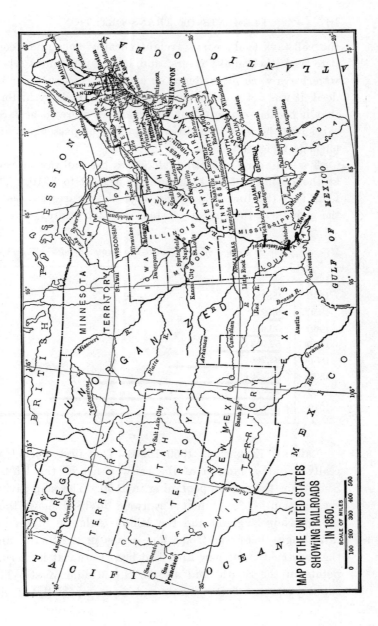

MAP OF THE UNITED STATES
SHOWING RAILROADS
IN 1850.

SCALE OF MILES

0   100   200   300   400   500

the railways could carry freight cheaply enough to compete with the canals, rivers, and lakes over routes where waterways were in existence or could be constructed. Indeed, it was not until the second decade of railway history, that it became evident that the railroads were to be large carriers of heavy commodities as well as of passengers and package freight.

The following charted table states the railway mileage at the opening of each decade from 1830 to 1910. The length of the lines illustrates what the figures say as to the growth in the railway system each ten years:

Mileage of the Railways of the United States by Decades—1830–1910

1830	23
1840	2,818
1850	9,021
1860	30,635
1870	52,914
1880	93,296
1890	163,597
1900	193,346
1910	240,000

Railway Expansion, 1850–1860.—The first period of really rapid expansion of the railway net of the United States was the decade beginning in 1850. The map giving the location of the principal railways in 1850 shows that, though New England and the Middle Atlantic States led in mileage, there were some long roads in the South and the construction of new lines had been begun at numerous points in the South, and also in the Middle West. The rapid progress of the South and more especially of the

West during the decade preceding the great Civil War,
caused the railway net to spread rapidly and the mileage
to rise from 9,000 to 30,000. Several causes readily account for this.

At this time the occupation of the Central West was
proceeding rapidly because of immigration from the Eastern States and also from Europe, where political troubles
were causing many people to emigrate to America. It was
in this decade, also, that the use of reapers and other labor-
saving farm machinery became general, and greatly aided
the spread of settlement. Moreover, the increased output
of gold from California, where it was found in 1848,
tended to make times prosperous, to stimulate business
activity in all lines and to hasten the construction of railways.

Early Railway Consolidations.—The decade following
1850 is a notable one in the history of railways, because it
was then that railroad consolidation began on a large scale.
Prior to this time most railroad lines were short. The line
from Albany to Buffalo consisted of seven connecting roads
owned and operated by as many independent companies.
Originally there had been eleven. In 1851, Commodore
Vanderbilt united the roads between Albany and Buffalo
and formed the New York Central; two years later, he
added the Hudson River Railroad; in 1858, five more lines
in New York State were acquired; and thus were laid the
foundations of the present powerful New York Central
System. The Pennsylvania Railroad Company, by constructing roads, and by purchasing and leasing State lines,
connected Philadelphia and Pittsburg in 1852. The Pennsylvania System to-day includes roads once owned by over
two hundred companies.

At this time—the decade of 1850—other railway systems were growing rapidly by construction rather than by consolidations. The Erie Railroad reached Lake Erie in 1851; the same year the Baltimore & Ohio entered Wheeling on the Ohio River; and in 1854 the Rock Island connected Chicago with the Mississippi River. Before the end of the decade, the Illinois Central, aided by a liberal land grant made by the United States in 1850, had reached a length of 700 miles.

The First Line to the Pacific.—The Civil War checked railroad building, and in most sections of the country it was not actively resumed until 1868 or 1869. One prominent exception to this was the building of the first road to the Pacific, the Union-Central Pacific line, which was begun in 1864 and opened in 1869. The carrying out of this great work at this time was made possible only by the aid, in the form of land grants and money advances, which the United States, for military and other reasons, gave the companies that constructed the roads forming the line.

The Five Years Preceding the Panic of 1873.—When the revival of railway building after the War came, in 1868, there followed a period of five years of feverish speculation in railway securities. There were 28,000 miles constructed, and the railway mileage was increased by forty per cent in five years. This rate of advance could not long continue unchecked; and the severe panic of 1873 was the natural result. During the next five years only 11,500 miles were added to the railway net.

The Wonderful Progress from 1870 to 1890.—By comparing the maps showing the railways of the United States in 1870 and in 1890, the main facts about the spread of our railroad net can be seen at a glance. In 1870, there was but one line to the Pacific, and it had been completed only a year. Railway building in Arkansas, Texas, and the

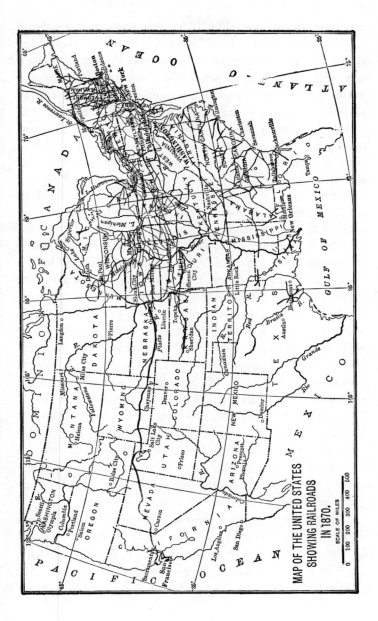

MAP OF THE UNITED STATES
SHOWING RAILROADS
IN 1870.

SCALE OF MILES

0 100 200 300 400 500

great Southwest had hardly commenced; comparatively few roads had crossed the Missouri; the vast region between the head of the Great Lakes and the Pacific Ocean was still without railroads; and even in the Southern States the lines were rather far apart. Twenty years later all this had been changed. Five roads had reached the Pacific and others were well on their way there; the lines in the Southern States had multiplied; Texas was well started upon the advance that has since put her ahead of all other States in railway mileage; while, from Maine to Colorado and the Dakotas, railroads had been added in such numbers that it is possible to include only the important lines on a small scale map.

The rate at which railway building progressed during the decade from 1880 to 1890 was marvelous. In those ten years 70,000 miles of new line were added! In no other country of the world could this have been done. Indeed, the people of the United States built more miles of railways in those ten years than the three leading countries of Europe had constructed in fifty years. Work was carried on in all parts of the country. Men with money were confident of the growth of the country, and they were encouraged in investing their funds in railways by the liberal assistance they had been receiving, since 1870, from the United States, the States, and the counties and towns. Oftentimes, railways were built into new sections of country ahead of settlement. Instead of waiting until traffic existed, the railroads opened up prairies and mountain valleys, and created travel and traffic.

Since 1890 it has not been necessary to build railways so rapidly as formerly. We are now adding from two to three per cent per annum to our railway mileage. Thus stated, the advance seems slow; but this rate means

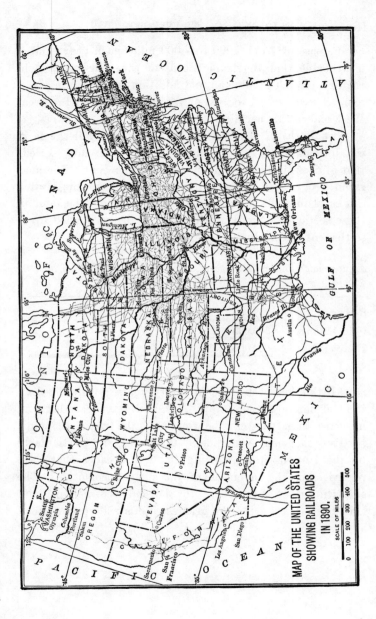

MAP OF THE UNITED STATES
SHOWING RAILROADS
IN 1890,

SCALE OF MILES
0   100 200 300 400 500

an increase of from 5,000 to 7,000 miles each year; and it is probable that the traffic needs of the near future will require a much greater annual addition to our railway system. The assured progress of the Southwest and the great West makes this certain.

Two Fifths of the World's Entire Railway Mileage is in the United States.—The length of our railroads exceeds that of those in all Europe by eighteen per cent. The most rapid progress in railroad building outside of the United States is in such countries as Canada, Argentine, and in those sections of South Africa that are being opened up to settlement and industry.

Approximate Railway Mileage of Europe, the United States, and the World in 1910

Europe.........	202,000
United States...	240,000
The World......	600,000

All this has been done in eighty years, within the lifetime of many persons now living. No truer index and measure than this can be found of the rapid economic progress that has been made by the world, and particularly by the United States, during the few decades that have passed since the invention of the steam locomotive. The substitution of mechanical for muscular power in land transportation started the greatest industrial revolution of all time.

CHAPTER III

THE PRESENT RAILWAY SYSTEM OF THE UNITED STATES

Railway Mileage and Companies in the United States.— There were 240,000 miles of railway lines in the United States at the close of 1909. Some of these roads have two tracks, a few of them have three and four, and all of them have sidings and yard trackage. Thus the railway tracks in the United States were 350,000 miles in length, long enough to reach around the earth fourteen times at the equator where its circumference is greatest. The companies owning these railways numbered about 2,800; but so many corporations were merely subordinate parts of other and larger ones that there were only 1,000 operating companies; and, as will be shown presently, most of these 1,000 organizations were federated into a small number of systems or groups of control.

Territorial Groups of the Railroads of the United States. —It is most difficult to comprehend the railway system of the United States as a whole, it is so vast and comprises so many parts. The task is made easier by dividing the railways into territorial groups corresponding with the natural physical divisions of the country, and by thinking of the leading railway systems with reference to their place in those groups.

The simplest and most general territorial grouping puts our railways into three divisions, those north of the Potomac and Ohio Rivers and east of the Mississippi, those

17

south of the Potomac and Ohio and east of the Mississippi, and those west of the Mississippi. The physical and industrial differences of these three sections of the country early made this a natural territorial grouping of American railways, and in time caused three distinct classifications of freight to come to be used—one for each of these regions.

It is also helpful to subdivide these three large railway groups into seven smaller ones:

The New England Roads.—The first of these seven divisions includes the roads in the New England States. Here, population is dense, passenger traffic is heavy, and there is an especially large volume of local freight. Most of the roads concentrate upon Boston, the great trading center and the chief seaport. Two railway systems are supreme in New England, the New York, New Haven & Hartford in the southern section, and the Boston & Maine in the north. Between them lies the Boston & Albany, which is a Vanderbilt road.

The Trunk Lines.—The second of these seven groups comprises the railroads north of the Potomac and Ohio and between New England and Chicago and St. Louis. This part of the United States, because of its coal and its manufactures, has the heaviest freight traffic of any section of the country. Its railroads also carry to the chief seaports of the United States the larger share of the commodities exported from our country, and take inland from those ports the major portion of our imports. The railways from the seaboard to the Great Lakes and the Ohio River are called the "Trunk Lines," because they were the first through or trunk lines in the United States. The main "Trunk Lines" have long since been extended to Chicago and St. Louis, and in so doing they have come to control the "Central Traffic Territory," the region between Buf-

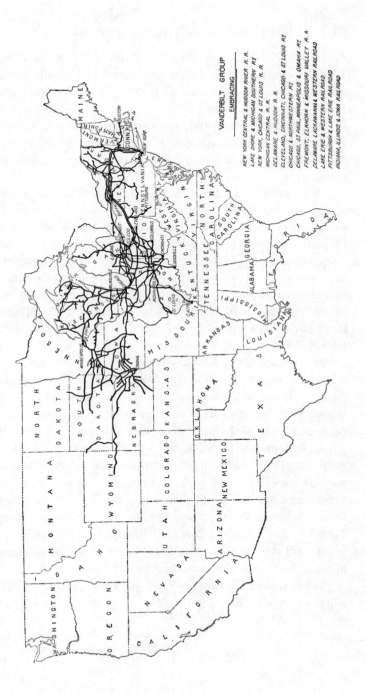

VANDERBILT GROUP

EMBRACING

NEW YORK CENTRAL & HUDSON RIVER R.R.
LAKE SHORE & MICHIGAN SOUTHERN RY.
NEW YORK, CHICAGO & ST. LOUIS R.R.
MICHIGAN CENTRAL R.R.
DELAWARE & HUDSON R.R.
CLEVELAND, CINCINNATI, CHICAGO & ST. LOUIS RY.
CHICAGO & NORTHWESTERN RY.
CHICAGO, ST. PAUL, MINNEAPOLIS & OMAHA RY.
FREMONT, ELKHORN & MISSOURI VALLEY R.A.
DELAWARE, LACKAWANNA & WESTERN RAILROAD
LAKE ERIE & WESTERN RAILROAD
PITTSBURGH & LAKE ERIE RAILROAD
INDIANA, ILLINOIS & IOWA RAILROAD

falo and Pittsburg on the East, and Chicago and St. Louis on the West. In this second territorial group, there are numerous strong roads with varying degrees of independence, but there are two great federations of systems—the Vanderbilt lines in the northern half of the region, and the Pennsylvania in the southern half—so powerful as practically to control the policy of all roads not in the federations.

The Southern Roads.—The railroads south of the Potomac and Ohio and east of the Mississippi constitute a third group. The chief traffic is coal, lumber, and cotton. The Southern Railway is the dominant road in the South, and its position is strengthened by the fact that other important roads, notably the Atlantic Coast Line on the East, and the Louisville & Nashville on the West, are controlled by the men who own the Southern. Paralleling the Mississippi River is the powerful Illinois Central, now controlled by the Southern Pacific interests.

The Southwestern Roads.—West of the Mississippi and southwest of St. Louis is the fourth group—the Southwestern Roads. Their tonnage consists most largely of wheat, corn, lumber, cotton, and livestock, which they transport partly to Galveston, New Orleans, and other Gulf ports, and partly to St. Louis and Memphis, where connections are made with lines to the East. Besides the various roads of lesser rank in this wide region there are three large systems that overshadow the others. In order from North to South, these three systems are the Rock Island-Frisco lines, the Missouri Pacific, with its affiliated roads, and the Southern Pacific, the last of the three being also the largest of the transcontinental lines.

The " Granger " Lines.—West of Chicago and West-Northwest of St. Louis is the fifth territory, that occupied

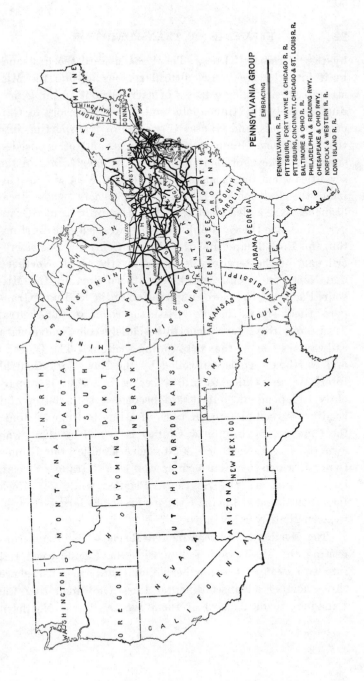

PENNSYLVANIA GROUP

EMBRACING

PENNSYLVANIA R. R.
PITTSBURG, FORT WAYNE & CHICAGO R. R.
PITTSBURG, CINCINNATI, CHICAGO & ST. LOUIS R. R.
BALTIMORE & OHIO R. R.
PHILADELPHIA & READING RWY.
CHESAPEAKE & OHIO RWY.
NORFOLK & WESTERN R. R.
LONG ISLAND R. R.

by the "Granger" lines. These roads were the first ones built into the great agricultural regions beyond the Mississippi; their traffic consists of carrying out farming products mainly to Minneapolis and Lake Superior, to Chicago, St. Louis, and Kansas City; and of transporting into the region coal, lumber, manufactures, and other needed supplies. They got their name of "Granger" lines in the seventies when the farmers of the Central West were organizing the Patrons of Husbandry, a society whose local branches were called granges. The most prominent "Granger" lines are the St. Paul, the Northwestern, the Burlington, the Rock Island and the Illinois Central. The northern part of the territory is served by the Great Northern and Northern Pacific, and the southern part by the Missouri Pacific. The mere enumeration of the leading "Granger" roads shows that they, like the roads in the Central Traffic territory, have come to be closely coördinated with railway systems in the surrounding sections. The Chicago and Northwestern is controlled by the New York Central interests; the Chicago, Milwaukee & St. Paul is apparently independent, but it has become a transcontinental road by the completion, in 1909, of a line to Puget Sound; the Chicago, Burlington & Quincy is owned by those who own the Great Northern & Northern Pacific; the Illinois Central, which is a Southern as well as a "Granger" road, is controlled by the Southern Pacific; while the Rock Island & Missouri Pacific Systems are more largely Southwestern than Northwestern.

The Northern Transcontinental Roads.—The roads connecting the Mississippi Valley with the Pacific coast fall into two groups, the northern and southern. There are three northern transcontinental lines (not including the Canadian roads). Two of them are the Great Northern

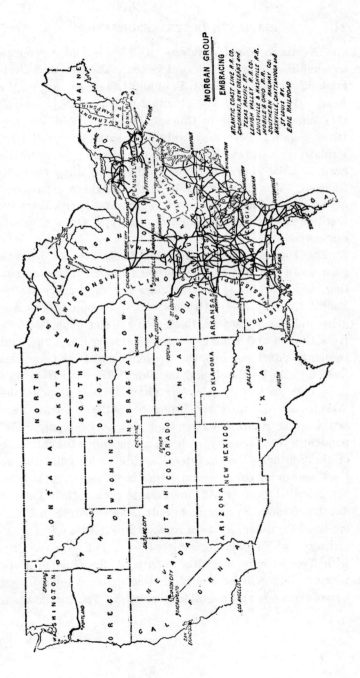

MORGAN GROUP

EMBRACING

ATLANTIC COAST LINE R.R.CO.
CINCINNATI, NEW ORLEANS and
TEXAS PACIFIC RY.
LEHIGH VALLEY R.R.CO.
LOUISVILLE & NASHVILLE R.R.
MOBILE & OHIO R.R. CO.
SOUTHERN RAILWAY CO.
NASHVILLE, CHATTANOOGA and
ST. LOUIS RY.
ERIE RAILROAD

and Northern Pacific Systems, which are under common ownership, and which connect Seattle, Tacoma, and Portland, on the West, with St. Paul and Lake Superior, on the East. By means of the Burlington which they control, they also have access to Chicago, St. Louis, and Missouri River points. The third transcontinental line is the St. Paul which now extends from Puget Sound ports to the head of Lake Superior, to St. Paul and to Milwaukee and Chicago. The through traffic of the northern transcontinental roads is made up largely of grain, flour, and manufactures westward, and lumber, fruit and Oriental goods eastbound.

The Southern Transcontinental Roads are the seventh group. In this section the Southern Pacific is the controlling factor. This system includes the original Southern Pacific line from New Orleans and Galveston to Los Angeles and San Francisco, the Union-Southern Pacific route from Omaha and Kansas City via Denver, Cheyenne, and Ogden to San Francisco, the Oregon Short Line from Salt Lake City to Portland, and the San Pedro road from Salt Lake City to Los Angeles—or virtually four lines to the West coast. Between the Union & Southern Pacific lines is the great Sante Fé System, which is nominally independent but supposedly, at least, much under the influence of the Southern Pacific interests. Two additional Pacific lines are under construction. One is the Western Pacific, being built by the Gould interests, to extend their Denver and Rio Grande System from Salt Lake City to San Francisco. The other is the Kansas City, Mexico & Orient Railway, which, when completed, will join Kansas City with Topolobampo near the mouth of the Gulf of California. This will be our ninth line to the Pacific Coast. Canada has one and is building another. The construction

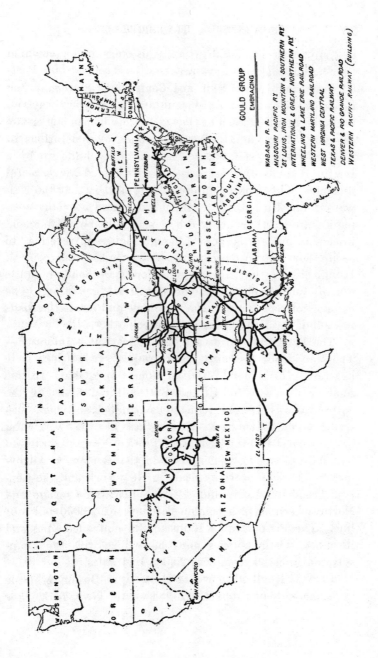

GOULD GROUP
EMBRACING

WABASH R. R.
MISSOURI PACIFIC RY.
ST. LOUIS, IRON MOUNTAIN & SOUTHERN RY.
INTERNATIONAL & GREAT NORTHERN RY.
WHEELING & LAKE ERIE RAILROAD
WESTERN MARYLAND RAILROAD
WEST VIRGINIA CENTRAL
TEXAS & PACIFIC RAILWAY
DENVER & RIO GRANDE RAILROAD
WESTERN PACIFIC RAILWAY (BUILDING)

of four transcontinental lines at the same time shows that the West is making rapid progress.

Grouping by Ownership and Control.—The account just given of the territorial grouping of American railways reveals the fact that each of the seven sections has one or two especially large and powerful systems or federations of roads. These systems have been severally built up by a few individuals of constructive genius, aided by powerful financiers and banking interests. Thus it is that the railways of the United States, though operated by many companies, are mostly controlled by a small number of financial interests; and it is possible, and highly instructive, to group our railways according to ownership and control. It will be seen that this classification corresponds broadly, though not closely, with the territorial grouping. The maps accompanying this chapter name and locate the roads in each of the large groups of control.

The Vanderbilt Roads and the Pennsylvania Interests.— The Vanderbilt & Pennsylvania railway federations have practical control north of the Potomac and Ohio. In this small section of the United States, three fifths of the entire railway freight tonnage is handled and here passenger traffic is heaviest. Hence, these are the two richest and strongest railway groups. The New York Central and its affiliated roads, which include the Boston & Albany in New England, various roads in New York and the Central Traffic territory, and the wide-reaching Chicago and Northwestern have a combined length of 23,006 miles of line. The Pennsylvania Railroad, its controlled lines and its allies, whose policies must harmonize with the Pennsylvania interests, comprise 20,385 line miles.

In New England, north of Boston, the Boston & Maine is paramount, but it is controlled by the New York, New

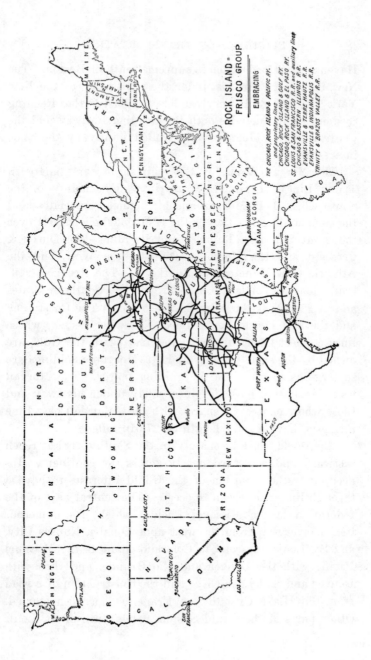

ROCK ISLAND =
FRISCO GROUP

EMBRACING

THE CHICAGO, ROCK ISLAND & PACIFIC RY.
CHICAGO, ROCK ISLAND & GULF RY.
CHICAGO, ROCK ISLAND & EL PASO RY.
ST. LOUIS & SAN FRANCISCO R.R. and auxiliary lines
CHICAGO & EASTERN ILLINOIS R.R.
EVANSVILLE & TERRE HAUTE R.R.
EVANSVILLE & INDIANAPOLIS R.R.
TRINITY & BRAZOS VALLEY R.R.

and proprietary lines

Haven & Hartford which is supreme south of Boston. The
New Haven, in turn, is under the joint sway of the New
York Central & Pennsylvania. Similarly, the Reading
System, which includes both the Reading Railway and the
Central of New Jersey, is controlled jointly by the same
interests.

The Morgan Roads, as the map shows, are partly in
Trunk Line Central Traffic territory, but mainly in the
South where J. P. Morgan and his financial associates hold
the commanding position as the result of their control over
the great Southern Railway and its allies—the Queen &
Crescent and the Mobile & Ohio on the West, and the
Atlantic Coast Line on the Southeast. The strongest railroad along the Atlantic seaboard of the Southern States
and in Florida is the Atlantic Coast Line. The Coast Line
and the still larger Louisville & Nashville System, whose
lines connect St. Louis and Cincinnati with the Gulf, are
owned by the same persons. and Mr. Morgan's holdings are
so large as to give him the guiding power. The Morgan
roads, including both the lines, solely under his sway and
those whose control he shares with the Atlantic Coast Line
interests, have a total length of 27,616 miles.

The Gould Lines lie mainly in the Southwest, but reach
eastward and westward nearly across the continent. Indeed, it is the ambition of the Gould interests to have a
through line from ocean to ocean. The central part of the
federation is the Missouri Pacific, which has numerous
lines converging from the west upon Omaha, Kansas City,
and St. Louis. A road to Colorado connects the Missouri
Pacific with the Denver and Rio Grande, and thus with
Denver and Salt Lake City; and the construction of a road
from Salt Lake City to San Francisco has been started.
Other parts of the Gould System reach south of St. Louis

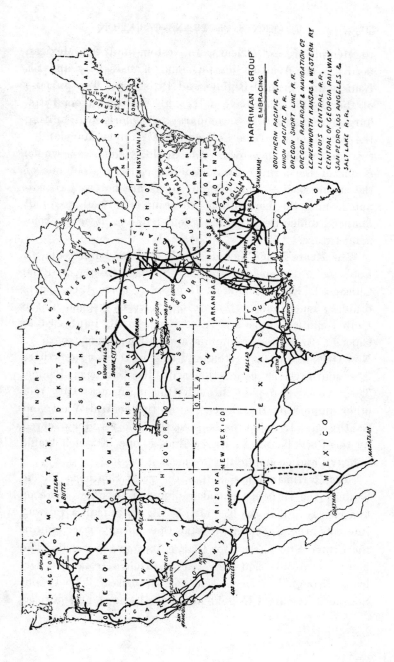

HARRIMAN GROUP
EMBRACING

SOUTHERN PACIFIC R.R.
UNION PACIFIC R.R.
OREGON SHORT LINE R.R.
OREGON RAILROAD & NAVIGATION Cº
LEAVENWORTH KANSAS & WESTERN Rº
ILLINOIS CENTRAL R.R.
CENTRAL OF GEORGIA RAILWAY
SAN PEDRO, LOS ANGELES &
SALT LAKE R.R.

to Memphis, New Orleans, Galveston, and the Mexican border. The Wabash joins Omaha, Kansas City and St. Louis with Chicago, Buffalo and Pittsburg. The purpose of the Goulds is to have a through line east from Pittsburg by constructing a comparatively short road uniting the Wheeling and Lake Erie with the Western Maryland— two lines which they own. The Gould System, as a whole, is one of the large railway federations, but is not one of the strong ones. The different parts are not well coördinated, and the controlling interests have had frequent financial difficulties. On the whole, however, it has a promising future.

The Moore Roads include the Rock Island lines, the St. Louis & San Francisco Railroad ('Frisco Lines), and the Chicago & Eastern Illinois Railroad. These three parts unite to make one of the strong railroad systems in the United States. Its roads reach north to St. Paul, east to Chicago, St. Louis, Memphis and Birmingham, south to New Orleans and Galveston, and west to Denver; and there is a southwestern connection with the Southern Pacific. These roads also pass through Omaha, Kansas City and other important traffic centers in the central West and Southwest. It will thus be seen that the territory served by the Rock Island & 'Frisco lines is one in which traffic is heavy and economic development is rapid.

The Harriman Lines include the great Southern Pacific System, the Illinois Central and numerous other more or less closely allied roads. Mr. E. H. Harriman's railway interests are more extensive than those of any other man in the United States, and, for that matter, in the world. The main line of the Southern Pacific extends from New Orleans through Los Angeles to San Francisco. The Union-Southern Pacific Line extends from Omaha and Kansas

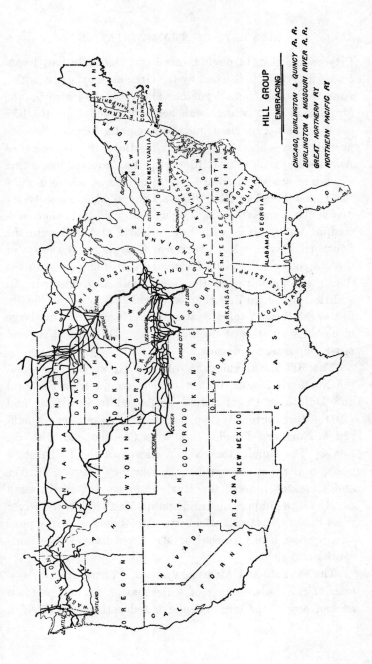

HILL GROUP

EMBRACING

CHICAGO, BURLINGTON & QUINCY R. R.
BURLINGTON & MISSOURI RIVER R. R.
GREAT NORTHERN RY
NORTHERN PACIFIC RY

City on the east, through Denver and Ogden to San Francisco. Portland is reached by the Oregon Short Line, which runs westward from Wyoming and Utah and also by the Mt. Shasta route which branches northward from the line between San Francisco and Sacramento. Ogden is connected with southern California by the San Pedro & Los Angeles Railroad. The Illinois Central System has a line extending westward from Chicago to Omaha where it joins the Union Pacific. The Illinois Central also connects Indianapolis, Louisville, St. Louis, Memphis and other Mississippi Valley cities with New Orleans, and thus with the Southern Pacific. The Central of Georgia, in the heart of the old cotton belt, gives Harriman a strong system in the South and an outlet to the South Atlantic seaboard. In addition to controlling the roads which belong specifically to the Southern Pacific System, Mr. Harriman owns large blocks of securities of the Baltimore & Ohio, the Erie and other important railroads.

The Hill Roads comprise (1) the Great Northern and the Northern Pacific, both of which extend from St. Paul and Duluth to Puget Sound ports and to Portland; and (2) the Burlington System, which unites the Great Northern & Northern Pacific lines with Chicago and with St. Louis. The Burlington System also gives the Hill lines a position of great strength in the territory between Denver and Chicago; indeed, the Burlington roads pass through nearly all the important traffic points on the Missouri River from Sioux City to Kansas City. Mr. James J. Hill's position is second only to that of Mr. Harriman in the transcontinental field.

The St. Paul and Atchison Systems.—There are two systems of railroads, neither of which has as yet been made a part of any of the large groups or federations described in

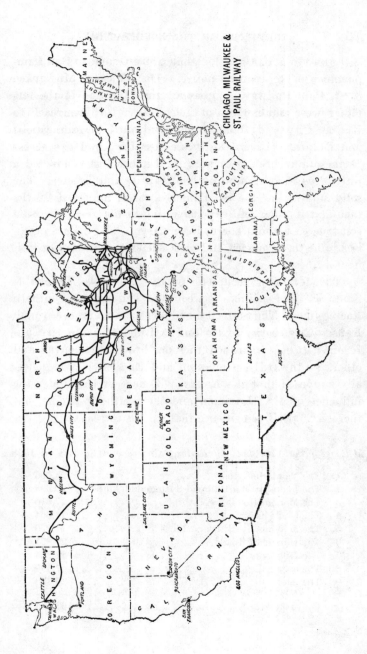

CHICAGO, MILWAUKEE &
ST. PAUL RAILWAY

the preceding paragraphs, that are of such size and importance as to require notice. The Chicago, Milwaukee & St. Paul Railway occupies a strong position in the territory west and northwest cf Chicago. Its lines reach to Kansas City and Omaha and northward to Minneapolis and Duluth. It has two lines across Iowa and two across Minnesota and South Dakota; and it has just completed a line to the Puget Sound ports of Seattle and Tacoma. The solid stability of the St. Paul System is indicated by the fact that its long and expensive line to the West has been constructed without borrowing money. The St. Paul promises to be the strongest and most efficient of the transcontinental lines.

The territory occupied by the Atchison, Topeka & Santa Fé lies mainly between the Union and Southern Pacific lines. The Santa Fé extends from Chicago through Kansas City, New Mexico and Arizona to southern California. It has a branch line northward to Denver and others southward to Galveston and El Paso. It is generally supposed that the Atchison is more or less under the influence of Mr. Harriman and the Southern Pacific, but there is no positive evidence that such is the case.

Mileage of the Nine Leading Railway Groups and Systems in 1908

1.	The Vanderbilt Roads	23,006
2.	The Pennsylvania Railroad System and Allies	20,385
3.	The Morgan Roads	27,616
4.	The Gould Lines	17,664
5.	The Moore or Rock Island Lines	14,270
6.	The Harriman Roads	22,821
7.	The Hill Lines	21,204
8.	The St. Paul	7,499
9.	The Atchison	9,430
	Total	163,895

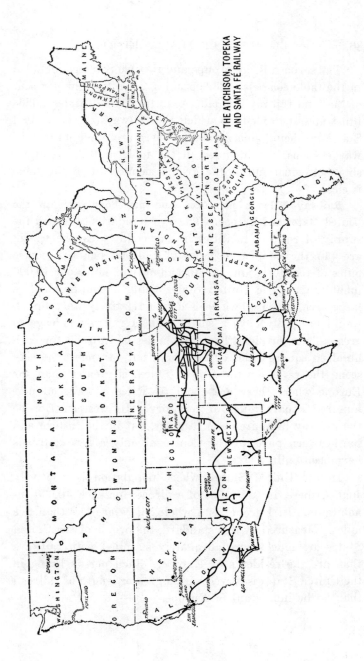

THE ATCHISON, TOPEKA
AND SANTA FÉ RAILWAY

The seven railway groups and the two Systems included in the table comprise 163,895 miles, or sixty-eight per cent of the total railway line mileage in the United States. This illustrates the extent to which the railways of the United States are being consolidated. There are other large railway systems, not included in the table and the relationship between some of the groups mentioned in the table is close.

Railway Mileage per Area and per Population in the United States and Europe.—The two standards by which the supply of railway facilities in any country can be tested, are (1) the number of miles of railroad per 100 square miles of territory, and (2) the number of miles per 10,000 inhabitants. The United States being a country with a large area, much of which is as yet relatively unoccupied, would naturally have a small ratio of railway mileage to area. There are less than eight miles of railroad for each hundred square miles of territory; but, strange as it may seem, the ratio for the United States is greater than for Europe where there are about 5½ miles of railroad per hundred square miles of territory. In western Europe the railway lines are close together, but in the eastern and southeastern parts of the Continent only a few railroads have been built.

In the United States, where population is relatively sparse, there are 27 miles of railroad for each 10,000 inhabitants. In Europe, as a whole, there are less than five miles. Measured by this standard, the people of the United States are much more adequately supplied with railways than are the residents of Europe. Each person living in the United States is served with a greater length of railroad than is the inhabitant of Europe.

CHAPTER IV

TRACK, CAR AND TRAIN—THE RAILWAY MECHANISM

The Parts of the Railway Mechanism.—The mechanism by which the railway service is performed includes the tracks, the cars, the locomotives and the trains. In the mechanical development of railway facilities, mankind has overcome great technical difficulties, and in no other field of human endeavor have civil and mechanical engineers shown greater ability in using the forces of nature to perform man's heavy work. In this chapter it will be possible to describe but briefly what has been accomplished.

TRACK WITH WOODEN STRINGERS, SURFACED WITH STRAPS OF IRON.

Early Track Construction.—At the beginning of railroad building different kinds of track were experimented with, but the one most generally adopted consisted of strong

37

wooden beams surfaced with strap iron and placed upon wooden cross-ties. Some roads tried using granite sills instead of wooden ones, but it was found that such a track was so rigid as to be injurious to the locomotives and cars. For the same reason the practice of placing the rails upon granite blocks instead of upon wooden cross-ties did not become general.

Improvements in the Rail.—Wooden rails were used first for two reasons: they were cheaper than iron, and the proc-

TRACK OF CAST-IRON RAILS RESTING ON GRANITE BLOCKS.

ess of rolling rails had not been worked out at the time the first roads were built. The first step forward in the improvement of the railroad track came with the use of the rolled iron rail, which became possible after 1840. The early iron rails were rolled in the shape of an inverted U, but by the middle of the century the T rail, now everywhere used, came to be preferred. The next great advance was made when steel rails began to be substituted for iron ones. This was shortly before 1870, when the Bessemer process so cheapened the cost of steel that it could be used in making rails.

The substitution of iron for wooden rails and of steel for iron was made gradually; as late as 1850, there were many railroads in the United States, especially in the

South, still having wooden rails surfaced with plates of iron. Likewise, it was not until near the end of the century that steel rails had entirely supplanted iron ones.

The Roadbed of To-day has rails weighing from 85 to 110 pounds to the yard, 100 pounds being the weight now most frequently used. Every possible effort is now being made, by careful ballasting of the track and by burnettizing the railroad ties to prevent their decaying, to strengthen the railroad track so that the track may safely bear the severe strain put upon it due to the use of heavy engines

ROLLED-IRON U RAIL, 1844.

and cars and to the high speed of passenger trains. Until recently the Bessemer steel rail was entirely satisfactory. It is now found to be too brittle; railroad companies are now insisting upon the use of open-hearth steel, and experiments are being made to produce a particularly tough rail of an alloy of a small quantity of other elements with steel.

Invention of the Locomotive.—The success of the steam locomotive dates from 1829 when George Stephenson built his celebrated "Rocket." To adapt the stationary engine to the requirements of a locomotive, Stephenson had to introduce two new features: one was to run a large number of tubes through the boiler from the fire box to the smoke-stack, in order to increase the heating surface; and the other was to have the steam from the cylinder exhaust into the smokestack, and thereby to increase the draught of air through the fire box and fire tubes within the boiler. The "Rocket" was a success because it had these two essentials.

Early American Locomotives.—But few locomotives were imported for use upon American railways. Our tracks

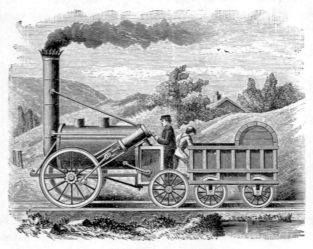

THE ROCKET, 1829.

were built with sharp curves and steep grades and were not so strong as those in England. A special type of locomotive was necessary and this was invented and constructed as early as 1830. In that year the West Point Foundry Works, within New York City, built two locomotives for the Charleston & Hamburg Railroad of South Carolina. The third locomotive constructed at these works was the "De Witt Clinton" engine shown in the illustration. In

1832, Mathias Baldwin, of Philadelphia, built the historic "Old Ironsides," and later established the locomotive

DE WITT CLINTON ENGINE AND TRAIN, 1831.

works, which, up to June 1, 1909, has turned out 33,446 locomotives. This great plant is capable of building about three thousand locomotives a year, or ten for each working day.

These early locomotives seem tiny in comparison with the monsters now in use. The "De Witt Clinton" weighed

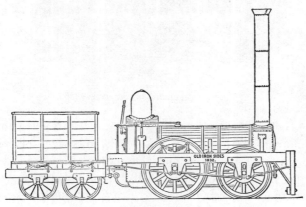

THE OLD IRONSIDES, 1832.

$3\frac{1}{2}$ tons; there are now numerous engines in use fifty times as heavy. The "John Bull" engine which was imported in 1831 for use on the Camden & Amboy Railroad, which connected Philadelphia and New York, was found too heavy for the track as first constructed, although it weighed only ten tons.

Some Steps in the Development of the Locomotive.—The general type of locomotive that has been found best adapted to use upon American railroad tracks was invented in 1836, by Henry R. Campbell, of Philadelphia. This locomotive had four connected driving wheels, with

FIRST CAMPBELL LOCOMOTIVE, 1836.

a four-wheel forward truck which was so attached to the locomotive as to permit the truck to swivel or swing through several degrees and thus permit the engine to go around sharp curves. Campbell did not invent the swivel truck, this had been in use for five years, his service consisted in designing the type of locomotive which was so generally used in this country as to be called the "American" type.

Another important improvement in the locomotive came in 1837 with the use of equalizing beams, which so distributed the weight upon the driving wheels as to permit each wheel to have a vertical motion independent of the other wheels. This keeps the pressure of each driving wheel fairly constant upon the track and enables the locomotive to run smoothly at a high speed.

At first the same locomotive was used for both freight and passenger services; but, after 1840, the Campbell type of engine was developed with reference to the passenger

"John Bull" Engine and Train on the Tracks of the Camden & Amboy Railroad at Bordentown, N. J. Photograph taken about 1870.

service, and other designs were brought out for handling the freight traffic. In time, three general classes of heavy locomotives came into use; the mogul, having six connected drivers; the consolidation, with eight drivers; and the decapod, with ten coupled driving wheels.

Among the many improvements made in the locomotive during recent years, two are worthy of special mention, one being the application of the principle of the double expansion engine to the locomotive. In these "compound" locomotives the steam, in passing from the boiler to the exhaust, is used in two cylinders in succession. This increases somewhat the power derived from the use of a given quantity of fuel. Another long step forward in the construction of high power locomotives was made with the introduction of the articulated engine, which, as the illustration shows, in reality unites two locomotives into one engine. Under the boiler there are two separately acting engines, each having six driving wheels. Each of these powerful engines weighs 596,000 pounds and has a

A High-Speed Compound Passenger Engine, Baldwin Locomotive Works.

tractive force of 94,600 pounds. They are especially adapted to steep mountain grades.

Early Passenger Coaches.—Almost from the start, the type of coach used in the United States differed from that favored in Europe. There, as the word coach implies, the old stagecoach body had been modified into a railway coach. The influence of this upon the passenger equipment used in European countries is still noticeable. In America, the tracks required the passenger coach to be mounted upon two four-wheel swiveling trucks. Consequently the "car" was made longer, and for the purpose of economizing space it was designed with end doors and a center aisle.

The first coaches were crudely constructed and have gradually been given their present comfortable design. One of the earlier betterments was that of raising the central half of the roof of the coach and inserting deck lights for ventilation; this was first done in 1836. Another addition to the passenger's comfort was made when the patent automatic coupler took the place of the old loose link coupling that had caused the jolting of cars, so annoying to the passenger. This was not invented until sometime after the Civil War.

Pullman Coaches.—George M. Pullman did more than any other individual to increase the comfort of travel. His

BALDWIN'S MALLET ARTICULATED COMPOUND LOCOMOTIVE. Weight of Locomotive and Tender, 596,000 pounds. Tractive force, 94,600 pounds.

first sleeping car, the "Pioneer A," was built in 1864. The sleeping car was soon followed by the buffet or hotel car; and after a few years, drawing-room and dining cars were introduced. When the dining car came into use and people were obliged to pass from their coach to the dining car, the vestibuling of cars was suggested. Pullman worked out and applied the vestibuling principle, the first train of vestibule cars having been run on the Pennsylvania Railroad in 1886.

Freight-Car Development and Specialization.—American freight cars, like those in Europe, consisted at first of four-wheel "wagons" with a loading capacity of about five tons. Our climate made necessary the use of large box cars, whereas in Europe the open car was, and still is, more largely employed. In improving the freight car two results have been accomplished: its carrying capacity has been increased to fifty-five tons, and it has been built in various types, each adapted to the performance of some special service.

For some time past, the standard box car in the United States has been of thirty tons capacity, but during the last few years the tendency has been to raise the standard to forty tons. Special cars for carrying coal, ore, and other heavy commodities are built with a capacity of fifty-five tons. When cars of this size and carrying capacity came into general use, it became desirable to use steel instead of wood in their construction. Nearly all of the heavy freight cars now being built are of steel.

The refrigerator car has made possible the shipment of perishable commodities long distances at all times of the year. This has brought about an enormous increase in production and has greatly enlarged the volume of high-class freight traffic. Until recently, regulation of the temperature of the air in the refrigerator car was solely by the icing of the car at the point of shipment and as often as necessary *en route*. Now, however, at some points the plan is being adopted of placing the loaded car within a precooling plant for such time, one or two days, as may be necessary to bring the temperature of the air and the commodities in the car to the temperature of the air in the precooling plant; then to ice the car and send it through to destination with such reicing *en route* as may be required. Precooling is a great improvement upon the former process of refrigeration.

Train Control.—The mechanisms for the control of passenger and freight trains have been greatly improved, and have had a large influence upon the services performed by the railroads. The introduction of the air brake, by means of which the train can be controlled by the engineer, was mainly the work of George Westinghouse. As early as 1868, it had been successfully applied to passenger trains, and by 1887 it had been so improved mechanically as to become of practicable use upon freight trains. It has revolutionized train control and train service. The power brake lessened the risks to which employees were exposed; and it decreased the danger of travel while making possible the handling of freight as well as passenger trains at a much greater speed.

The movement of trains is controlled by some form of signaling, of which there are two general kinds, manual and automatic. To install automatic signaling, the railroad line must be divided into short blocks and signals placed at the beginning of each block. Moreover, the lines must be supplied with an electric apparatus, which, automatically operated by moving trains, will control the signals.

The ultimate ideal to be attained is automatic train control. As long as the movements of a train depend upon the engineer's seeing and obeying all signals, accidents cannot be prevented—signals will be misread and engineers will sometimes be disobedient. It seems probable that it will not be long before some device for automatically stopping a train that attempts to enter a ''closed block'' will be so improved as to make it of practical use. It is to be hoped that the present destruction of life in railroad accidents may soon be checked and may in time be eliminated.

The installation of automatic signaling involves a greater expense than can easily be borne by railroads having relatively light traffic, but wherever the earnings of the railroads make possible the adoption of automatic signaling, it is being installed. As yet, however, only a small percentage of American railroads are thus equipped. It is not improbable that the United States Government will, in the near future, require practically all railroads to install automatic signaling.

CHAPTER V

THE RAILWAY COMPANY AND HOW IT DOES ITS WORK

Corporations Defined and Classified.—The railways are run by large corporations which unite the capital and labor of many men, and apply them to the performance of a complicated service. The railway corporations do their work under careful regulation by the Government; and are in many ways regarded as being different from most business companies. We shall better understand why this is so, if we hold in mind one or two definitions.

A corporation is "an artificial person, created by law, having a continuity of existence, either definite or indefinite, and capacity to do authorized acts, and capable, however numerous the persons that compose it may be, of acting as a single individual." (Dwight on Law of Personal Property). Individuals who unite in this "artificial person" called a corporation, are the stockholders, and in a large railroad or industrial company they may number tens of thousands. The stockholders, or such of them as can conveniently get together, have an annual meeting, at which they elect a small number of men as directors to run the company for the stockholders. The directors in turn choose a president, one or more vice-presidents, a treasurer, a secretary, and other necessary officers to carry on the administrative work of the company under the supervision and control of the directors.

Corporations are of two general kinds: private and public. The ordinary manufacturing concern is an example of the former kind, while the city or borough government is an instance of the latter. The railroad corporation partakes of the nature of both kinds. Legally it is to be classed as a private corporation, but the services it performs are of a public nature. The railroad corporation is created to perform a service which, in some countries, is in the hands of the Government, and which the various States and the National Government in this country would need to perform, if the railroad corporations were not created by the Government to carry on the business of transportation.

The Railroad Company is a Quasi-Public Corporation.—To distinguish the railroad company from other private corporations and to indicate the fact that its services are of a public nature, the railroad company is called quasi-public. Such corporations are subject to such control by the Government as the regulation of their service in the public interest may require; and it will be found, when we come to consider the Government regulation of railroads, that all of their services and charges are under the control of the Government. The only limitation upon Government interference is, that its rules and regulations must be reasonable and must not deprive the railroad companies of their property without just compensation.

The Railway Charter.—A railroad company derives its powers from a charter granted to it in accordance with general laws by some one of the States, or by the United States. Up to the present time most of the railroads in our country have been chartered by the States. Some of the companies that built lines to the Pacific were created by the United States Government, which has the power of requiring every railroad company engaged in interstate transportation to secure a federal charter.

The charter states what may and what may not be done by the railroad company which it creates. The policy of the States in granting railway charters has been liberal because the public was desirous of having the services of as many railways as possible. The result of this is that the charters do not carefully state what the railroads must not do; consequently, the railroad companies are regulated more by laws than by charters. Having been free to do practically what they chose to do, the railroad companies adopted certain practices which it was necessary to prohibit or prevent by law. This is what is meant by the "railroad question," of which more will be said later.

Size of Railway Corporations.—The railroad corporation, even of medium proportions, includes a great host of shareholders. In many companies there are more than ten thousand owners of stock, and in the Pennsylvania Railroad Company, which is probably the largest in the world, there were at the close of 1908, 58,739 stockholders. At that time, its capitalization was $314,594,650. This great body of stock is so widely distributed that the average holdings per person were only 107 shares. It is also an interesting fact that 28,000, nearly one half of the shareholders, were women. The great services performed by this and other large railroad companies in providing means for the profitable investment of the property belonging to the general public cannot be overestimated.

Careful Organzation and Strict Discipline Are Required in the railway service. The business activities of a railroad company are of many kinds and they are carried on over a wide territory, sometimes hundreds of miles in extent. To do the work, an army of employees, often num-

bering tens of thousands of men, is required. It is a difficult task for the railroad company to perform its services
with precision, to enforce its authority throughout all
grades of officials and employees, and to guarantee to stockholders that their property shall be honestly administered.
The line of responsibility must be continuous from the
track-hand to the president, and it must be maintained
in such a way as to keep the organization of the service
flexible enough to permit of the adoption from time to time
of new methods of conducting the service and managing
the company's finances.

The General Organization of a Railroad Company is like
that of other corporations except that there is, in addition
to the general corporate organization, a special one built
up to perform the services peculiar to the railway business.
This special organization has four general duties to perform: (1) It must provide and keep in good order the
roadway and all structures connected therewith; (2) it
must build or obtain and it must operate such cars, coaches
and locomotives as the traffic may require; (3) it must
conduct the business arrangements between the company
and passengers and shippers, and lastly (4) it must build
up a special and accurate system of accounting for the receipts and expenditures in a business which may annually
include millions of transactions and be carried on in many
States. In the case of a large railroad corporation, each of
these four general duties will be in charge of a vice-president; if the company is small, the same vice-president may
be responsible for more than one of the departments.

The Legal Department of a railroad company is especially important for two reasons: In performing its services, the company comes into business relations with a
great many individuals, and in the adjustment of its rela-

tions the services of counsel, or expert legal advisers, are constantly necessary. Moreover, the railroad being engaged in a service of a public nature is subject to Government regulation, and comes under the control of local, State and national authority. The enforcement of this authority makes it inevitable that the railway corporation should be a party to numerous proceedings in the courts and before State and national railway commissions. The largest railroad companies in the United States operate in ten to twenty States, and it will be readily seen that this gives its legal department more to do than would be the case if the company were subject to only one political power. The general counsel is always directly subject to the president of the company, and while he is seldom one of the vice-presidents, he ranks with them in authority.

The Operating Department and Its Subdivisions.—The largest department of the railway organization—the operating—includes four large divisions, all four being subject to the general manager: (*a*) the engineering or *construction* department, headed by a chief engineer, whose duty it is to bring the roadway and structures into existence; (*b*) the *maintenance-of-way* department, also in charge of a chief engineer, or engineer of maintenance of way, whose general duties are described by the name of his department; (*c*) the *machinery* department, under a general superintendent of motive power or a mechanical engineer, or both, whose duties are to see that the company is supplied with locomotives and other equipment of high technical efficiency. Some railroads, notably the Pennsylvania, construct a large number of the locomotives they use. The machinery department of the Pennsylvania Railroad is so important that the company has a chief of motive power, who is a technical expert ranking on a par with the general manager. (*d*) The *transportation* department, under the immediate control of a general superintendent of transportation. His duties are concerned with the operation of the trains, and if he is connected with a large company, he will have under him two superintendents one in charge of freight transportation and the other of passenger transportation. Unless the company be so large as to make a subdivision of duties necessary, all of these four large divisions of the operating department come immediately under the control of the general manager, who reports to one of the vice presidents.

The Traffic Department is the second largest branch of the railroad company's special organization, and is also usually headed by a vice-president. It naturally subdivides itself into the freight and passenger departments, each of which is under the supervision of a general agent. In the case of the larger railroad companies, the ranking officers below the vice-presidents are the freight traffic manager and the passenger traffic manager, under each of whom there may be one or more general agents. It is the duty of the traffic department to solicit business, to classify traffic, to fix rates and fares, to appoint and supervise local agents, to adjust the claims which passengers and shippers may have against the company, and in general to do all that can be done to increase the traffic and earnings of the company.

Financial and Accounting Departments.—The management of the company's finances is always intrusted to an experienced vice-president, who has the all-important duty of advising the president and the company as to its proper financial policy. Usually the treasurer of the company and his office are subordinate to the financial vice-president, as also are the comptroller and auditors who keep the books and accounts. In some railroad organizations, however, the financial and accounting departments are separate, each having a vice-president at its head.

Auxiliary Departments.—In addition to the large departments just described are several which are of lesser rank but of great service to the company. They are: (a) The purchasing department, headed by an agent who would ordinarily be subject to the general manager. Under the purchasing agent are the storekeepers from whom every department of the railroad must obtain its supplies upon a proper requisition. (b) The real estate department, also subordinate to the general manager, intrusted with the purchase and sale of real estate. The duties of this or its allied department is greater in the case of those western railroads that were aided with large grants of public lands. (c) An insurance department, headed by a superintendent. Not all, even of the larger railroad companies, find it necessary to have a separate department to take charge of insurance. (d) The relief department in charge of a superintendent. Only a few of the railroad companies have a separate relief department. When this department exists, it naturally comes under the general manager.

Organization of the Pennsylvania Railroad.—To illustrate the relation which the different departments of a railroad bear to each other, a table of the organization of the Pennsylvania Railroad is presented. It need hardly be said that the great size of this corporation makes necessary a greater subdivision of departments than is required in the case of a smaller corporation. The student will find it instructive to tabulate or chart the organization of those railroads with which he is individually most familiar.

Organization of Pennsylvania Railroad, 1909.

Stockholders, Directors, and President.

- **Secretary** ...... Assistant secretaries ...... Transfer clerk ...... Ass't transfer clerks.

- **General counsel** ......
  - General solicitor ...... Assistant general solicitors ...... Chief claim agent ...... District solicitors.
  - Assistant general counsel.

- **First vice-president** ......
  - Ass't to first vice-president.
  - Purch'g agt. and ass't purch'g agts. ... Ass't to purchasing agt.
  - Real estate agent ...... Ass't real estate agts.
  - Sup't insurance department ...... Ass't sup't insurance department.
  - Board of officers of Pension department.

- **Second vice-president** ......
  - Ass't to second vice-president.
  - Engineer of branch lines ...... Principal ass't engineer of branch lines.
  - Chief eng. and ass't chief eng ......
    - Assistant to chief engineer.
    - Engineer of bridges and buildings.

  (The second v.-p. has charge of the promotion of new lines and the construction of the N.Y. tunnels and station.)

  - Comptroller and ass't compts. ......
    - Assistant to comptroller.
    - Auditor and ass't auditor mdse. frt. receipts.
    - Auditor and ass't auditor coal frt. receipts.
    - Auditor and ass't auditor passenger receipts.
    - Auditor and ass't auditor misc. rec'pts and acct's.
    - Auditor and ass't auditor of disbursements.
    - Auditor and ass't auditor Union line.

- **Third vice-president** ......
  - Passenger traffic manager ...... General passenger agent ......
    - Ass't genl. pass. agt..Division ticket agts.
    - District pass. agents.
  - Freight traffic manager ......
    - Gen'l freight agent, through traffic ... Ass't gen'l freight agt .Division fr't agents.
    - Gen'l freight agent, local traffic.
    - Freight claim agent ...... Ass't freight claim agt.
    - Coal freight agent.
  - General coal freight agent ......
  - Manager of the Empire line ......
    - Western sup't, Empire line.
    - Western sup't, Union line.
  - Manager of the Union line ......
    - Eastern sup't, Union line.

- **Fourth vice-president** ......
  - Treasurer and ass't treasurers ....
    - Assistants to treasurer.
    - Cashier and assistant cashier.
    - Chief paymaster.
    - Registrars of bonds and ass't regist'rs.
  - Sup't employees' saving fund.

- **Fifth vice-president** ......
  - Chief of motive power.
  - General manager ......
    - Ass't to general manager.
    - General sup't of transportation ...... { Sup't freight tr'sp'n. / Sup't pass. transp'n.
    - General sup't of motive power ...... { Princip'l ass't eng'rs. / Sup'ts motive power.
    - Chief eng. of maintenance of way ... { Eng'r m'nt'ce of way. / Eng'r of signals.
    - Superintendent of telegraph.
    - General superintendents ...... Division superintendents ......
      - Assistant engineers,
      - Train masters.
      - Station masters.
      - Station agents.
      - Baggage agents.
      - Division operators.
      - Train dispatchers.
      - Master mechanics.
      - Road foremen of engines.
      - General foremen of car shops.
      - Foremen of car inspectors.
    - Sup't voluntary relief department.... Ass't sup't vol. relief department.

- **Assistants to president.**

CHAPTER VI

STOCKS AND BONDS, EARNINGS, EXPENSES AND PROFITS

Stock and Capital.—Railroad companies secure the funds for the construction, equipment and extension of their lines, mainly from the sale of stocks and bonds. These two kinds of securities constitute the capital invested. Strictly speaking, the capital of a corporation includes only its stocks, but inasmuch as the railways in the United States have been built largely from funds received from the sale of bonds, it is customary to include both bonds and stocks in the capitalization of railroads.

The shares or certificates of stock represent the investment made by the stockholders who own the company. The persons who loan money to the company receive bonds or certificates of the company's indebtedness to them, and those bonds are protected by mortgages which give the bondholders power to take over a part or all of the property covered by the mortgage if the company does not pay the interest and principal of the loans made to it in accordance with the terms of the bond. The bonds are the company's funded debt.

Main Classes of Bonds.—Bonds are of two classes: mortgage and debenture. The man holding a mortgage bond has a lien or claim upon some specified piece of property that he can take possession of, if the interest and principal of the loan are not paid by the company. These mortgage bonds are named in accordance with the kind of property to which they apply, there being equipment, terminal, and general or blanket bonds. Moreover, these several classes of bonds may give their holders a first, second, third, or fourth mortgage upon the property covered by the bonds. The holders of all but the first mortgage bonds are called junior lieners.

Debenture bonds differ from those secured by mortgages in that they give their holders a claim only upon the income received by the borrowing company from sources specified in the bonds. Sometimes the debentures have no other security than the credit of the company. In the United States mortgage bonds are mainly used, while in Great Britain the preference has been for debentures. Whatever the class of bond, the claim of bondholders comes ahead of the stockholders. No dividends can be declared upon stock until the interest on the mortgages has been met and the principal of the bonds that have become due, has been paid.

Capitalization of American Railways.—The stocks and bonds, or total capital of American railroads, amount to about sixteen billion dollars, somewhat over one half of the total consisting of bonds or funded debt. The capitalization per mile of line is very much lower than the average in European countries, the capitalization per mile in Great Britain being more than four times the average for American railways. This difference is due mainly to two causes: it cost very much more to build the British railways than it did those in the United States, because of the heavy expense of right of way and terminals, and also because the public required the British railways to be constructed as safe and strong as it was possible to make them. Moreover, British railway capitalization has increased more rapidly than American for the reason that

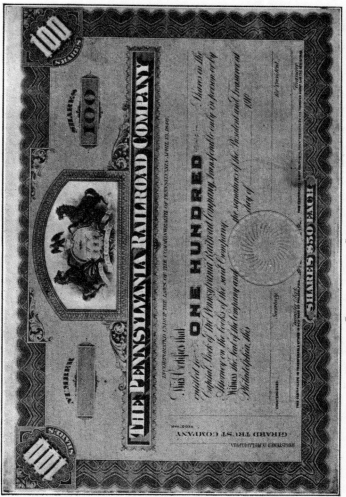

CERTIFICATE OF STOCK.

it is customary in Great Britain to charge all improvements to capital instead of paying for a large part of them out of current revenue, as is the general and wise practice in the United States.

The Watering of Stocks and Bonds.—In many parts of the United States the railroads were built mainly with borrowed money, i. e., from the proceeds of the sale of bonds. The stocks of these early companies were sold cheaply, and in some instances were given as a bonus to the buyers of bonds. This policy enabled the companies to borrow money more easily because those who received the stock for nothing, or at a very low price, were in a position to make large gains in case the railroad company proved successful and its stocks became valuable. Watered stock is that sold or issued for less than its par or face value, and the amount of water in the stock at the time of sale or issue is the difference between the selling and par value. While stocks have been watered more extensively than bonds, the policy of issuing watered bonds has also been frequently adopted.

The incentives for issuing railway securities at less than par value are strong. It is a well-known fact that investors prefer to buy securities that sell for less than par, because such stocks or bonds give an opportunity for speculative gains. It has been found by experience that more money can be obtained by the sale of five million dollars' worth of three per cent bonds than from the sale of three million dollars' worth of five per cent bonds, although the interest charges would be the same in each case. Furthermore, the men or banking firms who promote and underwrite railway securities are usually paid for their services in stock, the value of which depends upon the ability of the promoters to market the stock; and the promoter's opportunities for gain are greater when he handles speculative than when he deals in non-speculative securities.

The issue and sale of speculative securities, while often advantageous from the capitalist's or promoter's point of view, are objectionable from the standpoint of the public interest, and have come to be looked upon with disfavor

FORM FOR THE TRANSFER OF STOCK.   Printed upon back of a certificate of stock.

by conservative financiers. In several States the laws prohibit the issue of railway stocks and bonds at less than their face value, and permission to increase capitalization has to be obtained from the State Railroad Commission. It is not improbable that the United States Government will, in the not distant future, give the Interstate Commerce

Commission the power to regulate the capitalization of railroads.

The True Basis of Railroad Capitalization.—Before the State can intelligently regulate railway corporations it must decide what capitalization is fair or reasonable. Some persons think that the capital of a railroad should be based upon the cost of reproduction; it is held by others that the capitalization should correspond with the amount of the investment; while others think that earning capacity should determine the volume of stocks and securities that may be issued. The last is the basis advocated by most railroad companies, but it is not favored by the public generally because of the feeling that the earnings of the railroad should be a reasonable percentage of the investment or the cost of the property; in other words, that investment and not possible earnings should be the basis of capital.

The basis that has found most favor with courts and railway commissions has been the cost of reproducing or duplicating a railroad. This theory assumes that the owners of a railroad property are entitled to the natural increase in the value of their property, and that they should be permitted to issue securities to the amount of the present cost of another railroad similar to their own. Even this basis is subject to the criticism that it does not take into account the fact that the value of a railroad is to be found partly in its physical or material property—roadway, equipment, buildings, etc.—and partly in its charter, its business opportunities, and its value as a going concern, i. e., in the immaterial elements of its property.

Indeed, it seems logical to hold that the true basis of the capitalization of a railroad is the entire value of its property at any given time. This property, however, includes not only its roadway, equipment, and buildings, but also the value derived from its location and its right to do business. In determining what is a fair capitalization of a railroad, both of these elements and all its property—immaterial as well as material—should be valued.

Sources of Earnings. —Railroad companies have two general sources of income, the largest being the freight and passenger receipts or the revenue secured from the operation of trains; the other and minor items of income are interest on corporate loans and investments, and rentals derived from permitting tracks and structures to be used by other companies. The gross income of American railway companies during the year ending June 30, 1908, was nearly two and

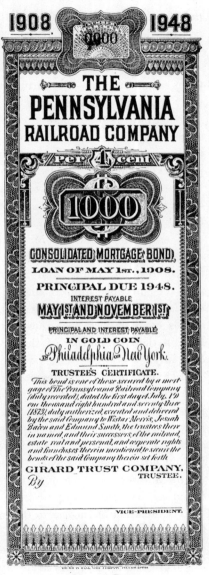

SAMPLE BOND.

and one half billion dollars, of which nine tenths was secured by performing transportation services and one tenth from other sources.

Gross and Net Earnings, Operating Expenses, Fixed Charges and Surplus.—The entire revenue of a railroad company constitutes its gross income. The term *gross earnings* is sometimes used to include earnings from operation and sometimes, though less accurately, it is held to be the same as gross income. There are three general classes of expenses that must be met by every railroad company. The first and largest of these is *operating expenses* which must cover the actual outlay for maintenance of way and structures, maintenance of equipment, conducting transportation, and general or administrative expenses. The next largest class of expenses is that of *fixed charges* covering the interest on funded and floating debts, rentals, taxes, and the sinking fund, if any. The third outlay is for *dividends* to the stockholders, those holding preferred shares coming first, and those owning the common stock last, in the distribution of the dividends or profits of the company.

Net Earnings from Operation are the earnings from operation less the operating expenses. This remainder, plus the income from other sources, is the company's *gross income,* out of which fixed charges (rentals, taxes, interest on bonds, and sinking fund requirements) are paid. What is then left is the *net income,* which the stockholders may use in adding to the company's surplus, and in the distribution of dividends.

The Relation of Income to Outgo.—In the chart showing the earnings and expenses of American railways for the eighteen years ending in 1907, the increase and variations in earnings and expenses are graphically shown. The effects of general business conditions are discoverable by studying the chart carefully.   Two things will be seen: first, that when the earnings fall off rapidly, operating expenses do not fall correspondingly.   The cause of this is that many operating expenses are independent of the volume of the traffic, i. e., they are the general outgo necessary to keep the road in operation.   Only a part of the expenses vary with

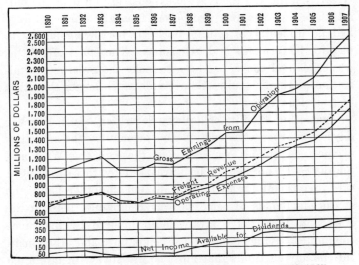

EARNINGS AND EXPENSES, AMERICAN RAILWAYS, 1890–1907.

changes in tonnage of freight handled and number of passengers carried.   A second fact shown by the chart is that when gross earnings rise rapidly the amounts paid in dividends do not increase with equal rate.   The explanation of this is that it is the policy of American railroads to use a part of their income during prosperous periods for improving their track, increasing their equipment, and making other useful betterments.   Instead of making these improvements and extensions entirely by selling stock and issuing bonds they are paid for in part out of the gross income. In this regard the practice of American railroads differs from that of the British. In our country, most of the roads were built as cheaply as possible and they have been improved as the traffic required, the expense for improvements being met in large part out of current income. In Great Britain, the roads were expensively built at the outset, the companies were prosperous from the start, and have had no difficulty in selling stock, or borrowing money to pay for betterments and extensions. The effect of this, as was explained above, has been to make the average capitalization of English railroads per mile much larger than that of American roads.

Increasing Stability of Railway Securities.—In the earlier days of railroad construction and promotion, the securities of most companies, especially of those in the West and South, could not wisely be purchased by those seeking a safe investment for their capital. On the other hand, the stocks and bonds of some railway companies, both in the East and West, have always been favored by insurance companies, savings banks, trust companies, and other institutions having funds that must be invested with minimum risk. The policy of our railroads to make betterments out of income, their growing tendency to discountenance speculative financiering, and, what is still more important, the growing publicity of the railroad business, as the result of more careful governmental regulation, are giving American railway securities increasing stability and are causing them to become safer storehouses than they formerly were for the savings of the masses.

CHAPTER VII

THE FREIGHT SERVICE

The Railway Services include the movement of freight, the carriage of persons, and the transportation of mail and express matter. Seven tenths of the total income of American railroads is derived from the freight services and a little over one fifth from the passenger business; the other one tenth of the revenue comes from the carriage of mail and express, and from "other sources."

The Freight Traffic.—During the year ending June 30, 1907, the railways of the United States reported a total freight tonnage of 1,796,336,659. This, however, was a greater number of tons than was actually shipped on the railroads, because of the fact that much of the freight was handled by two or more railroads, each of which reported its entire tonnage. After making the subtractions needed to eliminate duplications, it is found that 977,489,440 tons were actually turned over to the railroads by shippers. The average distance traveled by each ton of this freight was 242.05 miles. Thus the number of tons of freight carried one mile upon the railroads of the United States in 1907, reached the enormous total of 236,601,390,103 ton miles. To handle this traffic 41,337 freight and switching locomotives and over two million freight cars were used.

Commodities Carried.—Over one half (53.39 per cent) of this great volume of traffic was made up of minerals, mainly coal and iron ore. In no other country of the world

67

is the mineral traffic so great as in the United States, and
as this traffic must be carried at low freight rates, the average earning of the railroads for carrying a ton of freight
one mile is less in the United States than elsewhere. Manufactures make up somewhat more than one seventh of the
total tonnage (15.41 per cent), products of the forest include one ninth (11.38 per cent), and agricultural products one twelfth (8.62 per cent). These four commodities
include eight ninths of the total traffic, the other one ninth
being made up of animal products, general merchandise,
and miscellaneous articles.

Freight Classification.—In these few groups of commodities more than ten thousand distinct kinds of articles
are included. It is obvious that it would be impossible for
the railroads to make a rate for each of the ten thousand
articles; hence it is necessary to group the articles into a
small number of classes, and to make rates vary with
classes instead of by articles. Furthermore, it is desirable
that the railroad should give lower rates on commodities
when they are shipped in carloads than when they are
handled in less than carload quantities. These conditions
are met in the freight classifications which group the
articles into ten to fourteen classes, and which assign to
most articles a lower classification when shipped in carload
lots. A classification book divides each page into three col-
umns, the first column containing an alphabetical list of
articles, the second column giving the classification of the
article when shipped in less than carloads, and the third
column, the classification when shipped in carload quantities.

Classifications in Use.—Prior to the passage of the Interstate Commerce Act in 1887, nearly every large railroad
had its own classification, but in that year these various

classifications were consolidated into three. One of these, the *official* classification, applies in the territory north of the Ohio and Potomac Rivers and east of the Mississippi River. This originally grouped articles into six numbered classes, but these six classes have been raised to fourteen; nominally there are six classes, but their number has really been increased by grouping certain articles as one and a half, twice, or two and a half, etc., first class. South of the Ohio and Potomac, and east of the Mississippi, the *southern* classification is in force. It groups commodities into fourteen classes. West of the Mississippi the *western* classification prevails. It groups articles into ten classes. The class to which an article is assigned depends upon the value of the article, the expense of transporting it, the value of the service to the shipper, and many other factors. Inasmuch as the rate which an article pays is determined by the class to which it is assigned, the forces which control rates also control the classification.

Commodity Tariffs.—Not all articles of freight are included within the classification. Coal, livestock, lumber, grain, cement, and many other bulky commodities that are invariably handled in carload quantities are each given what is called a commodity tariff rate. Such commodities are "ex-class freight." Taking the country as a whole, the number of commodities thus designated is relatively large —between one thousand and two thousand—but they are less numerous than those within the classification.

Local and Interline Freight.—Railway companies designate freight as local or interline. That which does not leave the lines of the company is called local, and that which is received from another road or turned over to a connecting road is termed interline. The distinction between local and interline freight is made because interline

freight requires special billing and necessitates the employment of accounting methods that enable each railway company to keep a separate account with each of the roads
with which it exchanges traffic.

Local and Transfer Stations.—In every large city freight
is received and delivered at numerous local stations; the
Pennsylvania Railroad, for instance, has fifty-one stations within the city of Philadelphia. At the largest of
these local stations the freight received from shippers will
sometimes consist of carload quantities. In most instances,
however, the consignments are of less than carload lots,
and, of course, the shipments from every local station are
for many destinations. It thus becomes necessary for the
railroads to connect local stations with a large transfer
station to which the small shipments of freight are brought
in "mixed cars," containing different kinds of freight for
various destinations. At the transfer station, the mixed
cars are unloaded, as far as it is necessary, and freight is
so assorted as to make up "straight cars" containing shipments destined for only one point, or, at most, but few
points. Inbound freight is similarly handled, the trains
being broken up at the yards of the transfer station, from
whence cars loaded with freight for a single local station
are taken on to their destination. Such transfer of freight
as may be necessary to make up mixed cars to be switched
from the transfer to the local station is made at the
transfer station.

Shipping Papers.—There are many business papers that
must be used in performing the railway freight services.
Only a few of these papers have direct connection with
freight shipments. The principal shipping papers are the
receipt for freight, the bill of lading, the way bill and
freight bill.

Receipt for Freight.—When the shipper delivers his goods to the railway company at a freight station, he receives a receipt for freight. Business firms who ship regularly in large quantities, keep a supply of blank receipts in their offices and fill out these blanks in triplicate form, sending the receipt thus filled out to the station with the goods. The agent of the railroad company affixes his signature to the papers after he has checked up their contents.

Bills of Lading.—Ordinarily the receipts for freight are exchanged for a bill of lading, which is issued by the railway freight agent in triplicate form. One copy of the bill of lading is kept by the freight agent for his office records; the original and the other copy of the document are given to the shipper. Bills of lading are of two general kinds, "straight" and "order." When a straight bill of lading is used, the goods are billed to consignee, and the original bill of lading is sent by the shipper through the mails to the consignee. When the goods arrive at their destination the agent notifies the consignee who presents his straight bill of lading, pays the freight charges and obtains the goods. Straight bills of lading are not negotiable, and they are printed on white paper.

When the "order" bill of lading is used the goods are billed to the order of the shipper. The bill also states the destination of the goods and names the person to be notified when the articles reach their destination. The shipper of the goods attaches to the original bill of lading a draft on the purchaser of the goods to the amount of the purchase price of the commodities that have been shipped. The shipper then takes the order bill of lading with draft attached to his bank, which, after the shipper has made proper indorsement, purchases the draft and bill of lading. The bank then sends the draft and bill of lading to the

P. D. 3520

Pennsylvania Railroad Company

STRAIGHT BILL OF LADING—ORIGINAL—NOT NEGOTIABLE.

Shippers No. _____

Agents No. _____

RECEIVED, subject to the classifications and tariffs in effect on the date of issue of this Original Bill of Lading,

at _____ 19 ____

from _____ the property described below, in apparent good order, except as noted (contents and condition of contents of packages unknown), marked, consigned and destined as indicated below, which said Company agrees to carry to its usual place of delivery at said destination, if on its road, otherwise to deliver to another carrier on the route to said destination. It is mutually agreed, as to each carrier of all or any of said property over all or any portion of said route to destination, and as to each party at any time interested in all or any of said property, that every service to be performed hereunder shall be subject to all the conditions, whether printed or written, herein contained (including conditions on back hereof) and which are agreed to by the shipper and accepted for himself and his assigns.

The Rate of Freight from _____

to _____ is in Cents per 100 Lbs.

IF ... Times lar	IF 1st Class	IF 2d Class	IF Rule 25	IF 3d Class	IF Rule 26	IF Rule 28	IF 4th Class	IF 5th Class	IF 6th Class	IF Special per ___	IF Special per ___

(Mail Address—Not for purposes of Delivery.)

Consigned to _____

Destination, _____ State of _____ County of _____

Route, _____ Car Initial _____ Car No. _____

NO. PACKAGES	DESCRIPTION OF ARTICLES AND SPECIAL MARKS	WEIGHT (Subject to Correction)	CLASS OR RATE	CHECK COLUMN	
					If charges are to be prepaid, write or stamp here, "To be Prepaid."
					Received $ _____ to apply in prepayment of the charges on the property described hereon.
					Agent or Cashier.
					Per _____ (The signature here acknowledges only the amount prepaid.)
					Charges Advanced:
					$ _____

Shipper. _____ _____ Agent.

Per _____ Per _____

(This Bill of Lading is to be signed by the shipper and agent of the carrier issuing same.)

F. D. 2560

Pennsylvania Railroad Company.

ORDER BILL OF LADING—ORIGINAL.

Shippers No.

Agents No.

RECEIVED, subject to the classifications and tariffs in effect on the date of issue of this Original Bill of Lading,

at _____ 19____

from _____the property described below, in apparent good order, except as noted (contents and condition of contents of packages unknown), marked, consigned and destined as indicated below, which said Company agrees to carry to its usual place of delivery at said destination, if on its road, otherwise to deliver to another carrier on the route to said destination. It is mutually agreed, as to each carrier of all or any of said property over all or any portion of said route to destination, and as to each party at any time interested in all or any of said property, that every service to be performed hereunder shall be subject to all the conditions, whether printed or written, herein contained (including conditions on back hereof) and which are agreed to by the shipper and accepted for himself and his assigns.

The surrender of this Original **ORDER** Bill of Lading properly indorsed shall be required before the delivery of the property. Inspection of property covered by this bill of lading will not be permitted unless provided by law or unless permission is indorsed on this original bill of lading or given in writing by the shipper.

The Rate of Freight from _____

to _____ is in Cents per 100 Lbs.

IF .. Times 1st	IF 1st Class	IF 2d Class	IF Rule 25	IF 3d Class	IF Rule 26	IF Rule 28	IF 4th Class	IF 5th Class	IF 6th Class	IF Special per_____	IF Special per_____

(Mail Address—Not for Purposes of Delivery.)

Consigned to **ORDER OF**_____

Destination,_____ State of_____ County of_____

Notify_____

At_____ State of_____ County of_____

Route,_____ Car Initial_____ Car No._____

NO. PACKAGES	DESCRIPTION OF ARTICLES AND SPECIAL MARKS	WEIGHT (Subject to Correction)	CLASS OR RATE	CHECK COLUMN	
					If charges are to be prepaid, write or stamp here "To be Prepaid."
					Received $_____ to apply in prepayment of the charges on the property described hereon.
					Agent or Cashier.
					Per_____ (The signature here acknowledges only the amount prepaid.)
					Charges Advanced:
					$_____

_____Shipper. Per_____Agent.

Per_____ (This Bill of Lading is to be signed by the shipper and agent of the carrier issuing same.)

G–10–A. F. R.

Way-bill No. 4081 ....

Pennsylvania Railroad } and roads in { Inter-Line System.
Philadelphia, Wilmington & Baltimore Railroad
West Jersey & Seashore Railroad

October 1st, 190 ....

Inter-Line Way-bill of Merchandise forwarded from .... *Munhall, Pa.,* to .... *Rouse's Point, N. Y.,* Via *P.. V. & C. Jct., Lewistown Jct.,* Sunbury, Wilkes–Barre and D. & H.

When billing freight to a point reached via two or more routes, the agent must specify the route in the space provided above

CAR.		SHIPPER	CONSIGNEE, DESTINATION AND MARKS	DESCRIPTION OF ARTICLES	WEIGHT.	No. of Tariff or Rate Order.	CLASS.	RATE.	FREIGHT CHARGES.	ADVANCES.	PREPAID.	TO BE COLLECTED.
INITIALS.	NUMBERS.											
P. R. R.	17032	Henry Poe	Order Richard Roe,	56 Steel Beams	46100	I.C.C.J. 2271		20½ 15½	71 46			71 46
			Notify John Doe,									
			Montreal, Canada,									
			Via Grand Trunk Ry.									
			Totals of Weight and Money columns }		46100				71 46			71 46

The agent at destination must verify figures. He is held responsible for the correctness of the amounts collected.
An agent discovering an error must at once advise any other agent interested; also the Auditor of Freight Receipts.
When freight is shipped at a through rate or from a point beyond this road the through rate must be stated on the way bill. The route beyond the point to which the property is billed as above must be shown when final destination may be reached by more than one line.

.... a written copy, or the FIRST PRESS COPY of this way-bill, must be sent to the Auditor of Freight Receipts. Pennsylvania Railroad, and copies to representatives of other roads as directed.

W. L. McKeo, ... Agent.

SAMPLE INTERLINE WAY BILL.

bank with which it does business in the city to which the goods covered by the bill of lading have been shipped; and when this bank receives the bill of lading and draft, it collects the amount of the draft from the purchaser of the goods, who then receives the bill of lading which he must present to the carrier before he can obtain his goods. The original order bill of lading is printed on yellow paper, and for the two duplicates blue paper is used. It is thus impossible to substitute a duplicate for the original order bill of lading, or to change a straight into an order bill cf lading.

When either the straight or order bill of lading, just described, is used, the carrier is not liable for any loss or damage of the goods "caused by the act of God, the public enemy, quarantine, the authority of law, or the act or default of the shipper." The carrier is liable only for losses due to its own negligence. If the shipper desires to be guaranteed against all risk of loss while the goods are in transit, he must secure a "special" bill of lading and pay a higher rate of freight.

Way Bill.—The railway company's most important shipping paper is the way bill, a sample of which is shown in the illustration. Each shipment of freight is accompanied by a way bill which the forwarding agent either hands to the conductor of the freight train, or sends by mail to the freight agent at destination. If the way bill is forwarded by mail, a card way bill, such as is shown in the illustration, is given to the conductor in charge of the train upon which the goods are sent. When the goods are to be turned over to a connecting carrier, an interline way bill is used, and a copy is sent to the agent of the connecting carrier at the junction point. A copy of every way bill is also sent to the auditor of freight receipts.

Freight Bill and Notice of Arrival.—When the goods arrive at their destination the agent sends the consignee—or the person named to be notified in the order bill of lading—a " notice of arrival," the consignee then surrenders the bill of lading and settles the " freight bill " which contains a statement of charges due and which is receipted by the agent when the charges are paid.

Freight Lines.—Railroad companies are obliged to arrange for through shipment of carload freight to destination without transfer of the cargo *en route* from one car to another. In the early decades of the railway business, every railroad sought to keep its own cars on its own lines; and thus it was that freight lines came into existence to facilitate the handling of through or interline freight.

The first of these freight lines were *independent* of the railways, i. e., they were organized and managed by

---

P. R. R. Car No. *46.014*

To *Rouse's Point*

Via *P. V. & C. Jct., Lewistown Jct., Sunbury, Wilkes Barre and D. & H.*

Lading *186 Steel Billets,*

Combined Weight of Car and Lading for Engine rating, *42* Net Tons.

G—19—A. F. R.

PENNSYLVANIA RAILROAD,

Phila., Wilm. & Balto. Railroad,　West Jersey & Seashore Railroad, And Roads in Inter-Line System.

From *Munhall, Pa.*

Shipper *Henry Poe;*

Consignee *Order Samuel Koe;*

Notify John Foe;

Destination *Montreal, Canada;*

Via *Grand Trunk Railway*

Prepaid	To Collect
Marked Capacity of Car	*60.000* lbs.

ESTIMATED WEIGHT.	ACTUAL WEIGHT.
61.100 WEIGHED AT:	Gross *84.600* lbs.
Derry	Tare *22.900* lbs.
Oct. 1st, 1901	Net *61.700* lbs.

Date *Oct. 1st, 1901* *W. L. McKee* Agent.

Transferred to_____ Car No._____

At_____ Date_____190

SAMPLE CARD WAY BILL.

corporations distinct from the railroad companies over whose roads the cars of the freight lines were operated. These individual freight lines solicited business and provided through cars for handling the freight, and charged the shippers such rates as competitive conditions permitted. The only service performed by the railroad company was that of hauling the cars, for which it was paid by the independent freight lines.

It came to be the practice for railroad officers to form or become interested in freight lines, and, by controlling these lines, it was possible to make excessive profits at the expense of the income of the railroad. This led to the substitution of *coöperative* freight lines for the independent ones. These coöperative lines were merely a joint arrangement entered into by two or more railroads, each of which supplied its quota of cars for the freight line. The earnings of the coöperative line and all of its expenses were divided *pro rata* among the interested roads. Thus the coöperative freight line was primarily an inexpensive method of carrying on and accounting for interline business.

In course of time, as the result of the rapid consolidation of railways, many of the coöperative freight lines operated came to be owned or controlled by a single railroad company. This caused numerous freight lines to become *company* lines—they became a part of the freight organization of their railroad companies; and their principal services became soliciting and accounting for through traffic. There is a surprisingly large number of both coöperative and of company freight lines in existence at the present time, the business to and from the north Atlantic seaports alone being solicited and handled by over eighty freight lines.

Shippers' Cars.—The railroad companies supply most

FREIGHT BILL.

G—100—A. F. B.

Bill No. _____

Station, _____

Way-bill No. _____ Date, _____ 190

From _____

Car No. _____

To Pennsylvania Railroad Company, Dr.

For charges on the Articles named below :—

Shipped by _____

Original point of shipment _____

Original Car _____ No. _____

MARKS.	ARTICLES.	WEIGHT.	RATE.	FREIGHT CHARGES.	ADVANCES.	TOTAL.

Received Payment for the Company,

_____ 190

_____ Agent.

(DRAW CHEQUE TO ORDER OF THE PENNSYLVANIA RAILROAD COMPANY.)

Sample Freight Bill.

NOTICE OF ARRIVAL.

G—199—A. F. R.
5 65 5 x 16½ 4 8 1902.

Bill No.

.................Station, ...Date, ...190

Way-bill No. ....

From .... Car No. ....

Pennsylvania Railroad Company.

The property described below, consigned to you, is now ready for delivery at the above-named Station, on payment of charges due thereon. Please send for the same immediately.

Shipped by ....

Original point of shipment ....

Original Car .... No. ....

MARKS.	ARTICLES.	WEIGHT.	RATE.	FREIGHT CHARGES.	ADVANCES.	TOTAL.

To Freight Agent PENNSYLVANIA RAILROAD COMPANY

...............Station.

Please deliver the property above described to ....

...............190   Signature ....

CONSIGNEE.

Draw cheques to order of the Pennsylvania Railroad Company.
[OVER.]

SAMPLE NOTICE OF ARRIVAL.

but not all of the cars used by shippers. Many large shippers prefer to supply themselves with cars in order that
they may have an equipment especially adapted to their
particular needs. The shippers of packing house products,
of petroleum oil, and of various kinds of heavy machinery
are among those who make large use of their own cars.

Private Car Lines.—Some of the shippers using large
numbers of private cars have formed *private car lines;* as,
for instance, the Armour Line. The private car line handles the freight not only of those who own the line, but
of other shippers of similar products. Refrigerator cars,
of which large numbers are used, are owned and maintained mainly by private car lines. Formerly, the shippers
who used their own cars were unduly favored as compared
with other shippers, and the profits made by the private
car lines were, in many cases, unjustly large. These evils
are now under the control of the Interstate Commerce
Commission, which has the power to prevent unreasonable
discrimination.

Per Diem and Car Mileage.—When the railroad uses a
car belonging to another company it pays 25 cents a day
for the use of the car. Until 1902, the basis of payment
was the number of miles which the car was hauled. The
per diem system of payment was then adopted, and the
rate was first fixed at 20 cents a day per car. At the present time, while the prevailing rate is 25 cents, it may be
made higher by agreement among carriers whenever they
wish to secure the promptest possible return of cars to owners. The payment for the use of private cars is still on the
basis of mileage. The car mileage rates vary in different
parts of the country and with different kinds of cars; but
the usual payment is one cent or three fourths of a cent
per mile.

Demurrage and Track Storage Charges.—The consignee is usually given forty-eight hours in which to unload his goods; in the case of some special kinds of goods he may be given a longer time. At the end of the period allowed him, a demurrage charge of $1.00 per day per car is imposed. In some of the larger and more congested freight yards, the railroads have found it necessary not only to charge demurrage, but also to exact a track storage charge of the consignee when he requires the railroad to keep the cars standing a considerable period of time upon the company's tracks. These track storage rates begin with $1.00 a day per car, and may rise as high as $5.00 a day.

CHAPTER VIII

THE PASSENGER SERVICE

The Passenger Traffic. — In serving a population of ninety million people the railways in the United States have a large and rapidly increasing passenger traffic. In 1907, the number of trips taken was 873,905,133, while ten years earlier the figures were 489,445,198. If this rate of gain be continued for the present decade, the total for 1917 will be 1,559,920,662. The average length of the passenger trip or journey in 1907 was 31.72 miles; and the aggregate length of all the trips or the ''passenger miles'' was 27,-718,554,030. The volume of travel grows with the increase in the speed of trains and in the comforts of travel; while the average length of the trip taken on the steam railroads has become greater during recent years, because the electric railways now secure a larger share of the short distance traffic formerly handled by .the steam lines.

Passenger Revenues. — The income received by the steam railways from their passenger traffic in 1907 was $564,606,-343. In addition to this their passenger trains earned $120,386,794, mainly for carrying mail and express; and the operation of the passenger trains brought in about one fourth of the total income of the railways. In some parts of the United States, especially in New England where population is dense and travel frequent, and in the Rocky Mountain States where freight traffic is relatively light, the ratio of passenger earnings to freight receipts is much higher than the general average. On some of the New England roads the passenger earnings equal those received from the freight.

Extent of Travel.—The figures just presented indicate that the people of the United States travel frequently and extensively. It is an interesting fact, however, that there are several European countries where the yearly number of trips per person is greater than in the United States. This is not difficult to understand. The people in the United States are spread over a great extent of territory; and the distances from place to place in many parts of our country are so long as to limit the amount of travel for pleasure, and to cause men to do a larger part of their business by mail and by telegraph than they would do if they lived in a smaller country with a denser population. In the United Kingdom there are nearly one half as many people as there are in the United States, although the area of that country is no greater than three American States of average size. The resident of Great Britain takes, on an average, between three and four times as many railway trips per year as the American does; the people of Belgium and Switzerland take two trips to our one; the Germans one and a half, and the French one and a quarter. The length of our average journey is greater than the mean length of the trips in any European country, and thus the people of the United Kingdom are the only ones that travel more miles per year per person than the average American does.

Passenger Classification in Europe.—In the United States, as well as elsewhere, passenger services of dissimilar grades of excellence are offered for different rates of charges; but in our country the division of passengers into classes is not so distinct as in Europe. In the United Kingdom and most continental countries, there are three classes: first, second, and third; while in Germany there are four regular classes, besides special accommodations for the soldiers. Nearly thirty per cent of the travel in Germany is in the military and fourth classes, sixty per cent of the people ride in the third-class compartments, and less than ten per cent travel second or first class.

European railroads have found that the majority of the people wish to travel inexpensively and prefer economy to luxury. This demand for cheap service has been met by the railroads by furnishing the third and fourth classes, and by running slow trains upon which fares are lower than upon the express trains. During recent years the accommodations offered, particularly in the third class, have been made more comfortable and the trend of traffic has been from the upper to the lower classes. In general, in those countries where the railroads offer three or more grades of service, nine tenths of the passengers ride in the third and lower classes.

Classification of Service in the United States.—In our country, as in Europe, there are express trains upon which extra fares are charged and also ordinary trains upon which regular fares prevail. In addition to these two classes of service, there are four others that are coming to be fairly distinct. The first of these in point of excellence is the *Pullman* service which is now offered by the railroads upon nearly all of their express trains. The grade below the Pullman is the *first-class* service provided by the regular day coaches; probably 95 per cent of the entire travel is in the first-class day coaches. In some parts of the United States *second-class* tickets are sold at somewhat lower rates than first-class fares, but no special accommodations are provided for second-class passengers; it is customary to require them to ride in the smoking car.

Two other classes of service, which are practically on a par with the second class, are the *tourist* and cheap *excursion* accommodations. The tourist traffic is well-organized on the Pacific roads, and regular trains are run from Chicago to the Pacific coast, made up of tourists' sleepers which provide a fair degree of comfort at second-class rates. Cheap excursions of many kinds, particularly during the summer months, are run by the railroads in all parts of the country. In this traffic people are handled in train loads and the cars used are generally the older first-class coaches. The fourth grade of service is provided in the *immigrant* trains. The steerage passengers arriving at New York and other ports are taken through to interior destinations in full train loads. Old coaches are used and all the space in the trains is occupied.

The passenger traffic in the United States is being divided with increasing distinctness into well-organized classes. The Pullman and first-class services now provide two regular classes, between which most travelers may choose; as yet there is no well-organized class below the so-called first class. It is, however, probable that a grade of service corresponding to the European third class will develop as the railroads endeavor to induce the poorer people to travel more largely.

Relations of the Pullman Company and the Railroad Company.—With few exceptions the railroads do not own their sleeping, parlor, and dining-room cars, but secure them from the Pullman Palace Car Company of Chicago. Prior to 1899, this style of equipment was supplied to the railroads both by the Pullman and Wagner companies. In that year, however, the two companies consolidated under the name of the Pullman Company. The railroad pays the Pullman Company one cent per mile run for the use of the car, the maximum payment for the use of any car for a year being $7,500. The Pullman Company receives, in addition to this, the extra fares which the passenger pays for the privilege of riding in the parlor or sleeping car; in other words, the railroad company receives from the passenger the regular first-class fare, out of which it pays the Pullman Company for the car rental. On some especially fast trains, like the "Twentieth Century Limited" on the

"TWENTIETH CENTURY LIMITED" OF THE NEW YORK CENTRAL. Eighteen hours from New York to Chicago. Train photographed while running ninety miles an hour.

New York Central, and the "Pennsylvania Special" of the Pennsylvania Railroad, an extra fare is charged to cover the additional expense of running luxurious trains at high speed. Even then, these trains are not so profitable as those which are run at lower speed and carry day-coach passengers. It has been said with some degree of truth that "he who sits up all night in a day coach helps pay the fare of the man who rides in the Pullman car."

Reason Why Railway Companies Use Pullman Cars.—It is more profitable for the railroads to pay the Pullman Company liberally for the use of its equipment than for the railroads to supply themselves with their own sleeping, parlor, and dining cars. In some seasons of the year the railroad requires a larger equipment of these cars than at other seasons, and if it owned enough to provide for its

"Pennsylvania Special" of the Pennsylvania Railroad. Eighteen hours from New York to Chicago. Train photographed while running sixty miles an hour.

needs at all times it would have a large number of idle cars on its hands for a part of the year. A heavy demand of the railroads in one section of the country at a different season from that of the railroads in other parts of the United States enables the Pullman Company to distribute its cars economically, sending them from one part of the country to another with the variations in traffic.

The Baggage Service.—The baggage arrangements on American railroads are superior to those in most other countries, and our companies are especially liberal in the weight of the baggage which the passenger may take without paying an extra charge. Our checking system is familiar to every traveler. In the United Kingdom the passenger receives no baggage check. Upon arriving at the station his trunks are taken in charge by the station porter who sees that each piece of baggage is marked with the name of the station of destination. The porter also sees that the baggage is put into the "luggage van." Upon arriving at the end of his journey, the passenger identifies and claims his luggage. The British railways permit the passenger to take a large weight of free baggage; on the Continent, however, free baggage is usually limited to 56 pounds, and in a number of countries no free baggage allowance is granted. The checking system prevails on the Continent, the check consisting of a paper slip, the adhesive half of which is pasted to the piece of baggage and the other half given to the passenger.

Developing Passenger Traffic.—The passenger traffic on American railways can hardly be said to be highly developed. The average number of passengers per train in 1907 was only 51, and the increase in the average passenger train load had been 38 per cent in ten years. During this decade the average load of freight trains had risen from 205 to 357 tons, a gain of 75 per cent. It is evident that there might be a large increase in the number of persons carried per train without incurring a very great additional expense.

The traffic departments of our railways wisely devote much effort to increasing travel, and their advertising methods are matters of such common knowledge that they do not require explanation or recital. The work done by the agents who solicit the patronage of conventions and who arrange for the great variety of popular excursions is effective, and of profit to the railways.

People may be induced to travel in greater numbers by offering them an improved service or by reducing fares. In general, the policy of American railroads has been to increase traffic by improving the service; on the other hand, the practice of European roads has been to appeal to the masses of the people by offering an inexpensive third-class service at specially low fares. It must be admitted that the European method has proven more successful. There is unquestionably a large demand for a cheap passenger service, and it may yet be found advisable for American railroads to introduce a regular second-class service by running both first-class and second-class day coaches on their ordinary passenger trains.

The Ticket Scalping Abuse.—One reason why American railways have not favored the introduction of special classes of tickets, sold at less than regular rates, has been the difficulty of keeping these tickets out of the hands of "scalpers." Brokers in many cities do a large business buying and selling mileage books, excursion tickets of various kinds, the unused portions of through and return tickets, and all kinds of tickets which can be sold for less than the full fare and still yield the broker a profitable commission. This business is objectionable not only for the reason just cited, but also because it encourages dishonesty. Oftentimes it is necessary for the passenger to forge the signature of some other person in order to use the cut-rate ticket. In several States, ticket scalping has been prohibited—it should be by all of the States. Such laws, however, should require the railroads to redeem the unused portions of all railroad tickets; indeed, most rail-roads do this now, even though not compelled to do so by law.

The Electrification of the Passenger Service.—The most important fact regarding the present development of the passenger service is the rapid growth of the mileage of electric railways. Starting as street railways in the cities, the electric lines became suburban and interurban and in so doing took over from many steam railroads a large part of the short distance traffic. The construction of relatively long distance electric lines, such as the West Jersey & Sea-shore Railroad from Camden to Atlantic City, N. J., is becoming increasingly frequent. It is thought by many engineers that the time is not far distant when the local passenger services of the trunk line railroads will be elec-trically handled. There can be no doubt but there will be an increasingly large share of the traffic carried by electric lines and that this will result in a somewhat lower rate of fare. Heavy passenger trains, running at relatively long intervals and drawn by powerful steam locomotives, will more and more give place to trains of two, three or four motor cars operated upon a schedule of frequent ser-vice.

CHAPTER IX

THE EXPRESS SERVICE OF THE RAILWAYS

What the Express Traffic Includes.—The express traffic of the railways consists in general of the commodities, other than mail matter and passenger baggage, that are transported on passenger trains. Over a few routes, the traffic is heavy enough to cause the railroads to operate trains made up only of express, or of mail and express cars. The articles most frequently shipped by express are small parcels, valuable business papers and documents, printed matter too heavy for the mails, currency and coin, and perishable commodities requiring more rapid transportation and a quicker delivery than can be secured through the freight service. The companies doing express business in the United States have been able to secure the business of handling small packages, because up to the present time the United States Government will not accept domestic mail packages weighing more than four pounds. In most foreign countries packages weighing eleven pounds are regularly carried through the mails.

Relation of Express and Freight Traffic.—The shipper of a package whether large or small has the option of making his shipment by express or by freight. If the articles are sent as freight they will be handled at about fifteen miles an hour, and the consignee will be obliged to claim the articles at the railway company's freight depot. If the articles are dispatched as express, the express company will call at the shipper's residence or place of business for the packages which will be transported on trains that run from thirty to fifty miles an hour, and when the articles arrive at their destination they will be promptly delivered to the consignee. There is, however, little real competition between the express and freight services, because, by agreement between the railroad and express companies, the charges for the express traffic are made so much higher than freight rates as to limit the express business mainly to relatively small parcels of high value.

The Express Company.—In countries other than the United States, parcels are handled by the railroad companies themselves or by the Government post office; but in our country the railroads and the Government have thought best to allow most of the parcel traffic to be conducted by express companies; the main exception to this being that a few of the railroad companies have granted a monopoly of the express over their lines to subsidiary companies. Formerly, there were numerous large express companies, but most of these have been consolidated into six large ones—the United States, the Adams, the American, the Pacific, the Southern, and Wells, Fargo & Company. These six companies have, in a general way, divided the field among themselves, each company having most of the traffic in its particular section. Moreover, in so far as different companies are interested in the same section, or to the extent that they come into traffic competition, their relations are regulated by mutual understanding. There is no violent, and little active, competition among the express companies.

Agreements between Express Companies and Railway Companies.—Each large railroad company grants a monopoly of its parcel traffic to a single express company. The agreement between the two contractors stipulates that the express company shall handle, load and unload the parcels; shall assume the risk for loss and damage, and shall pay the railroad company forty per cent (sometimes a larger percentage) of the gross receipts from the express traffic for furnishing and hauling the cars used. When the volume of express traffic is relatively light, the portion of the rates paid to the railroad may be as much as fifty to sixty per cent; this, however, is unusual. The receipts obtained by the express company for the transmission of money, bullion and jewelry are usually exempted from the payments made to the railroads. Another important agreement between the two companies is that the express company may charge such rate as it may think best, provided that the minimum express rates shall be a fixed percentage (fifty to one hundred and fifty per cent) above the charges which the shipper would have to pay were the goods dispatched as freight.

Rates on Express Traffic average from three to four times what the freight charges would be, and are based upon the value and character of the goods, the quantity shipped, the distance and speed of transportation, and the kind of services rendered by the company in collecting and distributing the articles. Weight and distance are, however, the main factors in rate making. The minimum charge for a package is usually twenty-five cents, and the company assumes the risks against loss; but if the shipper places a value of over fifty dollars upon the package, an extra charge is made to cover the additional risks. For the transportation of money the charges vary according to the amount declared to be in the package; and, because of the greater weight and bulk of coin, the rate on gold is twenty-five per cent, and on silver, fifty per cent greater than for transporting paper currency.

The Organization of the Express Service is relatively simple. The older express companies have the partnership, and the later companies the corporate form of organization. Subject to the general officers of the company is a general superintendent, under whom there are division superintendents in charge of the company's business in different sections of the country. Station agents have charge of the receipt and delivery of goods, and messengers accompany the articles in transit. A small number of route agents is employed to examine the stations and agencies, and report to the superintendent.

The person consigning goods to an express company receives a receipt containing a description of the goods and a statement of their declared value. The express charges may be paid on receipt of the goods by the company (P. O. R.) or on delivery of the articles to the consignee (collect). The goods shipped are accompanied by a way bill similar to a freight way bill, stating the weight and value of each package, the consignor and consignee, destination, and charges, prepaid or unpaid. The messengers account to the station agents, and the agents to the auditor's office.

The Future of the Express Service.—Whether the railroads will continue indefinitely to turn over the parcels traffic to the express companies is somewhat uncertain. The separate express company came into existence and developed when the railway systems were small and when there were few facilities for handling traffic quickly over long distances. Those times are now past. The principal railroad systems each cover large sections of the country, and the volume of parcels traffic is so great that it would probably be profitable for many of our railroads to take over the service of collecting, billing, transporting and delivering parcels.

It is, however, highly probable that the United States Government will, in the near future, establish a parcels post, and thus admit to the mails a large share of the packages, which are now handled by express companies because the Government now refuses to admit into the domestic mails packages weighing more than four pounds. The arguments in favor of the parcels post are strong, and can hardly fail to prevail in the United States as they have in other countries. It, accordingly, seems probable that the present services of the express companies will, in the course of time, be divided between the post office and the railway freight department. Should this be done, the lighter parcels will be sent through the mails, and the heavier ones as fast freight. In foreign countries, the package traffic has long been handled in this manner.

CHAPTER X

THE DOMESTIC MAIL SERVICE

Volume and Growth of Mail.—Through the service performed by the post office department, the United States comes into daily touch with every citizen and with all classes of business; and the intellectual and material progress of the country may be accurately measured by the volume and growth of the mail traffic. The estimated number of pieces of mail handled in 1906 was 11,361,090,610, the increase since 1901 having been fifty-three per cent. The estimated weight of the mails in 1906 was 1,148,000,000 pounds, or 574,000 tons. These figures, moreover, include only the weight of the mail matter itself and not of the sacks, racks and other equipment necessarily used in transporting the mail. This equipment was heavier than the mail matter itself.

Classification of the Mails.—Mail matter, like freight, is classified but in accordance with different standards. In grouping commodities into classes, the railroads seek to facilitate the shipment of articles and to increase the company's revenues; whereas the aim of the Government is first of all to administer the post office in such a way as to promote public intelligence, and secondly to facilitate business. The railroads seek to make profits; the Government is satisfied if its revenues equal its expenses, which, as a matter of fact, they seldom do.

96

There are four classes of mail. The *first* class includes written matter and sealed packages, upon which the rate of postage is two cents an ounce. The *second* class is made up of newspapers and other periodicals issued at least four times a year. The rate on second-class mail is one cent for each four ounces, except when it is mailed by publishers, for whom the charge is one cent a pound. Local newspapers circulate free of postage within the county of publication, an exception being made in cities having free delivery service. The *third* class is made up of books and printed matter other than periodicals. The rate of postage is one cent for each two ounces. The limit of weight for a package of books is four pounds, except in the case of a single volume exceeding that weight. The *fourth* class is merchandise, upon which the rate is one cent an ounce. The weight limit of four pounds applies in this as in other classes.

Transportation of the Mails.—For the transportation of the mails the Government employs steam and electric railways, steamships, stage coaches, and messengers. Of the total weight of mail and equipment, over five sixths is carried by steam railroads. Three kinds of services are rendered by railroads in carrying the mails. Where the amount to be transported is small and where the mail is sent in closed pouches, the sacks are carried in the baggage car; while upon other routes, where the amount of mail is greater and where the mail is sorted *en route*, a car or part of a car is fitted up as a railway post office which is in charge of one or more postal messengers. Upon the routes where the traffic is heaviest, full sized post-office cars are run; and in a few instances two or more post-office cars may be attached to a train. When the amount of mail to be sent upon any train exceeds 50,000 pounds in weight, the Government may require the railroads to run a special mail train made up entirely of post-office cars.

Star Routes.—There are many post offices located away from the lines of railroads, and thus it is necessary for the Government to have the mails carried by wagon from the railway to the rural post offices. The contracts for these services are made for four-year periods and the routes over which these services are performed are called "star routes," because in the Government's list of postal routes they are starred with an asterisk. In 1908 there were 14,032 star routes. Persons living along the routes over which the star route messenger makes his daily trip have their mails delivered and collected by the messenger as he passes.

Rural Free Delivery.—The most important extension of the postal service during recent years has resulted from the introduction of the rural free delivery, which has proven so popular and has spread so rapidly that there are now more than 40,000 routes over which mail is daily taken to those living in the country. The rural free delivery service differs from the star route service, in that the star route messenger carries the mail between one post office and another and delivers and collects mail only for such persons as may live along the highway connecting the two offices; whereas the rural free delivery messenger starts out from the railway post office and makes a circuit by various roads back to the post office from which he started, delivering and collecting the mail on the way. The star route messenger usually passes the same point twice daily— going and coming. The rural free delivery carrier passes each place on his route only once in making his round.

Railway Mail Payments.—Any railway may be required by the Government to carry the mails and upon such of its trains as the Postmaster-General may select. The railways furnish the equipment needed by the Government, and when the mails are not heavy enough to require the services of a postal messenger the employes of the railroad company are obliged to load and unload the sacks of mail.

When the mails are carried in the baggage car or in the postal compartment of a car, the railroads are paid for their services in accordance with the weight of the mail and the distance it is carried. When the Government requires special post office cars there is an additional payment for the use of the car. The following table shows the rates paid by the Government to the railroads for carrying the mails:

Rates Based on the Weight of the Mails.

Average Daily Weight of Mails Over Whole Route.	Pay per Mile per Annum.	Rate per Ton per Mile.
200 pounds.........................	$42.75	$1.171
500 pounds.........................	64.12	.702
1,000 pounds.......................	85.50	.468
1,500 pounds.......................	106.87	.390
2,000 pounds.......................	128.25	.351
3,500 pounds.......................	149.62	.234
5,000 pounds.......................	171.00	.187
5,000 to 48,000 pounds, per ton..........	20.30	.058
Above 48,000 pounds, per ton..........	19.24	.052

The additional pay received by the railroads when full-sized post office cars are supplied the Government is shown by the following table:

Rates Allowed for Full-sized Post Office Cars.

Length of Car.	Rate per Annum per Mile of Track.	Rate per Mile Run by Cars.
40 feet..............................	$25.00	3.424 cents.
45 feet..............................	27.50	3.767 cents.
50 feet..............................	32.50	4.460 cents.
55 to 60 feet........................	40.00	5.479 cents.

The rates given in the table are for a daily round trip. If a car makes the trip but one way each day, the payment is one half the sum named in the table. In 1908, there were 1,342 full-sized post office cars in use and in reserve.

It will be noted that the rate of compensation per pound or per ton received by the railroads for carrying the mails grows less with the increase in the weight of daily mails. The pay per ton per mile for a daily mail averaging 2,000 pounds, or one ton, is only one half the rate for a daily weight of 500 pounds. As the mail carried grows in weight the pay received by the railroad increases, but not in proportion to the volume of traffic.

It would be too much trouble and would cause delay to weigh the mails every time they are sent. For that reason the Government determines the weight of mail over any route once in four years by having the mails weighed for ninety or more consecutive working days. The average for this period is assumed to be the daily average for the four succeeding years, but the weight normally increases year by year; and it is probable that the railroads are required to carry about ten per cent of the mails free during the last year or two of the four-year period.

The Postal Deficit.—The post office department makes a profit upon first-, third-, and fourth-class mail, but it incurs a very large deficit in handling the second-class mail, most of which pays the very low rate of one cent per pound. About sixty-four per cent of the total weight of mail has the benefit of the cent-a-pound rates, and the receipts therefrom are but 5.19 per cent of the total post office revenue. This is the main cause of the large annual postal deficit. Another cause for this deficit is the expense of the rural free delivery services which is only partly met by the postage on the mail matter handled over those routes. The postal deficit could easily be changed into a surplus by slightly increasing the rates on second-class mail and by the introduction of a rural parcels post.

The Parcels Post.—It is difficult to understand why the United States Government should be the last one of the great nations of the world to introduce a parcels post. If the Government were to accept packages weighing up to ten pounds in weight for delivery in cities, and up to twenty-five pounds in weight for delivery by rural carriers, there would unquestionably be a large increase in the postal revenues; and, what is more important, the public would obtain a much needed service. The private express companies naturally are opposed to a parcels post, and they are supported in their opposition by retail merchants in the smaller cities who are afraid that the large mail-order houses in Chicago and other big cities will secure an undue share of the rural trade. The arguments of the express companies hardly ought to prevail, and if it should be deemed wise to protect the local merchants, the Government can do so by restricting the rural parcels post to the transportation of packages between points along the rural route. After experimenting with the rural delivery parcels post thus restricted, the question of establishing an unlimited parcels post can be decided more intelligently. Ultimately, we shall doubtless follow the practice now prevailing in other countries, and open our mails liberally to the parcels traffic.

CHAPTER XI

RELATIONS OF RAILWAYS WITH EACH OTHER, COMPE-
TITION, POOLS, AND TRAFFIC ASSOCIATIONS

Public Nature and Unity of Railway Services.—Railroad
corporations are created by the State to perform a service
which would otherwise be done by the Government. Although the railroad company is legally a private corporation, its services are of a *public nature,* and the nature of
the service is in no wise changed by the fact that the Government chooses to have the work done by a corporation.
Another important characteristic of the transportation service is that although it consists of many parts performed
by numerous and separate corporations, it requires *unity
of action* on the part of these agencies. Carriers must work
together, if the public is to be well served; and it is the
duty of the Government to promote and enforce such measures of coöperation as will secure unity and harmony of
action on the part of those engaged in the transportation
business.

Relations Coöperative and Competitive.—While railways
must coöperate with each other in performing their services, they are also competitors. Every railroad company
desires to secure an increasing volume of traffic because it
can add to its traffic without proportionately enlarging its
expenses. Its net profits rise with the growth in the volume of business. This is a permanent cause of inter-railway competition. There is, however, another cause which

is even more powerful. Every large railroad company performs the transportation work required to connect the industries in the section of country which it serves with the markets where the products of those industries are sold. It is well known that every large market of the world can be and is supplied from many regions of production. This results in an inter-regional competition among producers to place their goods upon the important markets; and thus the railroads that carry the products to the markets are bound up with this competition; because no railroad company can afford to permit the industries which it serves to decline or to develop more slowly than do the industries served by other railway systems.

When two rival railways compete for the same traffic, their struggle is often so intense as to be called a rate war. A railroad will prefer to take traffic at rates which but little more than cover the extra expenses incurred by handling the particular traffic in question; because anything above this extra expense is profit to the company and contributes something, although but little, towards defraying the general expenses for maintenance, repairs, equipment, structures, and office administration. Stated otherwise, the expenditures of any railroad company are partly of a general character quite independent of particular traffic services, and are in part directly the result of handling traffic. About all a railroad company can save by refusing to take particular shipments are the train costs resulting from handling that particular traffic; and as long as receipts from any class of business cover the train costs and yield a small surplus to be applied to the company's general expenses, every railroad will naturally seek to hold business against competitors.

Agreements to Restrain Competition.—The experience

railroads have had in trying to avoid disastrous rate wars has clearly proven that it is necessary for them to unite on some method of restraining competition. There are four possible methods by which railroad companies may check their rivalries: (1) They may make hard and fast agreements with each other to maintain certain *rates*, each company being left free to secure as much business as possible at those rates; (2) They may contract with each other to divide up their competitive *traffic* according to agreed percentages, each company taking such a share of the total competitive business as it has previously demonstrated itself to be entitled to; (3) The companies may agree to divide up their total *earnings* from competitive traffic according to agreed ratios; (4) The rival roads may divide up the *field*, each company thereby receiving a section of the country within which it is to be allowed to conduct and develop its business unmolested by the other railroads party to the agreement.

Rate Agreements.—The first of these four plans for restraining competition—rate agreements—is much the simplest. As early as 1858, when the leading railroads in the East had become of great enough mileage to be able to engage in competition with each other they began the practice "of agreeing upon remunerative rates." Such agreements worked with fair satisfaction until about 1870, when some companies secured control of through lines from the Atlantic seaboard to Chicago, and began to struggle violently for the control of the traffic to and from the great Mississippi Valley. Then a higher form of inter-railway organization became necessary.

Traffic Associations.—During the decade following 1870, traffic associations were formed to regulate in detail the relations of railway companies with each other. From 1874 to 1876, the powerful Southern Railway & Steamship Association was built up by the genius of Albert Fink. This was immediately followed by the organization of the Trunk

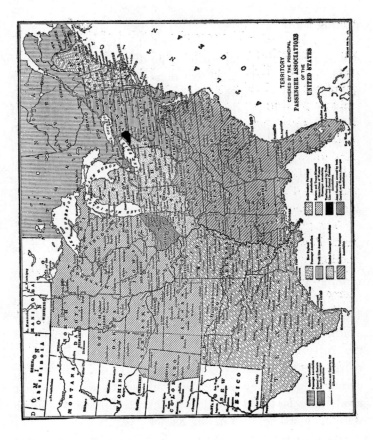

Line Association, the Central Traffic Association, the Western, the Southwestern, the Transcontinental and various others. Usually separate associations were formed for the regulation of freight and passenger traffic. Most of the

original traffic associations have been reorganized once or several times; but they still exist and are an important factor in railway management. The two most salient features of these traffic associations were rate agreements and pooling contracts.

Railway Pools.—The second and third of the four methods of regulating competition—the division of competitive traffic or the division of earnings from that traffic—are popularly called railway pooling. Between 1870 and 1887, railway pooling became general in all parts of the United States. *Pools were agreements among railroads whereby their competitive traffic, or the receipts from that traffic, were divided among the companies according to stipulated ratios.* The arrangements for the division of the business were called traffic pools; those for the distribution of the receipts, money pools.

The public was strongly opposed to railway pooling, because it was thought that the railroads entered into these pooling contracts for the purpose of charging and maintaining extortionate rates. Thus, when the Interstate Commerce Act for the regulation of railroads was passed in 1887, common carriers were prohibited from pooling their competitive profits or earnings thereof. This provision of the Interstate Commerce Act compelled the railroads to reorganize their traffic associations and to omit all pooling arrangements; they were then obliged to regulate their rivalries as best they could by their rate agreements which were made as rigidly binding as possible.

Rate agreements proved ineffective for the regulation of the intense competition that developed during 1893, and the succeeding years of serious business depression. The railway situation was extremely unsatisfactory at this time; and, in 1897, the outlook for the future was made increasingly doubtful by a decision of the United States Supreme Court whereby rate agreements among railroads were held to be in violation of the antitrust law that had been passed in 1890. It now became unlawful for the railroads to decide upon and enforce common rates upon competitive traffic; at the same time, it was clearly impossible for the railroads to carry on their business without having an understanding with each other as to rates on traffic free to move by more than one railway line. For each company to work independently of all others, would be to inaugurate constant warfare and establish transportation chaos. The railroads continued to confer with each other as to rates, and sought to bring about unity of action by informal understanding rather than by formal agreement. Fortunately, this was made possible by the return of prosperous times in 1898, which brought about a rapid increase in the traffic earnings of all railroad companies.

Railway Consolidations.—After 1898, railway consolidation became rapid. This was mainly due to the necessity the railroads felt of controlling their traffic rivalries and of avoiding the waste of competition. There were, however, other contributory causes, the chief of which was the desire of ambitious financiers and large banking firms to build up and control extensive railway systems. Consolidations were brought about (1) by the purchase of one or more railroad companies by those owning another; (2) by long term leases, and (3) by the working out of "community of interest" in the management of distinct companies. The extent to which railway consolidation had been accomplished by 1909 has been explained in Chapter III. The first and second of these three methods of consolidations are self-explanatory; the third calls for a brief description.

Community of Interest.—After numerous large railway systems had been built up by consolidation, it became the practice for the directors of each of those systems to elect to their board, directors or officers from one or more of the other large companies. Thus community of interest was established. Usually community of interest is accompanied by community of ownership, the principal owners of one company being financially interested in other rival roads. In other words, there is ordinarily a community of interest both in ownership and management.

This plan of securing harmonious action among rival interests was well illustrated in the construction of the Board of Directors of the Northern Pacific in 1901. The Great Northern and Union Pacific were each trying to secure control of the Northern Pacific. The struggle also involved the control of the Burlington· System, and thus concerned the interests of the Chicago & Northwestern System, a competitor of the Burlington having close traffic relations with the Vanderbilt or New York Central System. The Chicago, Milwaukee & St. Paul, another competitor of the Burlington, and a road closely connected with the Pennsylvania System, was also interested in the outcome of the contest. The rival parties placed their interests in the hands of J. P. Morgan, who settled the struggle by placing on the directorate of the Northern Pacific the president of the Great Northern, the chairman of the Executive Committee of the Union Pacific, a director of the Chicago, Milwaukee & St. Paul, a director of the Chicago & Northwestern, and a vice-president of the Pennsylvania Railroad.

CHAPTER XII

RAILWAY RATES AND FARES EXPLAINED

Consolidation and Monopoly Charges.—The chief purposes railroad companies have in forming associations and in consolidating are to regulate their services, and to agree as to the rates to be charged upon competitive traffic. As has been explained in the previous chapter, the railroads have not been allowed to coöperate legally in rate making, and for this and other reasons they have proceeded rapidly with consolidation. They have united chiefly to restrain competition and to lessen expenses.

To what extent, it may be asked, does the coöperation of railroads or their consolidation enable them to establish a monopoly. Are railroad rates competitive or monopolistic, or do they partake in part of both characteristics? In order to answer this question it is necessary to agree upon what is meant by monopoly. A manufacturer or a railroad company having the power to fix the prices which the buyer must pay has a monopoly; *monopoly is the power to fix prices.* Any individual or combination having the full power to decide what the producer must pay possesses a complete monopoly. This condition, however, does not exist in many kinds of business. Usually the buyer of commodities or of transportation services has more or less power to determine what prices he shall pay. In such cases, the producer has a partial monopoly and not a complete one; but whether the monopoly which the producer

109

has is partial or complete, the essence of his monopoly is his power over prices. Any business enterprise, whether it be large or small, is monopolistic to the extent that those who manage it can determine what the buyer must pay.

Railway Charges are a Partial, Not a Complete Monopoly. —While it is clear that our great railway systems, some of which own and control practically all of the lines in wide sections of the country, must have large power to determine what transportation charges the public shall pay, it is none the less true that there are competitive forces which railroads cannot control and which prevent them from establishing a complete monopoly in the making of rates and fares:

(1) Every railroad company, as was stated above, is eager to increase the volume of its business, because the net profits upon each ton of freight or upon each passenger are larger the greater the traffic. This being true, every railroad company is careful to keep its rates low enough to permit a steady increase in business.

(2) An even greater influence upon railway charges is exerted by the "competition of markets," by which is meant the efforts of producers in different sections of the country to supply common markets. Every railroad company is a joint producer with the farmers, the manufacturers, miners and lumbermen, helping them to get their products into the world's market at a total cost for production and transportation that will permit the commodities to be sold in large and increasing quantities. It is especially to be noted that this "competition of the markets" is not affected by the consolidation of railroads. The real competition is between the regions of production; and the railroads, whether operated separately or in combination with each other, are involved in the struggle of producers for the

control of, or a share in, the markets. For the trade of the Southern States, for instance, there is active competition between the manufacturers of the New England States and those in the upper Mississippi Valley. Producers shipping from Pennsylvania, New York, or New England to the South secure desirable rail rates, because it is also possible to ship coastwise by water. The manufacturers in Chicago and other cities in the upper Mississippi Valley are able to secure as low rail rates to the South as eastern shippers obtain; because, if the railroads did not grant such rates, the manufacturers in the Middle West would be debarred from southern markets, and the traffic would be lost to the railroads.

(3) The local shipper served by only one railroad is not completely at the mercy of the carrier, since his rates are not permitted by law to be higher than those granted to producers shipping past him to common markets. Furthermore, the traffic officials know that if they make their local rates too high new industries will not be established along their line, but along the roads of rival carriers that offer favorable rates and services.

This brief analysis of the competitive forces in railroad charges shows that the railroad company, however large and powerful it may be, possesses only a partial monopoly in making rates. It is seldom possible for the railroad to compel its patrons to pay *all* they would pay rather than go without the transportation services desired; in other words the railroad company possesses a partial and not a complete monopoly.

Upon What Rates May Be Based.—In most lines of business the charges for services are fixed with reference to the cost of performing the service, and it might be supposed that railways would fix their rates and fares in accordance with the expenses incurred in transporting freight and passengers. If this were the general practice, charges for services of various kinds would vary according to the differences in the cost of performing the several tasks. As a matter of fact, however, railroad charges are based quite as much upon the value of the service to the shipper and upon the value of the article transported as upon the carrier's costs.

Terminal and Line Costs.—Various standards are adopted in fixing charges; and rates and fares must also cover two distinct expenditures, i. e., terminal and line costs. Every railroad company must provide itself with stations and yards, and in large cities these are very expensive. It must, also, load and unload most freight traffic. Experience shows that it costs on an average from 40 to 50 cents per ton to perform necessary terminal services. The maintenance of a roadway between terminals and the operation of trains give rise to the line costs. It will be seen that terminal expenses do not depend upon length of haul or the distance traveled by passengers; while, on the contrary, line expenses vary with, although not strictly in proportion to, the distance.

The Cost of Service Basis of Rate.—While rates and fares are influenced by the cost of the services, it is impossible to make cost the sole or main basis of charges, because the cost of particular transportation services cannot be ascertained. Every railroad carries thousands of different commodities; a single freight train will usually have a large variety of articles in its cars and often many kinds of goods are shipped in the same car. To run its trains and to handle its cars, there must be a roadway, depots and yards, and thousands of dollars of general expenses must be incurred to maintain and operate the railroad as a whole. The gross receipts from passengers and shippers must cover all expenses, but no one is able to say just what part of the company's total expenses results from transporting a hundredweight or carload of goods, or from carrying a passenger a given number of miles. Most of the expenditures of a railroad company are joint costs, only a part of its outlay can be charged against individual services. In other words, the cost cannot be made the exact basis of railroad charges, because the cost cannot be determined.

The Value of Service Basis.—If a bushel of wheat is worth 90 cents in Chicago and $1.00 in New York, the transportation of wheat from Chicago to New York adds 10 cents to its value, i. e., the value of the service to the Chicago shipper is about 10 cents; and the railroad company can, if it chooses, make that increase in value the basis of its rates. Similarly, if travelers on an average value a railroad trip from Philadelphia to Chicago at $15.00, the railroads can make that value the basis of their fare. In all rate making, traffic officials study carefully the value of the service to shippers and travelers, and seek to charge "what the traffic will bear."

Value of Commodities Basis, or Taxation Principle.—It will be found in studying railroad rates that the value of the commodity also has much influence upon the charge made by the carrier. Articles of high value, like silks, can pay a high rate, while charges on cement, coal and iron must be low; often the low rate on such a commodity as coal may be thirty per cent or forty per cent of its value, at point of production, while the high rate on silk may be less than one per cent of its value at the mill. If rates were fixed mainly in accordance with the value of the articles, railway charges would be similar to taxation, and the carriers would secure their necessary revenues by taxing producers and shippers certain percentages of the value of their goods. The tax principle, however, cannot be carried so far as this in the making of rates.

Competition and Rate Making.—It is the duty of the traffic official to make such rates and fares as will hold traffic against competitors; and, in the case of an extensive railway system, competition exists in many forms and at many places. The traffic will not bear a higher rate than is offered by a competing railway line or water route; and, while the traffic official will be influenced in fixing his rates: (1) by measurable differences in cost of service; (2) by the value of the service to the shipper, and (3) by the value of commodities transported, he will, to a considerable extent, be obliged to disregard all of these standards and make his rates conform to competitive conditions. Whatever he does, he must, if possible, secure an increasing volume of traffic for his company.

Rates Must be Reasonable and Just.—In making rates to meet competitive conditions, some localities are certain to receive more favorable treatment than others do. The discriminations, however, between persons, places, and different commodities must be reasonable; the rates must be just. The railroads must not so discriminate against any place as to prevent its healthy development. The chief purpose of Government regulation of rates is to prevent the competitive struggles of railroad companies from resulting in unreasonable discriminations in rates. It is the business of the State to see that localities and shippers are treated with absolute and relative justice.

What is a Reasonable Rate?—There is no mathematical formula by which a reasonable rate may be determined. It is certain, however, that rates cannot be lower than the extra cost resulting from the performance of the particular services for which the charges are made. If the State were to fix rates below that point, it would soon destroy the value of the railroad property. It is equally true that railway charges cannot be greater than the value of the service to the shipper or traveler. If the railroads were to attempt to make the rates higher than the value of the service, the traffic would rapidly decline. Thus the additional cost of performing a particular service fixes the minimum below which the railroad charges cannot go; and the value of the service fixes the maximum beyond which they cannot rise. The *reasonable rate* is somewhere between these two extremes, and *must be determined for each class of traffic or each important commodity with reference to measurable costs of service, and with regard to the value of the article.* The actual fixing of rates by traffic officials and their regulation by the Government involve an exercise of human judgment rather than the solution of a mathematical problem.

CHAPTER XIII

HOW RATES AND FARES ARE MADE

Rates More Important than Fares.—The conditions controlling the making of freight rates are so different from those that prevail in determining passenger fares that it will be well to consider the two separately. It is much easier to decide upon and enforce passenger fares than it is to fix freight rates, and the policy of the railway company in regard to freight charges is of much greater importance. It will, accordingly, be best to devote the larger part of this account of how rates and fares are made to freight charges.

Classification of Freight the First Step in Rate Making.—Inasmuch as every railroad company is called upon to transport many thousand kinds of articles, it is necessary for the railroads to group the commodities into a limited number of classes, and to base the rates as far as possible upon classes instead of upon individual articles. The manner in which the classification of freight was worked out was briefly described in Chapter VII. Efforts have been made from time to time, but thus far unsuccessfully, to prepare a satisfactory classification to apply to the entire country. It has, however, been found practicable to reduce the number of freight classifications in the United States to three—the Official, which is in force north of the Ohio and Potomac and east of the Mississippi; the Southern, south of the Ohio and Potomac and east of the Mississippi;

and the Western, west of the Mississippi. In each of these
territories there is a classification committee of which the
several railroad companies are members, and the classification of freight in each section is decided upon, or is
amended, by action of the classification committee and not
by any individual railroad company. As has been explained above, the classification does not include articles
like grain, livestock, coal, and other articles that are
shipped in bulk and usually in train-load lots. This bulk
freight goes at commodity rates, and the commodities outside of the classification, because of their great volume and
weight, make up more than half of the total tonnage.

Officials Intrusted with Rate Making.—The task of making rates belongs to the traffic department of the railroad.
At the head of this department, there is a vice-president
of the company; and under him, if the company is large,
there will be a freight traffic manager and a passenger traffic manager. Subordinate to the freight traffic manager is
the general freight agent. Large railway systems find it
necessary to subdivide the work of the general freight
agent's office and to have a general freight agent in charge
of local traffic and another to supervise through traffic;
and sometimes there is a third agent in control of coal
freight.

The rate sheets are prepared and issued by the general
freight agent and he is the official to whom the company
looks for the actual making of the rates. The rate sheets
he issues are signed by him and by his immediate superior,
the freight traffic manager. The general freight agent is
controlled as to his general policy of rate making by the
freight traffic manager, who in turn consults with the vice-
president at the head of the traffic department concerning
important questions of policy. Some of the largest, but

only the most important, questions of traffic policy will be brought to the attention of the president and the board of directors.

The making of railroad freight rates for a large railroad system is a difficult task, involving a knowledge of a multitude of details; and it is necessary for the general freight agent to obtain his information from those under him, the division freight agents and their subordinates, the freight solicitors, who come into closer touch with business in different sections of the country served by the railroad, and who have personal acquaintance with the larger patrons of the company.

Rates on Local Traffic.—If the traffic upon which the rates are made according to the method just described is local to the lines of the company making the rates, the general freight agent publishes and issues his rate sheets without consulting with competing carriers. All rates on interstate traffic must be filed with the Interstate Commerce Commission at Washington and do not become effective until thirty days after they have been thus filed. Many companies have such a large coal traffic that the making of coal rates is in the hands of the general coal freight agent whose method of procedure in the determination of actual charges is similar to that for other kinds of traffic.

Competitive and Through Rates—Functions of Freight Traffic Associations.—In the making of competitive and through rates, the general freight agent, or the traffic manager, will not reach a final decision until he has consulted the traffic officials of other railroads that may be affected by the proposed rate. The conferences in regard to these rates take place at meetings of the freight traffic associations. Every railroad company is a member of one or more traffic associations. Formerly, competitive and through rates were decided by formal action of the traffic association, which imposed penalties upon its members for violation of the rate agreement; but, in 1897, the Supreme Court held such agreements to be a violation of the antitrust law. Since that time, it has been necessary for each railroad company to act independently in the making of its rates; as a matter of fact, however, competing and connecting lines have to be consulted with, and rates are informally decided upon at the meetings of the traffic associations. The rates thus found to be acceptable to all interested carriers are put into effect by separate action of the individual companies. No attempt is made to enforce these informal rate agreements by fines and penalties.

Rates in Trunk Line & Central Traffic Association Territory—The Percentage Tariff System.—In the Trunk Line & Central Traffic Association territory east of the Mississippi and north of the Ohio and Potomac, the through rates on classified traffic over the numerous competing lines to and from the many centers of industrial competition have been worked out by taking for a basis the rate from Chicago to New York by the shortest line. East-bound class rates to New York from other points than Chicago are fixed percentages of the rate from Chicago to New York. On west-bound class rates, likewise, the New York-Chicago rate is the base, and the rates from New York to other cities than Chicago are percentages of the base rate.

The principle may be illustrated by referring to the west-bound class rates. The rates from New York to Buffalo, Pittsburg and Erie, that is, to the Lakes and the Ohio River, are tariffs established by each of the trunk lines, acting nominally independent, and the charges are, in general, in accordance with distance. To points west of

Buffalo, Erie and Pittsburg another system of rate making, the percentage plan, applies. The rate from New York to Indianapolis, for instance, is ninety-three per cent of the rate from New York to Chicago; to places west of Chicago, the charge is greater than to Chicago— Peoria, Ill., for example, having a rate from the Atlantic seaboard of one hundred and ten per cent of the rate to Chicago.

The same general principle applies east-bound on class traffic. In Central Traffic Association territory, the east-bound rates to points as far east as Buffalo, Erie and Pittsburg are the distance tariffs of the Central Freight Association; while from all points other than Chicago in Central Traffic Association territory to New York and other places east of Buffalo, Erie, Pittsburg and Wheeling, the charges are certain percentages of the Chicago-New York rate. From Detroit to New York the rate is seventy-two per cent of the Chicago-New York rate. From Chicago to Albany the rate is ninety-six per cent of the Chicago-New York charge; from Indianapolis to Albany, ninety-three per cent of the Chicago-Albany rate.

The map of the Central Traffic Association territory and of a portion of Lower Canada marks the boundaries of the districts having like percentages of the Chicago-New York (east-bound) rates. The percentage rate system is in reality a zone tariff system; because the same rates to New York apply from irregularly concentric strips or zones of territory. The map is adapted from one in Ripley's *Railway Problems*, where a full account of the Trunk Line and Central Traffic rate system is given.

Rates in Southern Territory—The Basing Point System.— South of the Ohio and east of the Mississippi, the main feature of rate making is the basing point system. The rates to each of the larger cities where competition prevails is made the basis of the charges to local points adjacent to such centers. The principal cities of the South, which are the main centers for the collection and distribution of traffic, are called basing points. Rates at basing points are

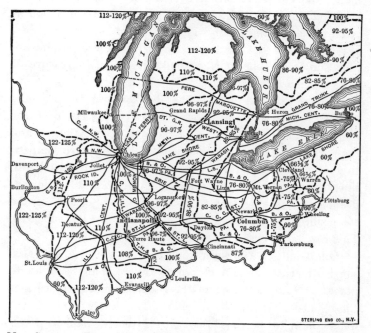

MAP SHOWING RATE PERCENTAGES IN CENTRAL TRAFFIC ASSOCIATION TERRITORY ON EAST-BOUND TRAFFIC. The map states the percentage of the Chicago-New York rate applying in each section.

fixed subject to competition of alternate routes to and from those cities. The rate from a distance to local towns in the region about a basing point city is the sum of the rate to the basing point, plus the local tariff from the basing point to the local town. For instance, the rate from Philadelphia to a town within twenty-five or fifty miles of Atlanta, Ga., is the rate from Philadelphia to Atlanta, plus the rate from Atlanta to the adjacent town. If this local point is on the way from Philadelphia to Atlanta, it pays a higher rate than Atlanta for a shorter haul. This discrimination against the smaller town has been held to be legal because of the greater competition at Atlanta, the basing point. This system of rate making does not apply to quite all the southern territory, but its application is so general as to make it the main feature of the southern rate policy.

Transcontinental Rates—The Blanket System.—For the traffic moved east and west between the section of the United States adjacent to or near to the Atlantic and the region bordering on the Pacific, there is active competition of two kinds. The numerous transcontinental rail lines compete with each other and they, as a whole, endeavor to hold the traffic against the competition of the steamship lines handling traffic between our two seaboards. This has had two results:

One result is a lower rate from points east of the Missouri River to the Pacific coast States than is given to places *en route* situated in the States immediately east of those bordering on the Pacific. The lower rate on the longer haul to the coast than on the shorter haul to places in Utah, and Nevada, etc., is given to meet the competition of the steamship lines. The other result has been to cause the rate to the Pacific seaboard terminals, from San Diego to Seattle, to be the same from all points east of the Missouri River. The charge from New York to San Francisco is no higher than from St. Louis or Kansas City to San Francisco on practically all kinds of freight.

This is called the *blanket system* of rate making, by

which is meant that the whole territory east of the Missouri River is blanketed by the same west-bound rate. The rate from any point east of the Missouri River to an intermediate point, as Reno, Nev., just east of the Sierra Nevada Mountains, is determined as follows: to the blanket rate from the eastern point of shipment to the nearest Pacific terminal, which in this case would be Sacramento, is added the local rate from Sacramento to Reno. The traffic is hauled only as far as Reno, but the rate is the sum of the rate to Sacramento, plus the rate from Sacramento to Reno.

Transcontinental rates east bound are not blanketed over so wide a territory in the east as are those on traffic moved in the opposite direction. Local or distance tariff rates prevail from the Pacific terminals to the Missouri River points; then all places in the territory between the Missouri and Mississippi rivers pay a fixed sum or differential above the rate to the Missouri River. All places between the Mississippi River and Chicago have the same differential above the rate to the Mississippi. This rate is again increased by a fixed sum for shipments to all points between Chicago and Pittsburg, and the rates to points between Pittsburg and the Atlantic seaboard are a fixed amount above the rate to Pittsburg. In other words, the rate from the Pacific seaboard to points east of the Missouri River are graded up by relatively wide zones.

The Making of Passenger Fares.—Each large railroad company has a passenger traffic manager under whose immediate supervision is the general passenger agent, who is the man that decides upon and issues the schedules of fares. If the fares apply only upon the lines of his own company, they are probably made without consulting competing and connecting carriers; if, however, the fares apply to competitive traffic in which rival lines are interested any proposal regarding such fares is brought to the attention of the passenger traffic association, where it is considered by all lines interested in the proposition. When the members of the traffic association have agreed informally, the general passenger agent, acting solely for his own company, files the rate sheets with the Interstate Commerce Commission, and at the expiration of thirty days required by law, the fares that have been informally agreed upon by all parties in interest become effective through the nominally independent action of the carrier filing the rate sheet.

Special Fares for Special Traffic.—It is well known that the railroads seek to increase travel by offering special fares of many kinds. The most important of these are the commutation rates given to residents in the suburbs of large cities. In this manner, the local traffic of railroads has been greatly stimulated. Excursions of many kinds with largely reduced fares are run at all seasons of the year. Practically every large convention secures special rates, and the railroad solicitors are always eager to secure the convention traffic. Among the other many forms of exceptional traffic, and one that is growing rapidly, is that to winter and summer resorts. The increasing number of people spending the winter in Florida and other southern sections, and the travel to the sea coast and mountains, to New England, to Canada, and to other sections having a cool summer climate, grows year by year with the increase in population and the improvement in transportation facilities.

CHAPTER XIV

PUBLIC AID GIVEN AMERICAN RAILWAYS

The Government Must Both Aid and Regulate Railways.—
This chapter and the three succeeding ones are concerned
with the relation of the Government to the railways. It is
necessary for the State both to aid and to regulate the
railways, and this is true whether the railroads be built
and operated by the Government or by corporations. Regulation, as will be shown later, may take the form of Government ownership and operation, or it may consist of
controlling the services and charges of the corporations
which the Government intrusts with the performance of
the railway transportation business. If the roads are constructed and managed by railroad companies, they must
first be aided by the State with a charter giving them a
large grant of powers. To secure a right of way, it is necessary for the corporation to exercise temporarily the
State's "right of eminent domain." Moreover, in addition to these necessary forms of aid, it has been the practice of both the central and local governments in most
countries to give financial assistance to companies constructing railways. This chapter has to do with public
aid in the United States.

Aid Given by the Several State Governments.—Although
the railways in the United States were built mainly with
private capital, the companies received liberal aid from
the States, from the Federal Government, and also from

counties and cities. The first aid was given by the States. Their assistance began to be active as early as 1837, when the United States Government deposited its surplus revenue with the States. At that time, the aid given to transportation by the States went mainly toward constructing canals and highways, but after 1850, the assistance of the Government was given principally to the railroads. The financial help which the States gave to canals and railways was more liberal than was warranted by their revenues. The ideas of the public at that time in regard to banking and financial methods were crude; and, as a consequence, many States contracted such heavy debts that they were seriously embarrassed for a long time. Some States even went so far as to repudiate their debts.

The assistance given by the States to railroad construction consisted most often of the purchase of the stocks of the corporations. Sometimes the States bought and paid for them either in cash or in State bonds. In some instances loans were made to the companies; but most of the sums thus advanced were never repaid, and the loans became gifts. The amount of aid given by the States is not definitely known. There were, in all, nineteen States which gave or advanced public funds for railroad construction, and among those that contracted especially large debts were Illinois, Indiana, Michigan, Georgia, Tennessee, North Carolina, South Carolina, Missouri, Virginia and Louisiana. Missouri, for instance, invested $32,000,000 in railroads and received back into the treasury only a little over $6,000,000 of that sum; Tennessee's railroad debt amounted to $29,234,000. The total investments of the States in railroads must have run into the hundreds of millions.

The Results of State Aid were comparatively small. This was due in part to the disastrous financial methods followed by the States, and in part to the aid given to railroads that were built in advance of the needs of the sections they were intended to serve. Some of the States built railroads as government works, but most of the State lines were subsequently turned over to corporations for a mere fraction of the original cost. It is not, however, to be inferred that the State funds were altogether wasted. Many parts of the United States were served by railroads earlier than they could have been without public aid. The resources of the Central West and the South were developed somewhat earlier than they could have been without State aid to railroads.

Federal Assistance to Railways: Land Grants.—The United States began to aid railroad construction on a large scale in 1850 by grants from the public domain. The first grant was made to assist the building of a railroad from Chicago to the Gulf. It was thought at that time that the United States did not have the constitutional power to make grants of land directly to corporations to build railroads within the States; accordingly, the grants in 1850 were made to Illinois and other States as trustees, the land to be turned over by the States to the railroad company in accordance with the terms of the grant. During the twenty years beginning with 1850, about eighty such grants as these were made to the States to be used by them in assisting railroad construction in the Mississippi Valley.

In 1862, the United States entered upon a second phase of its land-grant policy by donating large tracts of land directly to various railroad companies, to use in building a continuous railroad from the Missouri River through to the Pacific Ocean. The total area of land granted to aid in the construction of the first transcontinental railroad was 33,000,000 acres—an area considerably greater than the State of Pennsylvania. Much of the land, however, in this and the other grants to Pacific lines was of small value, because of its location in mountainous and arid regions.

Between 1862 and 1871, when Congress made its last land grant, twenty-three companies received direct donations from the public domain. The total area of land placed at the disposal of the railway companies from 1850 to 1871 was about 159,000,000 acres, an area more than five times that of Pennsylvania. The railroad companies did not meet, nor have they yet fulfilled, all the conditions which have to be met before the land granted is actually patented or turned over to the companies. Up to June 30, 1908, 110,861,353 acres had been patented to the railroad companies from the lands previously granted. The original grants gave assistance to about 15,000 miles of railroads.

Aid by National Loans.—The seven companies which undertook to build the first transcontinental line received, in addition to the 33,000,000 acres of land, large blocks of United States bonds. These companies came into existence during the Civil War, and probably for that reason were given financial assistance. Most of the money went to the Union Pacific Company, which built a line from Omaha to near Ogden, and to the Western Pacific and the Central Pacific companies which constructed a road from Sacramento eastward to the neighborhood of Ogden. These three companies received over $55,000,000 of United States six per cent bonds; while the other companies interested in this first transcontinental line obtained assistance which brought the total to the seven companies up to $64,623,512.

The aid given was the right to sell United States thirty-year six-per-cent bonds. The companies were to pay the interest on the bonds, and to return the principal to the

United States at maturity. The railroads did not prosper as was expected, the United States had to pay the larger part of the current interest; and it was supposed for a long time that the companies would not be able to pay the principal when the bonds became due. The Government had a second mortgage on the railroads, and could have taken over the lines had it chosen to do so. Fortunately, this was not necessary; for the properties had become valuable enough when the bonds fell due, between 1895 and 1899, to enable the United States to secure from the companies all of the principal of its loans and the larger part of the interest which it had advanced for the companies during the life of the bonds.

The results of the Federal aid to railways were most unsatisfactory. It can be seen now that Congress was too eager to dispose of the public lands which have already become so scarce as to make us wish that they had been held for sale only to actual settlers. The Mississippi Valley was, it is true, connected with the Pacific coast much earlier than would have been possible without national aid to railroads, but to secure this result unnecessarily large assistance was given by Congress. Moreover, there were shameful scandals connected with the legislation to aid the Pacific railroads.

County and Municipal Aid.—Throughout the Central West, and to some extent in the East, the counties and the cities were so eager to secure new railroads that they issued bonds to secure funds with which to assist the railroad companies. In the State of New York, the counties and municipalties voted $30,000,000 to aid railroads; in Illinois the sum equaled about $20,000,000. The exact amount given by the counties and towns and cities in the various States is not known, but it probably amounted to several hundred million dollars. The sum is much larger than is realized by those who have not studied the subject.

The communities that made these large sacrifices did so because they felt that their economic progress depended entirely upon their securing access to markets. Their farms were productive, their manufactures were promising; but industry could not thrive unless the products could be marketed. The railroads shrewdly took advantage of this situation. A favorite method by which the companies secured a large bonus was that of surveying two alternate routes—a route through each of two rival towns or counties—for the purpose of getting the towns or counties to bid against each other for the railroad.

Other Public Aid.—The aid given by the public was by no means all in the form of Government assistance. Enterprising and public-spirited farmers and merchants living along the line of a proposed road were easily persuaded by the company to buy stocks and to assist in the building of the road. In some instances, the stocks thus bought proved to be good investments; but often they did not, because the companies which built the lines were so financed during the period of construction that bankruptcy of the company and the sale of the property followed closely upon the completion of the road. In this way, the original investors lost all or much of their capital.

The injustice of this resulted from the fact that the railroads thus aided by individual investors consisted mainly of branch lines, or feeders of the main lines. When a branch line was to be constructed, the company really interested in the line often did not directly finance and build it; but created a subsidiary corporation whose stock was sold to individual investors. The bankruptcy of the road that built the branch line, enabled the larger company for which the branch line was really being built to secure its feeder for a relatively small actual investment.

The foregoing brief account of public aid to railways in the United States shows that in many sections of the country the early lines were built largely at the expense of the communities and individuals the roads were constructed to serve. In this fact is to be found a partial explanation of the intense opposition to the railroads which developed in the seventies when the people of the West and South realized that the railroads, whose construction they had aided, were giving lower rates to the big cities and the large shippers than they were to the merchants and farmers living in and about the smaller towns.

CHAPTER XV

RAILWAY REGULATION BY THE STATES—THE STATE COMMISSIONS

The Powers of the States and Nation Over Railways.—The Constitution of the United States gives Congress the power "to regulate commerce with foreign nations and among the several States and with the Indian tribes." The commerce carried on entirely within a State is subject to State authority. International and interstate commerce and carriers may be regulated by Congress; while intrastate commerce and carriers are under the control of the States. Thus, in addition to the Federal Government, there are forty-six States and two territories having power to regulate railroad transportation.

Early State Regulation.—Railway companies, with the exception of those which have built roads within Federal territory, have received their charters from the States; thus the States have always had it within their power to decide what the railroad companies might or might not do. Some of the early charters attempted to regulate railroads in detail; but this practice was not continued and there was, as a matter of fact, but little regulation of the railroads by the States prior to 1870. Indeed, from 1850 to 1870, the prevailing political theory in the United States was that that Government was best that governed least. This theory worked fairly well while the railroad and other corporations were small concerns; but, when they became

132

large and powerful, the public realized that the Government must be something more than a policeman. It was found to be necessary for the Government to regulate the relations of railroads with each other and to the public; and, since 1870, the tendency has been towards increasing public supervision and control of the services and rates of public carriers.

The Legislation of the Seventies.—It was shortly before 1870 that the public demand for Government regulation of railways became insistent. The main cause of this demand on the part of the public was the discrimination in rates and fares which favored the large cities and big shippers to the real or supposed detriment of the small towns and shippers. It was also felt, particularly in the Central West, that railway charges were not only unjust in their discriminations; but that they were higher than they ought to be. The farmers of the West had come to have a large surplus of grain and other farm products which they were eager to market in the East and to export to Europe. Thus they began to clamor for lower rates. The agitation for the regulation and control of the railroads brought about the establishment of State Railroad Commissions. Most of those in the East were given power only to supervise the carriers; while those in the West and South, for the most part, had authority to issue orders to the railroads and to make and revise rates.

The Commission with Power to Supervise and Advise.— The first commission of the advisory type was created by Massachusetts, in 1869; and the other States that adopted commissions of this kind were largely influenced by the provisions of the Massachusetts law. The commission created by Massachusetts consisted of three men appointed by the Governor with the consent of the State Council; the term of office was three years, one man being appointed each year. The commission was given authority (a) to ascertain whether the railway companies were living up to the terms of their charters and were obeying the laws; (b) to supervise the roads with reference to the security and accommodation of the public; (c) to investigate the railroads either upon the commission's own motion or upon complaint of some shipper or traveler; (d) to prescribe and enforce a system of keeping accounts; (e) to act as a board of arbitration to settle disputes between the corporations and the public; and (f) to make an annual report, with recommendations, to the Legislature. It will be seen that the Massachusetts commission had no authority to issue orders or to enforce its decisions. The theory of the law was that the railroads would be regulated by the force of public opinion and by enactment of such laws as the Legislature might think necessary.

The Commission with Power to Issue Orders and to Make and Revise Rates.—The railway problems in the Southern, and, particularly in the Western, States were more acute than in the East; and it was believed by the people of the South and West that the railroad corporations, being public carriers engaged in performing a service of a public nature, should have their services and the charges therefor regulated by public authority. To accomplish his, the so-called "granger" laws were passed. The legislation for the control of railroad rates was given the name of "granger" laws; because in the early seventies an association of the farmers by the name of the Patrons of Husbandry, the local chapters of which were called granges, was being organized and rapidly built up in the West and South. The agitation for the Government control of the railroads was a movement that started with the people of the smaller towns as well as with the farmers. After this movement was under way it was taken up and carried forward by the "grangers."

The " Granger " Laws were of two kinds: those which fixed railway rates by stating in acts of legislation what the rates should be; the other and more usual practice was for the State to establish a railroad commission with power either to prescribe and enforce schedules of rates, or with power to revise the rates after the charges had been put into force by the railroad companies. The so-called Potter law, passed by the State of Wisconsin in 1874, was a type of the laws fixing rates by act of Legislature. The State of Illinois, by laws which it passed in 1871 and 1873, created a railroad commission whose duty it was to prescribe a "schedule of reasonable maximum rates of charges for the transportation of passengers and freight." This Illinois law, which may be taken as a type of those which created "commissions with power," gave to the railroad commission all the authority possessed by the similar body in Massachusetts; and, in addition thereto, the power to prescribe rates and to prosecute the railroad companies in the courts for failure to obey the orders of the commission either in regard to rates or concerning other matters over which the commission was given jurisdiction.

Naturally, the railroad companies opposed the granger laws in the courts, and every effort was made to prove the laws unconstitutional; but, in 1877, the United States Supreme Court held the laws to be valid and declared that the States had authority to regulate railway services and charges. The main principles for which the "grangers" contended were then upheld, and have since been extended by State and national legislation and by judicial decisions.

The Present Commissions.—At the present time, as is

shown by the accompanying map, there are only six States
—Delaware, Maryland, West Virginia, Idaho, Wyoming,
and Utah—and two territories, Arizona and New Mexico,
that have no railway commissions.   The map shows the type
of commission established by each State.   There are but a
few States now having the Massachusetts type of commission with only advisory powers.   By far the greater number
have commissions with power to fix or revise rates; and of
such commissions there are three subclasses: The largest of
these three subclasses is that in which the commission has
jurisdiction only over steam railroads; the second subclass
of commissions with power is represented by Virginia,
North Carolina and Oklahoma, which States have given
their commissions authority over corporations generally.
The third and latest form of the mandatory commission
is one having jurisdiction over public utilities—steam and
electric railways, telegraph and telephone companies, and
other municipal public service corporations.   Wisconsin
and New York have public service commissions.

The Public Service Commission.—The establishment of
State commissions with authority over street railways and
municipal and other public service corporations as well as
over steam railroads, marks a distinct step forward in dealing with the large problem of public regulation of corporations.   The American people are indebted to New York
State for having been the first one to create a public body
of this character.   In 1906, New York established two public service commissions, one with jurisdiction over the city
of Greater New York and the other with authority over
the remainder of the State.   These bodies are intrusted
with the regulation of the services and the charges, the
finances and the accounts of steam and electric railways
and gas and electric lighting corporations.   Much has al-

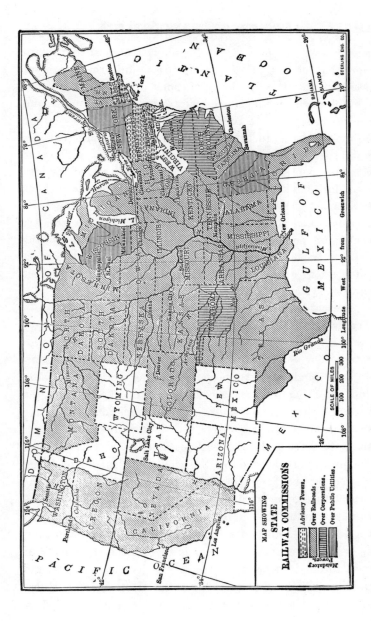

MAP SHOWING

STATE

RAILWAY COMMISSIONS

Mandatory Powers.
Advisory Powers.
Over Railroads.
Over Corporations.
Over Public Utilities.

SCALE OF MILES
0 100 200 300

ready been accomplished. Possibly, the most important work has been that of prescribing a uniform system of accounting, whereby the operations of the railways and their financial methods are made known to the public, and are thus subjected to regulation both by law and by public opinion. It was fortunate for Greater New York that this public service commission was created shortly before the company controlling the surface street railways of the city went into bankruptcy as the result of its previous reckless financiering. The interests of the public are being safeguarded, and the transportation facilities of this greatest center of population in America will be better in the future; because there has been a commisson with powers sufficient to enable it to assist in reconstituting the street railway system of New York.

Present Tendencies in the State Regulation of Railways.— Nearly all of the commissions established since 1890 have been given power to enforce their orders and to revise rates. The States are disposed to give their commissions greater administrative powers, such as those prescribing and enforcing uniform accounting, and of regulating the issue of stocks and bonds. The commissions now have from three to five members; the salaries are much larger than were formerly thought necessary; and the members are usually appointed by the Governor instead of being elected by the voters of the State as was frequently the case with the early commissions. These changes have resulted in inducing men of higher standing to become members of State railroad commissions. The most important, as well as the latest tendency is to give the same body of men authority over steam railroads, electric railways, and public utilities generally. As the State commissioners are given larger powers and wider authority, their dignity is enhanced and their opportunities for serving the public are increased. The States are unquestionably making real headway in the needful work of bringing public service corporations under conservative but effective Government regulation.

CHAPTER XVI

RAILWAY REGULATION BY THE UNITED STATES: THE INTERSTATE COMMERCE COMMISSION

Railway Regulation a National Problem.—Not long after the States took up the work of railway regulation, which was in the early seventies, the people of the United States began to realize more and more clearly that the problems the States were endeavoring to solve were in large part inseparably connected with interstate commerce over which the Federal Government had sole jurisdiction. It was seen to be necessary for the States and the National Government to coöperate in the work of railway regulation; because the authority of each State was limited to the services connected with, and charges for, traffic that did not pass its boundaries. It is true that some of the State laws, passed before Congress took action, really applied indirectly and more or less directly to interstate as well as intrastate railway traffic; but, in 1886, the United States Supreme Court, in a case involving the authority of the Illinois Railway Commission, held that the authority of the State was limited to the regulation of traffic within its boundaries.

The Movement for Federal Regulation of Railways.—Upon a recommendation made by President Grant in his annual message in 1872, the Senate of the United States appointed a committee which made a thorough investigation of the question of Federal railway regulation. This committee reported, in 1874, in favor of Federal Legislation. Action, however, was not taken by Congress until 1887, by which time the problem of railway control had been thoroughly investigated by another Senate committee, whose report was submitted in 1886. This Cullom report, so named from its chairman, was accompanied by a bill for the Federal regulation of railways, and this bill with various amendments became the Interstate Commerce Act which was enacted in 1887.

The Interstate Commerce Act.—The act of 1887 has been strengthened from time to time by amendments, the most important of which were the Elkins Act of 1903 and the Hepburn Act of 1906. The former law was aimed particularly at the prevention of discriminations; whereas the Hepburn Act gave the Interstate Commerce Commission, which had been created by the act of 1887, the power to revise railway rates and to prescribe uniform accounting. The main provisions of the Interstate Commerce Law, as now amended, are as follows:

The law applies to passenger and freight traffic carried by railways or by a joint rail and water route; to express- and sleeping-car companies, to pipe lines, and to private car lines. It does not apply to the traffic carried upon all water routes.

It is made unlawful to charge extortionate rates or those which unjustly discriminate between places, persons, or commodities. Free passes are prohibited, and railway companies are not allowed to be producers of any commodities they carry, with the exception of lumber.

It is unlawful for a carrier to " receive any greater compensation in the aggregate for the transportation of passengers or like kinds of property, under substantially similar circumstances and conditions, for a shorter than for a longer distance over the same line, in the same direction, the shorter being included within the longer distance.'' But the commission has power to suspend the enforcement of this provision in the case of carriers that have to meet exceptional conditions of competition. This is known as the ''long-and-short-haul'' clause.

Railways are not allowed to pool their freight traffic or the earnings from their freight or passenger business.

All railroad rates and fares must be printed and filed with the Interstate Commerce Commission. No rates can be put into force until thirty days after they have been filed, nor can they be changed except upon thirty days' notice to the commission, unless the commission gives permission to the carriers to change the rates in less than thirty days.

The penalty for violating this act is a fine of $5,000 for each offense. If the offense be an unlawful discrimination in rates or charges, this penalty may be increased by imprisoning the guilty officials for a term not exceeding two years, and the offending corporations may be subjected to a fine of $1,000 to $20,000 for each day during which the offense is committed.

The administration and enforcement of the act is intrusted to an Interstate Commerce Commission of seven members. One member is appointed each year for the term of seven years at a salary of $10,000 per annum. The principal office of the commission is in Washington, D. C.

The commission has the power to investigate the railways either upon complaint or upon its own motion. The commission cannot prescribe rates; but, upon complaint and after investigation, it can require the carriers to change the fares or rates that have been found to be unreasonable. The equity of the commission's order as to rates can be tested in a Federal Court by formal proceedings instituted by the carriers.

Carriers must obey the orders of the commission within thirty days, unless the carriers can secure from a Federal Court an injunction suspending or annulling the commission's order.

Railways subject to the act must make monthly reports to the commission regarding accidents, operating revenues, and expenses; and must submit an annual report containing detailed information concerning practically every phase of their operations and finances.

All the accounts kept by railway companies must be in accordance with a uniform system prescribed by the commission, which has the power to inspect the books of the railways, and thus to enforce its system of uniform accounting.

Railway Regulation by the Interstate Commerce Commission.—The Interstate Commerce Commission accomplishes its difficult task of regulating the railways by means of three general classes of powers:

The first and most important of these is its power of *investigation*. In the fullest sense of the word, the railway business is now public and not secret. The commission is able to inform itself, the Congress, and the public fully in regard to the services and practices of interstate carriers. This enables the commission to correct abuses, and, what is probably of more consequence, it enables an enlightened public opinion to exercise a large corrective influence over the transportation business.

The hearing of complaints and *the adjustment of rates and fares* is the second great function of the commission. It may not only investigate and recommend, it can also correct. There is no economic problem of greater importance to the people of the United States than an equitable adjustment of railway charges among competing localities. Justice cannot be secured except by public regulation, and Congress has wisely given the commission the power to adjust rates and fares.

The Interstate Commerce Commission *regulates the services and accounts*, and thus exercises a positive, constructive influence upon the management of the railway business. Having been given authority over the accounts of railway companies it has been put in a position where it can improve the business and financial methods of our railway companies. Every company is óbliged to conform to the accounting standards of the best companies. The commission was given control over accounting in 1906, but several years earlier it had been given supervision over equipment as regards safety appliances. Recently, Congress has given the commission the duty of seeking to bring about a more rapid introduction of an effective system of block signaling and of train control on all railroads in the United States. Thus the commission is developing administrative duties as regards railway operations as well as concerning railroad accounting. The Congress has not yet given the commission power to regulate the issue of railroad stocks and bonds and to supervise financial methods; it is probable, however, that these powers also will be given to the commission in the near future.

Results Accomplished—The Future Ideal.—The problem of regulating the vast transportation business of the country seemed almost impossible of solution twenty years ago; but efforts, begun in 1887, have met with more than expected success. Publicity has been given to the railway service, unjust practices have been made illegal, and the laws have become enforceable. Our present ability to enforce law is due to a change in public sentiment. In America only those laws can be enforced that give expression to public opinion. In order to make unjust railway discriminations impossible, it was necessary that the public should condemn, as immoral, secret discriminations and other illegal practices of common carriers. It augurs well for the future that our ethical standards now are such that we are disposed to apply to the public service corporation the same standards of business conduct that we apply to the Government in its dealings with its citizens and with different sections of the country.

CHAPTER XVII

THE COURTS AND RAILWAY REGULATION

The Courts Determine the Meaning and Scope of Laws.—
Although the State laws are made by legislatures and the
governors, and the Federal laws by the Congress and the
President, it is the courts that decide what those laws
mean and to what they apply. It thus comes about that
the laws on some subjects are, to a large extent, '' court
made,'' and this is particularly true of the laws regulating
railroad services and charges.

This fact may be illustrated by reference to a decision
of the United States Supreme Court, in 1897, in which it
was held illegal for the Trans-Missouri Freight Association
to fix and enforce rates on the competitive traffic of the
roads that were members of the association. The court
reached this decision, because it decided that the Sherman
antitrust law, passed July 2, 1890, to prevent the restraint
of trade by the trusts, applied to railroad rate agreements;
although it is quite certain that Congress did not have the
railroads in mind when the law was enacted. The meaning
of practically every section of the Interstate Commerce
acts of 1887 and subsequent years has been passed upon
by court decisions, and the scope of these laws has, in
many particulars, been narrowed, and in others widened
by court interpretation.

Sources of the Courts' Authority.—The courts derive their
authority from the constitution, from the statutes, and

146

from the accepted body of legal precedents which is called
the common law. The basis of the power of the Federal
courts is the United States Constitution; whereas a State
court is subject both to the Federal Constitution and to the
constitution of its own State. Statutory laws are increased
and amended year by year, and they deal with the major
share of individual and corporate rights and duties.
There are, however, numerous relationships, not covered
by statute law, which are regulated by the courts through
the equity powers which they exercise in accordance with
the principles of common law. The authority which the
courts have been given by statutes is definite and fixed;
but the scope of equity jurisdiction, except where determined at certain points by law, may be extended at the
will of the judiciary.

Equity Powers of the United States Courts over Rates.—
This helps to explain why it has been in the exercise of
their equity powers that the courts have had much influence upon the governmental regulation of railways. Every
law fixing a railroad rate involves a question in equity as
to the reasonableness of the rate thus fixed, and this is
equally true when the rates are fixed by State commissions
or by the Interstate Commerce Commission. The fifth
amendment to the Constitution of the United States stipulates that no person '' shall be deprived of life, liberty, or
property without due process of law.'' This limits the
power of Congress. The fourteenth amendment limits the
authority of the States by stipulating that no State '' shall
deprive any person of life, liberty, or property without due
process of law; nor deny to any person within its jurisdiction the equal protection of the laws.'' It has been decided that the word '' person,'' as used in the Constitution,
applies to those artificial persons created by law which we

call corporations. It will thus be seen that neither the
Congress nor State legislatures can pass a law fixing railroad rates so low as to destroy the value of the property
of railroad companies; and the courts have decided that
the property rights of the railroads under the Constitution
include the right to a reasonable profit from the property.
In other words, railroad rates cannot be so low as to prevent the railroads from securing a fair return on their investment.

The Doctrine of Judicial Review.—The principles laid
down in the preceding paragraph are popularly called the
doctrine of judicial review. In its present form this doctrine is that the United States courts have the power to
pass upon the reasonableness of any rate fixed by a State
or by Federal authority. If a State legislature or State
railway commission fixes rates so low that the carriers
think the rates unreasonable, the carriers may now appeal
directly to the United States courts for the annulment of
the State laws on the ground that they violate the Federal
Constitution. It goes without saying that the United
States courts can determine the reasonableness or constitutionality of any rates which may be fixed either by the Congress or by the Interstate Commerce Commission acting
for and under the authority of Congress. All legislative
rates, State or Federal, must be reasonable; and the United
States courts can decide what rates are and what are not
reasonable.

Prevention of Extortionate Railway Rates.—If a railroad
charges a shipper an extortionate rate on traffic from one
point to another place in the same State, the shipper may
sue the railroad company in the State courts to recover
damages. This is a case between two " persons " of the
same State, and can be finally settled by the State supreme

court. If the shipment be from one State to another, the
case against the railroad company must be brought in the
Federal courts; because the United States Government has
jurisdiction over interstate commerce.

If a railroad company announces an increase in rates
that the shippers think will make the charges extortionate,
the persons whose business is in danger of injury from the
proposed rates may appeal to the courts for an injunction
ordering the railroad not to make the proposed increase
in charges. If the court thinks that the prayer for an injunction is justified, it may issue a temporary injunction
ordering the railroads not to increase the rates until the
matter can be argued before the court; after such argument, the temporary injunction will be dismissed if not
found to have valid reasons back of it, or will be made permanent if the court decides that the public interests will
suffer by the higher rates proposed by the carrier. Stated
in a word, the courts may enjoin railroad companies from
charging extortionate rates.

Prevention of Rate Wars.—A violent rate war with the
consequent excessive cutting of rates may be as destructive
of property as extortionate rates would be. If the roads
leading to one city reduce the rates and fares below those
prevailing to and from another competitive city, the latter
place may lose its business, and its merchants and manufacturers may suffer heavy losses. A prolonged war of
rates between two railroads, furthermore, may so reduce
the revenues of the contestants as to destroy the market
value of their bonds, and the creditors of the companies
may thus lose their investments. Such violent and prolonged rate wars as would produce those results seldom
occur at the present time, but formerly they were frequent.
The courts have the same power to prevent the railroads

from charging destructively low rates that they have to order them not to make their rates extortionate. A violent rate war between the Seaboard Air Line and the Southern Railway Company in 1896 was stopped by injunctions of the courts.

The Powers of the State and Federal Courts over Railway Charges may be summarized as follows: The State courts, having jurisdiction over controversies between citizens of the commonwealth, may pass upon the reasonableness of the rates charged by the railways upon traffic moved entirely within the State. The State courts may also pass upon the constitutionality or reasonableness of the rates fixed by a State Legislature or a State Commission—this question, however, may also be decided by the Federal courts. The United States courts may determine the reasonableness of rates fixed by the railroads upon interstate traffic; and may pass upon the constitutionality of charges fixed by Congress, by the Interstate Commerce Commission, by State legislatures, and by State railroad commissions. As explained above, the courts may also be appealed to for injunctions to prevent carriers from charging extortionately high, or destructively low, rates.

Court Injunctions in Labor Disputes.—It is lawful for men, who have not made a contract to give their employers notice of intention to quit work, to quit employment at any time; and men may do this either individually or in a body. It is lawful for men to strike, provided they do so to better their condition, and without a declared intention to injure their employers. The courts, however, may enjoin strikers from doing anything to injure their employers and from using force to prevent men from taking the places formerly held by strikers. This is the general law of strikes.

The powers of the courts to issue injunctions in disputes between railroad companies and their employees is strengthened by the fact that the United States Government has the power to regulate interstate commerce. The Federal courts may enjoin men from interfering with trains engaged in handling interstate commerce; and the law furthermore provides specific penalties for interfering with the transportation of the United States mails. Back of the Federal courts, is the entire army of the United States under the command of the President. It is thus a serious matter for strikers to disregard the injunctions of the United States courts issued to preserve order during railway labor strikes.

Management of Insolvent Roads; Railway Receiverships.— When a railroad company becomes insolvent—i. e., when it cannot pay the interest on its debt or meet its other financial obligations—the creditors of the road may ask a court to take possession of the property. If the court grants the request of the creditors, the property is taken from the management of the directors and officers of the company and put in charge of an officer of the court called a receiver. If the company is not hopelessly insolvent, the road will be operated by the receiver, who will coöperate with the creditors and the owners of the road in reorganizing the company and placing it on a solvent financial basis. If, however, the liabilities of the company are found to be so great as to make impossible a return to solvency by means of reorganization, the court will instruct the receiver to sell the property for the benefit of the creditors; but whether the property is sold or not every effort will be made to keep the railroad in operation, because the value of the property invested in a railroad depends almost entirely upon what it can earn as a railroad. It cannot be used for other purposes.

Railroad construction in the United States was carried on with great rapidity and without any Government supervision of stock and bond issues. Many roads were overcapitalized, and not a few of them were built ahead of business needs. The result of this has been that during periods of financial crises, as from 1873 to 1878, and from 1893 to 1898, a large number of railway companies have become insolvent, and have thus been brought temporarily under the management of the courts. During the eighteen months ending July 4, 1894, 43,000 miles of railroad—twenty-four per cent of the total mileage in the country—was taken in charge by the courts. With the return of prosperity, most of the roads became solvent; but even under the present improved conditions, a business depression such as began in the latter part of 1907 and lasted through the following year, may force several thousand miles of railroad into receiverships. However, as our railroads become stronger and their financial methods more conservative, the duties of the courts in managing insolvent roads will be steadily lessened.

CHAPTER XVIII

GOVERNMENT REGULATION AND GOVERNMENT OWNERSHIP OF RAILWAYS

Government Regulation of Railways a Permanent and Double Problem.—The regulation of the railways is a problem with which the Government of every country has to deal; moreover, it is a problem, which, like poverty, cannot be finally disposed of. In dealing with this question the State has two duties to perform: one is properly to adjust the relations of the carriers with each other, and the other is to bring about and maintain equitable treatment of the public by the carrier.

This twofold problem may be dealt with in either one of two ways: the Government may own and operate the railroads, or it may regulate the services and charges of corporations created by law to perform the work of public carriage. The former method has been adopted by a majority of the countries, but in the United States the plan of private ownership and Government regulation has prevailed.

The Problem of Government Regulation Defined.—The essence of the problem of Government regulation consists in harmonizing as far as possible the interests of private corporations of a *quasi* public character, engaged for profit in the performance of a service of a public nature, with the interests of the individuals, the localities, and the general public served by the carriers. Such a problem as this

153

must necessarily be a permanent one, because it involves the enforcement of equity. Equity is a matter of relationship, and thus varies with changes in the things compared. What is equity to-day may not be equity to-morrow; a rate that was reasonable five years ago may be unjust at the present time; a service that was adequate and reasonable in 1900 may be quite otherwise in 1910. These are the questions which the Government has to decide in regulating railroads; hence this work of the Government can never be completed—it remains a permanent duty.

Government Ownership a Question of Expediency, Not of Principle.—Whether the railroad problem shall be dealt with by State ownership or Government regulation is a question of expediency. In Germany, the several States of the empire have succeeded admirably with the ownership and operation of the railroads. Other countries have had a fair degree of success. On the other hand Government regulation of railway corporations has been successful in Great Britain, and promises to prove so in the United States. There are so many factors involved in reaching an accurate decision as to which of the two policies it is wise for any particular Government to adopt, that it will be well to summarize the arguments for and against State ownership and operation of the railways. The arguments will be stated with particular reference to the United States.

ARGUMENTS IN FAVOR OF GOVERNMENT OWNERSHIP AND OPERATION OF RAILWAYS IN THE UNITED STATES

(1) The leading argument in favor of State ownership and operation of railways is that unjust discriminations between persons, places, and commodities can thereby be

prevented. It is reasonable to suppose that the Government will manage the railroads with the same impartiality that it conducts the post office. In a well-conducted Government, it is probable that favoritism will not exist; and that the Government will tolerate only such discriminations as are in the public interest.

(2) When the Government operates the railroads it can adjust charges with reference to the maximum development of industry and commerce, or with regard to the promotion of social progress, or with a view to increasing the strength and efficiency of the army. In Prussia the Government has sought with remarkable success to promote all three of these aims. Railroad rates are made a part of the protective tariff system, and they are so adjusted as to favor foreign trade, to build up the iron industries of the western part of the country, and to further the agricultural development in the eastern and southeastern portions of Prussia. Passenger fares have been arranged with reference to increasing the travel for educational purposes and to relieving the congestion of population in the cities. From the early days of Bismarck's power to the present time, the construction and operation of the railroads of Prussia and other German States have been made to serve the military strength of the country.

(3) It is argued that rates and fares can and will be lower under Government ownership and operation; for the reasons that the Government will not seek to make more than fair profits, and, having a monopoly of the entire system within the country, it can avoid many of the expenses due to competition and to the maintenance of a large number of separate and rival corporations. In connection with this argument, however, it should be remembered that the Government cannot charge lower rates

than private corporations unless it is equally efficient in the management of the railroads. Unless the Government administration is both honest and efficient, its expenses will be greater than they are under private management. It is a well-known fact, moreover, that the Government, particularly in democratic countries, usually pays higher wages and exacts a shorter working day than corporations do. This may be desirable from a social point of view, but it helps to increase the expenses of Government operation, and tends to prevent a reduction of rates and fares.

(4) The nationalization of the railroads converts the more or less speculative stocks and bonds of railroad corporations into sound investment securities. Railway capital takes the form of Government bonds in which individuals, insurance, and trust companies may safely invest their accumulating surplus.

(5) The substitution of Government bonds for the securities of corporations takes those securities out of the stock market and thus limits the field of speculation. It is believed by many that the influence of the stock market is demoralizing and that anything tending to limit its operations will be a public benefit.

(6) The nationalization of the railroads has the support of the advocates of socialism and also of others who feel that the present unsatisfactory distribution of wealth among different classes of people calls for vigorous corrective measures on the part of the Government. To take $18,000,000,000 of railroad property out of private control and place it in the ownership of the public as a whole, would unquestionably limit somewhat the present inequality in the wealth of different social classes. There is, moreover, no other large body of wealth that could be more readily socialized.

ARGUMENTS AGAINST GOVERNMENT OWNERSHIP AND OPERATION OF RAILWAYS IN THE UNITED STATES

(1) With minor exceptions, the policy of both the United States and the States has been to interfere as little as possible with private management of transportation. Formerly, there was much opposition even to Government regulation of the corporations engaged in performing the public service of railway transportation; latterly, we have come to realize that efficient Government regulation is necessary; but a majority of the American people still hold to the political theory that interference should not go beyond the point of absolute necessity; accordingly, the nationalization of railroads would be considered a radical step and one opposed to our traditional policy. This argument, however, has lost much of its force during recent years with the unavoidable extension of the functions of the National Government.

(2) The nationalization of railroads in the United States would increase the number of Government employees by nearly a million and a half, most of whom are voters. It is claimed that this throng of men might be so manipulated as to corrupt the ballot. The danger of this is much less now than it would have been under the old spoils system, and the possibilities of political leaders controlling the votes of Government employees is growing less with the increase in the intelligence and independence of the individual voter.

(3) The opponents of the nationalization of railways argue that the Government would develop our railways more slowly than private corporations would, and that the

Government would be apt to construct new lines mainly in those sections of the country having the greatest political influence. This might be true in some countries but probably would not be in the United States.

(4) The advocates of private railways assert that the rates upon the Government roads are too rigid. It is claimed both that the rate systems worked out by corporations are more flexible and that their charges are kept in closer harmony with economic conditions. It is true that rates ought to be kept in adjustment with economic needs, but a close study of the question will convince an impartial student that rates may be too flexible as well as too stable. The increasing tendency at present in countries where the railroads are operated by private corporations is toward a greater stability in rates. Moreover, it is equally true that the Government machinery may bring about an excellent adjustment of railway charges to industrial conditions. The Prussian Government, with the assistance of advisory councils made up of representatives of the business interests in all the sections of the country, has succeeded admirably in rate making; and there is surprisingly little complaint on the part of the shipping and traveling public in that country.

(5) The strongest argument against the nationalization of railways in the United States is that our Government would be less economical and less efficient in the management of the railroads than the private corporations are. Ordinarily, Government works are more expensive than private works. The corporation usually gets more for each dollar expended than the Government does. The employee of the corporation is held up to a higher degree of effort than is the public servant. Thus while some of the expenses which corporations now incur would be avoided by

the nationalization of railroads, the total expense would probably be increased under Government management.

(6) While the pressure for a reduction of rates would be strong, it is not probable that the Government could perform the transportation service at lower rates and fares than now prevail; indeed, it is probable that the ultimate, if not the early, effect of Government management in the United States would be higher charges than well-regulated private corporations would need to exact of the public.

Nationalization of Our Railways Not Now Expedient.—In order to decide whether the United States ought to acquire and operate the railroads within the country it is necessary to answer three questions: (1) Could the Government administer the railways honestly? (2) Could it do this as efficiently as private corporations can? (3) Can the Government regulate private railways satisfactorily and adequately?

The answer to the first of these questions must be an uncertain one. The nationalization of our railroads would place an immense strain upon the administrative machinery of the Federal Government; whether honesty could be maintained is questionable—it would at least be a dangerous experiment. The answer to the second query must be negative. Private corporations in the United States are unquestionably more efficient than the Government could be. The answer to the third question is affirmative. Satisfactory progress is being made by the United States Government and by several of the States in the regulation of the railways. In a word, the success of Government regulation in the United States, while incomplete, is sufficient to justify the belief that the control of our railroads can be accomplished by regulation, and that nationalization is neither necessary nor desirable at the present time.

PART II

ELECTRIC RAILWAY TRANSPORTATION

CHAPTER XIX

ORIGIN AND GROWTH OF ELECTRIC RAILWAYS

Importance of Electric Railway Transportation in the United States.—At the end of two decades of growth the electric railways carried 9,533,080,766 passengers in one year, many times the number transported on steam railways; and, although the fare paid by each passenger on the electric cars is only a few cents, the earnings of electric railways are about two thirds the income received by steam roads from their passenger traffic. The advance made by electric railways is the result of the growth both of urban transportation and also of suburban and interurban traffic. The rapid transit which the electric lines gave to the cities enabled the cities to grow rapidly and spread widely, and this in turn has brought an ever enlarging volume of traffic to the street railways. The economy with which electric roads could be built along highways and the frequency of the service they could offer to the public caused such a large number of interurban lines to be constructed as to give the electric railways a greater mileage in some States than the steam railroads have.

The substitution of the electric for the steam locomotive within the limits of large cities has been begun on an extensive scale in New York, and in course of time will be carried out in all the other great cities. This, in turn, will doubtless have a large influence upon the use of electric power for the passenger service on trunk-line railroads where the traffic is heavy. The electric railway is developing much more rapidly than the steam railroad and it is still in the early stages of its growth. The main facts regarding electric railway transportation will be presented in this and the three following chapters.

The Predecessors of the Electric Railway.—The first organized service for the transportation of passengers in cities was supplied by omnibus lines, which began to run in New York City in 1830, and in Philadelphia the following year. About twenty years later the street railway and horse cars made their appearance in New York. The first street railway line in Boston received its charter in 1853; five years later the first line began operation in Philadelphia; and in 1859 Chicago had a street-railway service. These horse-car lines provided a service of four or five miles an hour, which answered very well in cities of moderate size. By 1870, however, several American cities had become so large as to have urgent need for rapid transit.

Surface cable lines and elevated roads with steam locomotives began to be constructed about 1870 to furnish more rapid transit than could be secured without animal traction. The first city to construct a cable line was San Francisco whose hilly location made horse cars impracticable on many of its streets. San Francisco's first cable line was opened in 1873. The next city to have cable traction was Chicago, whose first line began running in 1878. Philadelphia's cable line was opened in 1884.

New York City took the lead in the use of elevated railways. The long distance from the lower end of Manhattan Island to the residential portions of New York, and the congested condition of its streets made it absolutely necessary to provide rapid transit by elevated roads. The first franchise for an elevated street railway in New York was granted in 1867, other lines followed in quick succession, and by 1879 New York City's system of elevated roads was nearly completed. The first plan was to use cable traction upon these elevated lines, but it was decided to adopt dummy locomotives which were used for twenty-five years until displaced by electricity. In Chicago the construction of elevated railroads began in 1888; Boston's excellent system of elevated roads was opened in 1903; and Philadelphia's line in 1907.

The Origin of the Electric Railway: The Invention of the Motor.—It was the dynamo which was invented in 1864 that subsequently made possible the use of electricity to propel railway cars; but nearly twenty-five years were required to improve the dynamo and adapt it to the street-railway service. Among the men who did the most to accomplish this important work were Stephen D. Field, Thomas A. Edison and Frank S. Sprague in the United States, and Siemens & Halske in Germany. Experiments with short electric-car lines were being carried on by different people in various places after 1880. In 1888, Sprague began the successful operation of an electric trolley in Richmond, Va. This same year, Bentley & Knight installed an electric line in Allegheny City, Pa., and the Thompson-Houston Company started a service in Washington. The success of these roads, although not complete, was sufficient to induce the officers in charge of the great West End System in Boston to replace horse cars with electric instead of cable traction. After 1888, the growth of electric mileage was rapid.

The Improvement of the Motor.—The first motors were naturally crude and of low-power efficiency. Experience early showed that the motor must be carried on the trucks —not in the cars—and that the truck carrying the motor must be separate from the body of the car. It was thus necessary to devise a motor of sufficient power that was small enough to be placed between the floor of the car and the axles of the trucks. This problem was solved by making the motors small, running them at high speed and gearing them down to the axles, at first by double reduction and later by a single gearing. The motor had to be sup-

BALDWIN-WESTINGHOUSE ELECTRIC LOCOMOTIVE. Weight 70,000 pounds.

ported flexibly in order to prevent destructive jolting, and yet be suspended concentrically with reference to the axle. Numerous improvements were made in the motor year by year whereby its power was increased without adding to its size and whereby greater efficiency at low motor speed was made possible. The inertia of moving parts was lessened and sparks were prevented by better commutation. Among the many important improvements introduced was the controller, by which the motorman regulates the speed of the car; and the magnetic circuit breaker for the protection of the dynamos against lightning and the motors against excessive currents.

The Electric Car.—By 1870, the standard two-horse car was sixteen feet long, had relatively large windows, a monitor roof, and a seating capacity for twenty-two persons. Subsequent to this, only minor improvements were made in the designs of the horse cars; but when electric traction was introduced there was an immediate demand for longer and more spacious cars. It was found by experience that the limit for the length of four-wheel closed cars was 20 feet, and for open cars, 25 to 30 feet, with a total weight of 20,000 pounds for body and trucks. Early in the nineties, the demand for larger cars led to the introduction of street cars with eight wheels and two trucks. The general design of these cars is similar to the steam railway coach. In Europe, the double-deck car is popular in many cities, but it has not been used in America, because the length of time taken by passengers to dismount from the roof seats reduces the speed of the car below the average necessary in American cities, where distances are exceptionally great.

The Track.—The early street-railway tracks had rails consisting of wooden stringers surfaced with iron. After 1880, light T rails, weighing 25 to 60 pounds per yard, were used in many cities. With the introduction of electric cars, the use of girder rails, the heaviest of which now weigh 141 pounds to the yard, became general. Of the several designs of girder rails, the grooved rail is the one most favored; because wagons may easily pass to and from the rails without difficulty. Suburban and interurban lines are laid with T rails such as are used on steam railroad tracks.

The underground trolley requires a track of special

construction. The metal conductor for the electric current is placed in a conduit which is framed in, and supported by, large metal cross-yokes that carry the rails of the track. Thus each cross-yoke forms a section of the conduit and also serves as a cross-tie. The use of the conduit came later than the overhead trolley, because of the great expense and also because of the difficulty of insulating the conductor in the conduit. The insulation of the conductor bars is secured by placing them near the top of a conduit large enough to carry the water that may enter the conduit off to the street sewers with which the conduit is connected at frequent intervals. The conduit system is much preferable to the overhead trolley, because overhead wires are dangerous and disfigure the street. New York, Washington, and some other cities have wisely refused to permit overhead trolleys in their streets.

The Electric Locomotive and the Multiple Unit Train.— There are three methods by which electricity may be employed to move cars: (1) The cars may be run singly as is most customary in the surface street-railway service. (2) An electric locomotive may be employed to haul a train of cars or "trailers." (3) Two or more cars, each supplied with motors, and capable of being operated singly, may be united into a train, and the train may be managed as a unit by a single motorman. This was named the multiple unit system by its inventor, Frank J. Sprague. It might also be called the electric train.

As early as 1882, electric locomotives were used for hauling cars in mines. The next use was for subways and tunnels. When the City & South London Railway was opened for traffic in 1890, it was decided to adopt electric locomotives instead of cables for handling trains. The success of this London subway caused the electric locomotive to be used in other subways and tunnels where the avoidance of smoke and gases was necessary.

Upon elevated street railways and on interurban lines where electric cars are run in trains, the Sprague multiple unit system has been generally adopted. The power being applied to each truck of the train, high speed may be obtained quickly without any motor being of high power. Moreover, the motors being distributed throughout the

BALDWIN-WESTINGHOUSE ELECTRIC LOCOMOTIVE . FOR MINE SERVICE.
Weight, 30,000 pounds.

train, none of the cars needs to be so heavy as a locomotive must be. The multiple-unit train became a possibility about 1900, and it marked an important step forward in the progress of mechanical traction.

Transmission of the Current.—The most important advances now being made in the application of electricity to transportation and industry are in connection with the transmission of the current. It has now become possible to transmit a high voltage alternating current from 50 to 150 miles, and to transform the current locally at many points into a continuous current at a low voltage. Where water power is available, electricity can be generated economically and can be distributed over a wide area.

The Triumph of the Electric Railway.—In 1890, seven-tenths of the total single track mileage of street railways in the United States was operated by animal power; to-day,

WESTINGHOUSE ELECTRIC LOCOMOTIVE USED BY NEW YORK, NEW HAVEN & HARTFORD RAILROAD.   Weight, 204,000 pounds; 1,000 horse power.

with the exception of a few short cable lines, electric traction occupies the field. The transition from animal to mechanical traction was quickly made, because of the greater economy and efficiency of the electric railway. This may be illustrated by reference to the operating expenses of the street railways of Massachusetts before and after the adoption of electricity. In 1888 there were 553 miles of horse-car lines in that State and no electric roads. At that time the ratio of operating expenses to gross receipts was 81.07 per cent. In 1902 there were no horse-car lines in Massachusetts and there were 2,484 track miles of electric roads. At that time, the operating expenses had fallen to 69.5 per cent of the gross receipts; and this was true in spite of the fact that one half of the electric-railway mileage was in rural districts and small towns where the ratio of operating expenses was higher than in the large cities where the traffic is heavier.

This reduction in the ratio of operating expenses to gross receipts has also been the result of another factor. The electric railway has brought about such a large increase in traffic that gross receipts have risen more rapidly than have operating costs. In the street-railway service, as in most lines of business, the cost per unit of service or product grows smaller with the increase in the volume of business.

CHAPTER XX

URBAN ELECTRIC RAILWAYS

Mileage and Services of Street Railways.—Although electric railways have become interurban, their chief services still consist of carrying passengers through the streets of cities and between the cities and their important suburbs. The line mileage of the street railways in a large city is surprisingly great. In New York there were at the beginning of 1908, 603 line miles of surface electric roads, 67 line miles of elevated roads, and 22 miles of subways. The passengers carried on these roads of New York were 1,330,776,165. In Philadelphia the street-railway mileage is 620, and the number of passengers carried in 1908 was 512,869,023.

In the largest cities, three classes of street railways are employed for the transportation of passengers—surface lines, elevated roads and subways. While the surface lines will always have the largest mileage, and in most cities the greater volume of traffic, New York and Chicago have long been obliged to make extensive use of elevated roads; and, during recent years, such roads have been constructed in Boston and Philadelphia. The elevated road is a permanent part of our urban transportation system. Subways also will be used more and more in the future. The pronounced success of the subways that have been opened in New York, Boston and Philadelphia, and the even greater success of subways in foreign cities, make it certain that

wherever the traffic is heavy enough to warrant the investment, the tendency will be to construct subways to provide rapid transit over the longer routes within crowded
cities.

Consolidated Management of Street Railways.—In every
large city of the United States, many street railway companies have received charters for street railways and have

PHILADELPHIA ELEVATED RAILWAY. Section along harbor front.

constructed lines. It was supposed in the earlier decades
of street-railway construction that if the State granted
charters to a number of companies to build the roads in a
city, the companies would compete with each other and
thus give the public better service and cheaper fares as a
result of competition. It was soon found, however, that
these several companies tended to consolidate; and at the
present time, in practically every large city the various

street-railway companies have been brought together under a single control. In Philadelphia, for instance, all the street railways are owned by the Philadelphia Rapid Transit Company; in Boston, the Boston Elevated controls all the lines; and in New York the Interborough-Metropolitan Company has absorbed all the lines.

Financial Methods Employed in Consolidation.—In most States, with the exception of Massachusetts, financiers have been allowed to employ such methods in consolidating street railways as they chose to adopt. The promoters of financial syndicates discovered as long ago as 1880 that the rapid growth of cities and the consequent increase of street-railway traffic made it possible for them to issue securities much in excess of the actual investment in street railways. Moreover, when the traction company consolidated a number of formerly independent roads, it was found possible for the traction company to float large blocks of stocks or bonds in addition to the securities of the consolidated roads. Thus, step by step, the capitalization of street railways has been increased, except where prevented by public authority; until at the present time the traction company in nearly every American city is struggling along under an exceptionally burdensome load of capital. Meanwhile, the public is being less efficiently served than it might be had those formerly in control of the street-railway business been prevented from issuing unlimited quantities of stocks and bonds.

The Street Railway Service and Fares are a Monopoly in Each City.—Street-railway transportation has always been a monopoly service even when there were several companies operating in the same city. At the present time, the consolidation of the street railways in each city strengthens this monopoly, not because the nature of the monopoly has been changed, but because the consolidated company possessing the monopoly is more powerful than its several predecessors individually or collectively were.

Street-railway monopoly rests upon four bases. (1) The charter derived from the State necessarily gives a street-railway company the exclusive right over certain streets and thus within certain sections of the city. (2) Street-

A TYPICAL STATION OF THE PHILADELPHIA ELEVATED RAILWAY.

railway companies serving different sections of a city cannot compete with each other to much extent, because people living in a particular section of a large city must patronize the company serving that municipal district. (3) Street-railway transportation is a service for which there is universal demand and for which there is no substitute. Conditions of life in our cities are now such that the street railways—surface, elevated, and subway—must be used by practically everybody. (4) Competition in so far as it is possible among street railways, is readily set aside by agreements as to fares or by the consolidation of the lines. In Philadelphia, for instance, thirty-nine companies were chartered between 1857 and 1874, and most of these companies constructed lines. But in 1859 there was organized the Board of Presidents of City Passenger Railway Companies and this board so completely regulated the fares that they were always uniform on every line in the city.

Street Railway Fares.—In the United States, the street-railway fare is usually five cents for a single ride within the city limits regardless of distance. In many cities, six tickets are sold for twenty-five cents; and there are some places where tickets are sold at reduced rates during the morning and evening rush hours. In some cities, free transfers are given; but in several of the large cities a transfer ticket costs from six to eight cents instead of five cents.

In Europe, with few exceptions, street-railway fares vary with distance. The fare for the shortest trip is from one cent to two and a half cents, and for the longest rides seldom more than six cents. This plan of grading street-railway charges with reference to distance works admirably in the cities of Europe where many people live at or near their places of business, and where the average distance people ride upon the street cars is much shorter than the average length of the trip on American street railways. Our cities spread out over large areas and most persons live in residential sections well away from the centers of business. These differences between American and European cities account for the dissimilar systems of street-railway charges.

Public Regulation or City Ownership Necessary.—From

what has been said in this chapter, it is evident that the street-railway service when performed by private corporations must be carefully regulated by the public. Whether it is a better plan to have the service performed by carefully regulated public-service corporations, or to adopt municipal ownership and operation of street railways depends almost entirely upon whether the city government

PHILADELPHIA SUBWAY. Tracks emerging from subway and rising to the elevated section.

is or is not honest and efficient. Since 1890, two thirds of the street railways in Great Britain have been taken over by the cities, and the ratio of municipal to private undertakings has steadily increased. City ownership and operation work admirably in Great Britain where the city governments are carefully and wisely administered.

In the United States, the universal policy is to charter corporations to perform the street-railway transportation services. Had it also been our policy from the start to regulate these public-service corporations carefully as regards their systems of accounting, their capitalization and financial methods, their charges and their services, the results would doubtless have been satisfactory. In most States, however, the practice has been to grant public-service corporations large powers and to provide for little effective control over their actions. In consequence of this

THE TWO-TRACK SECTION OF THE PHILADELPHIA SUBWAY.

mistaken practice, we have a serious street-railway problem, the solution of which is yet to be found in most of our States and municipalities.

American System of Street Railway Regulation.—A company desiring to build and operate a street railway in any city applies to the State for a charter, and having obtained the charter it secures a franchise from the city in which the street railway is to be constructed. It is customary for the State to impose relatively few charter restrictions upon street-railway companies and to permit the local governments to exact such franchise conditions as they may think best. In granting the franchise, the city may stipulate what the maximum fares shall be, may require the companies to pay to the city a certain percentage of their gross or net receipts and may compel them to pave and keep in repair the part of the street occupied by the railway tracks.

THIRTEENTH STREET STATION, PHILADELPHIA SUBWAY. Entrance to Wanamaker Store at level of station platform.

Massachusetts has been more successful thus far than the other States have been in the regulation of street railways. The franchises are granted in perpetuity, but the franchise concessions may, with the approval of the state railroad commission, be revoked by city and town governments, if the companies fail to carry out their obligations to the public. The State railroad commission of Massachusetts is given large power over the street railways. Its approval of the location of a proposed line must be secured before the railway can be constructed. The commission regulates the amount of stocks and bonds that may be issued, and its consent must be secured to the terms of a lease, sale, or consolidation of roads. It also has supervision over the fares and services of street railways and has power to make investigations and to recommend such additional State legislation as the commission may deem desirable.

The State of New York is making amends for the past neglect of its duty to regulate street railways. In 1907 a Public Service Commission for Greater New York and another for the rest of the State were established and these two railway commissions were given much larger powers than their predecessor had. They have control over the location, capitalization, accounts, and services of public service corporations. It will take some time for public regulation to correct the mistakes that have been committed in the past in Greater New York and the other cities of the State, but the prospects for the future are at least encouraging.

Under the influence of Massachusetts, New York and other progressive commonwealths, progress is being made with the solution of the problem of public regulation of street railways; and it seems reasonable to expect that it will become customary in the not distant future for all States to require publicity of accounts of all public-service corporations, to subject their capitalization and financial operations to public regulation and to control their charges and services so as fully to safeguard the interests of the cities and the welfare of the public.

CHAPTER XXI

INTERURBAN AND RURAL ELECTRIC RAILWAYS

The Increase in Interurban Lines.—During the five and one half years ending with 1907, the total mileage of electric railways, urban and interurban, increased 53.4 per cent, and while the spread of lines within the cities was continuous, the growth of extramural and interurban lines was at an even greater rate. The construction of interurban lines has been going on in most parts of the United States but their progress has been exceptionally rapid in New England, New York, in the Central West, and in southern California.

In the small State of Massachusetts, there are 2,223 miles of electric lines and this exceeds the line mileage of steam railroads by 112 miles. The map of the electric lines of this State shows how completely they connect the principal cities in the eastern and central part of the State with the surrounding cities and adjacent country. For a number of years, it has been the policy of the New York, New Haven & Hartford Railroad Company to absorb the electric lines with which it has competition, and also to build electric roads as feeders to its main line. The map of electric railways controlled by the New Haven gives an indication of the extent to which the interurban roads have been developed in southern New England.

The construction of electric lines has been pushed with vigor in Ohio, Indiana, southern Michigan, Wisconsin, and in portions of Illinois. The accompanying map of this section of the United States shows that interurban electric roads in large number radiate from Milwaukee, Chicago, Indianapolis, Cincinnati, Dayton, Columbus, Detroit, Toledo, Cleveland, and from numerous other cities of smaller size. Several electric lines are operated over relatively long routes, there being a regular service of electric trains from Toledo to Dayton, from Toledo to Cleveland, and over several other lines. In some instances, sleeping cars are operated. Another important center of interurban electric roads is Los Angeles, Cal. From this city, as also from Indianapolis, lines proceed in several directions from a large electric terminal station. The Southern Pacific Railroad interests now control all the electric lines about Los Angeles.

Character of Electric Roads Now Being Built.—The first suburban lines were constructed in the highways leading from one town to another. Such roads were cheaply built and they necessarily provided an unsatisfactory service, because high speed was impossible. Moreover, the steep grades of ordinary highways made the expense of operation excessive and limited the development of traffic. The electric lines now being built have their own exclusive roadway and are constructed as well as the best steam railways. Many of the early electric roads which, like the first steam roads, started with as cheap construction as possible, have been rebuilt in accordance with the best standards. This has reduced the expenses of operation, and has enabled the electric lines to develop new traffic and to compete more successfully with steam railroads.

Passenger Service of Interurban Lines.—The electric railways have the great advantage of being able to provide a frequent passenger service; the steam railroad train must

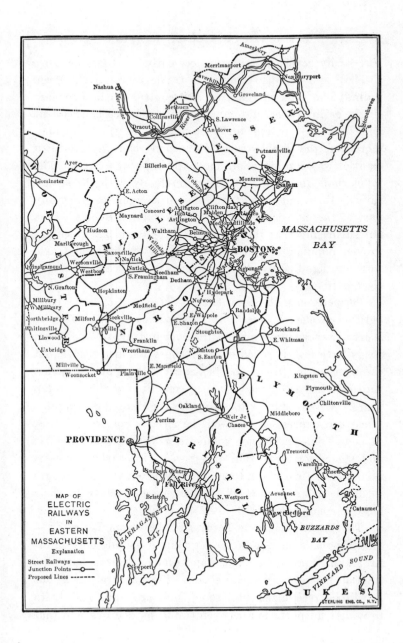

MAP OF
ELECTRIC
RAILWAYS
IN
EASTERN
MASSACHUSETTS

Explanation

Street Railways ————
Junction Points —O—
Proposed Lines ------

STERLING ENG. CO., N.Y.

necessarily consist of a heavy locomotive and two or more coaches, and it must handle its traffic in relatively large units. The electric road, on the contrary, can run cars singly or in trains, and can provide a service as frequent and in such varying units as the traffic may demand. Moreover, the double-track interurban road with its own right of way can offer both local and express services. The interurban lines always coördinate closely with the street-railway lines and thus enable their passengers to reach any part of the city conveniently with minimum delays. It is not surprising that the service of the interurban lines has proven popular, and that a large part of the local traffic formerly handled by steam railroads is now carried by the electric lines.

Competition with Steam Roads.—The most effective competition of electric lines with steam roads has been for the short-distance suburban and interurban traffic. The steam roads have lost so much of their short-distance traffic that the average length of the passenger trip upon the steam railroads has risen eighteen per cent during the past ten years. We are now witnessing the beginnings of long-distance and express services on the electric roads; and this, of course, means keener competition between the electric and steam services. The progress of interurban lines is certain to be rapid, and the steam railroads must prepare to divide a larger part of the passenger traffic with their electric competitors.

The Electric Lines as Feeders of the Steam Railroads.—Electric roads outside of the city limits include both interurban and rural lines. It is impossible to draw a sharp distinction between these two classes of extramural lines; but it will be recognized that some lines are built mainly to provide transportation between two or more cities, and that other less expensive lines are constructed mainly to connect the smaller-sized towns with the surrounding villages and rural communities. These rural lines must be looked upon as feeders to the main lines with which they connect. For the most part, these main lines are the steam railroads, but to some extent they are interurban electric roads. Moreover, the interurban roads are often to be regarded as branches of steam railroads—branches that have been constructed where a steam road would probably have otherwise been built. As the interurban lines reach out from the trunk-line steam roads, through one town after another, and as the rural lines extend from town through rural villages and communities, the general transportation system is made more complete and of greater economic and social advantage to the public.

Fares on Interurban Roads.—The charges of the electric lines average lower than those of the steam railroads. When the first interurban roads were built along the country highways, the fares were made especially low; but with the construction of electric lines on private rights of way, and with the improvement of the service, it has been necessary for the electric roads somewhat to increase their fares. On the shorter interurban roads, a zone tariff prevails, five cents being charged and collected for each distance zone into which the line is divided. The long interurban roads, which approach the characteristics of steam railroads, sell tickets, and have a system of fares not unlike the passenger charges of the steam lines.

Freight Services of Electric Lines.—Although the electric lines have in all cases been constructed to handle passenger traffic, and although their main services consist of the transportation of persons, three classes of freight traffic are being developed:

The first and most important of these freight services is the handling of parcels and the lighter grades of package freight into and out of the large cities. This service may be illustrated by reference to the Detroit United Railways which is now one of the many large electric railway companies that have well-organized freight services. This service, which dates from October, 1901, is typical of that of other electric companies. The three electric systems controlled by the Detroit United Railways have a joint freight and express depot in Detroit. Freight stations are built along the company's lines which extend to a point nearly one hundred miles from Detroit. The traffic handled includes milk, general express matter, parcels from the markets and stores, and various kinds of package freight. To some extent the territory tapped by the Detroit United Railway lines has no other railway facilities, and this fact made it easy for the electric roads to build up a freight traffic. There is, however, successful competition with the steam railroads for a small part of their general freight business.

The second class of freight service is performed by those electric roads that are feeders of the steam railroads. Usually these electric feeders extend from relatively large towns, located upon a steam railroad, through smaller towns having no railway connections. Several large steam-railroad systems are encouraging the construction of electric branch lines to serve as feeders both for their passenger and freight business.

The third class of electric freight services is performed by the rural trolley lines, which gather up and take to market the farm products and perform a large part of the transportation business of the country villages. These rural lines are inexpensively built, mainly along the high-

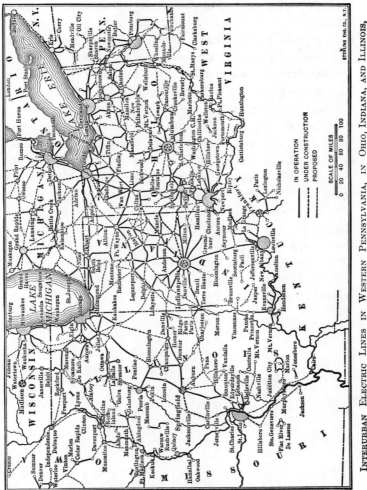

INTERURBAN ELECTRIC LINES IN WESTERN PENNSYLVANIA, IN OHIO, INDIANA, AND ILLINOIS, AND IN SOUTHERN MICHIGAN AND WISCONSIN.

ways; and with the development which they are certain to have in the near future, the steam- and electric-railway transportation system will be brought into immediate connection with an increasing number of rural communities and with the people of a greater number of small towns.

Economic and Social Advantages Resulting from Electric Railways.—The desire to travel is universal; and the rapid increase of suburban and interurban railways has made it possible for men to travel much more easily and cheaply than they formerly could. There has been an enormous development of travel for pleasure and for education, but the chief effects of the electric railways have been industrial. Most travel is undertaken for business reasons, and the chief function of the electric road has been to enable the people to do their work more easily. Moreover, with the spread of electric lines generally through the country, production and trade will be carried on more economically, and the general well-being of the masses of the people will thereby be improved.

CHAPTER XXII

ELECTRIFICATION OF STEAM ROADS

The General Problem.—Electric railways have met with great success in short-distance passenger traffic, and they are beginning to be used to some extent for the transportation of passengers over routes 100 to 200 miles in length; indeed, it may be said that an electric railway 100 miles in length is nothing unusual at the present time. A beginning has also been made in performing a light freight service, and there are a few instances of the handling of heavy freight upon electric roads. In view of these facts, the question may well be asked whether electric power will, in the near future, largely or entirely take the place of the steam locomotive. If both steam and electric power are to be employed, what are the special services that will be taken over by the electric lines?

The General Electrification of all Steam Railways is not Probable.—Careful studies have been made by engineers and transportation experts to determine whether it would be economical for the steam railroads as a whole, or for the more important railway systems, to equip their lines electrically and to abandon the use of steam locomotives. The results of these calculations do not indicate the early, general abandonment of steam power. A change to electricity necessitates a heavy investment of capital which can be justified only under special traffic conditions.

Electric power is well adapted to two very different

classes of services: one is the existence of a passenger or freight traffic heavy enough to require a frequent service. The heavier the traffic the more economical does electric power become. On the other hand, railway lines having relatively light freight traffic and but a moderate volume of passenger business which can be handled in small units at relatively frequent intervals, can also use electricity to advantage. It needs no argument to show that these two traffic conditions prevail only to a limited extent upon American railways, and that consequently the conditions do not warrant the early abandonment of the steam locomotive.

The Electrification of Steam Railroads will be in Particular Sections and it will be done for special purposes:

1. The first service for which the electric locomotive was used in place of the steam engine was to haul engines through tunnels and subways. Reference has already been made to the adoption of the electric locomotive, by the City and South London Railway, in 1890, to handle traffic through the Thames tunnel. In 1895, the Baltimore & Ohio Railroad began hauling freight trains through its new tunnels in the city of Baltimore with heavy electric locomotives. Electric locomotives will be used in the Pennsylvania Railroad tunnels into and under New York City. These are but the beginnings of the general use of electricity wherever possible for tunnel work.

2. One of the largest substitutions of electricity for steam is in the electrification of the big city terminals of the railroads. The equipment of the New York terminals of the New York Central and the New York, New Haven & Hartford railroads, the electrification of the lines of the Long Island Railroad in the western part of Long Island, and the use of electric locomotives in the Pennsyl-

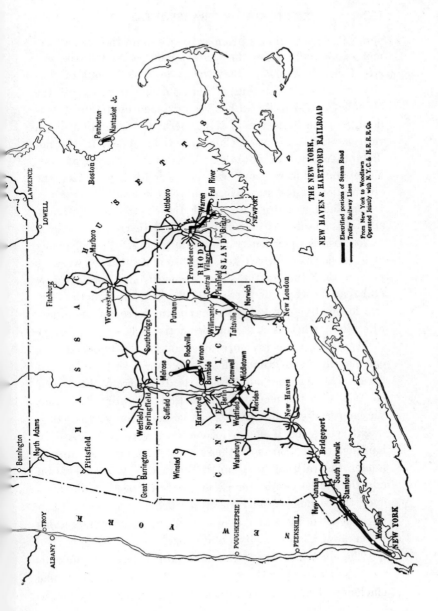

THE NEW YORK,
NEW HAVEN & HARTFORD RAILROAD

━━━ Electrified portions of Steam Road
━━━ Trolley Railway Lines

From New York to Woodlawn
Operated jointly with N.Y.C.& H.R.R.Co.

vania Railroad tunnels promise to eliminate the steam locomotive not only from the central part of New York, but
also from the railway lines for some distance out of that
city. The electrification of the Chicago terminal of the
Illinois Central Railroad has been decided upon, and this is
doubtless the first step in the general electrification of all
railroads in the city of Chicago. Other cities in the not
distant future will doubtless follow the example of New
York and Chicago, and we may confidently expect the
elimination of the steam locomotive from our cities.

3. Another service for which the electric locomotive is
specially adapted is that of handling both freight and passenger trains upon heavy mountain grades. The efficiency
of electric locomotives for exceptionally heavy work is
greater than that of the steam locomotive. There are several reasons why this is so: (a) One cause is that the electric locomotive can exert its maximum force for an indefinite time; whereas a steam locomotive has such difficulty
in keeping up the pressure of steam in the boiler that it
can handle its maximum load only for a short period of
time. (b) Another advantage resulting from the use of
electricity in the mountainous sections of railroads is that
the length of summit tunnels can be made longer than they
might wisely be if steam locomotives were to be used in
hauling trains through them. By making the tunnels
longer the railroad line can be kept at a lower elevation
and the grades can be correspondingly reduced. (c) Moreover, the economy of electricity is much greater when it can
be generated by water power, and in mountain sections
water power is generally obtainable.

The electrification of the mountain sections of our railways will doubtless decrease costs and increase the traffic
efficiency of most of the railroads which have heavy moun-

tain grades to overcome. The Chicago, Milwaukee & St. Paul is considering using electric equipment over the Bitter Root Mountains and through the tunnel in that section of its line. The Northern Pacific has announced its intention to install electricity upon its heavy mountain grades; and other railroad companies having lines across the Rocky Mountains are making investigations with the view to electrifying certain sections of their roads.

4. Beginnings have been made with the electrification of sections of trunk-line railroads for the purpose of handling electrically the local passenger traffic over those portions of the road. Instances of this are the electrification of the Rochester branch of the Erie Railroad, and of the main line of the West Shore Railroad between Utica and Syracuse, N. Y. Over these sections thus electrified, through traffic, freight and passenger, is handled by steam locomotives, while the local passenger services are performed by electric cars. By handling local passenger traffic in this way a more frequent service can be given, the volume of business can be increased; and, what is also important, these sections of the Erie and the West Shore railroads can closely coördinate their local passenger traffic with that of the connecting urban and interurban electric lines.

The Adoption of Electricity instead of Steam on New Railways.—Many railways are being built with electrical equipment that would have used steam locomotives had they been constructed a decade ago. Indeed, the rapid growth of new interurban lines is doing more to bring about a substitution of electricity for steam than is the electrification of existing trunk-line railways. This movement will continue, and in the future we may expect to see the transportation services divided between steam and electric roads, each performing the work for which it is best fitted.

The change from steam to electricity promises to be gradual. There is little prospect that the heavy freight traffic will be moved electrically, except through tunnels, over mountains, or into and out of large city terminals. The change, in the near future, will be confined mainly to an increasing use of electricity for the passenger services. New interurban lines whose traffic will consist largely of handling passengers will almost surely be electrically equipped. A partial, but not a general, electrification of main line steam railroads may be expected, first to handle the local passenger traffic; later, possibly, for the through freight and passenger business.

PART III

OCEAN TRANSPORTATION

CHAPTER XXIII

TONS AND TONNAGE. HOW VESSELS AND TRAFFIC ARE MEASURED

Uses of the Words Ton and Tonnage.—In describing the various types of vessels, and in discussing ocean transportation, frequent use must be made of the words "ton" and "tonnage," and, in order to avoid confusion and error, it is necessary to keep clearly in mind the several meanings in which these terms are employed. Tonnage may refer either to the size of the vessel or to the amount of the ship's cargo; accordingly, there are two distinct kinds of tons: the vessel ton and the cargo ton. Each of these two kinds of tons is used with several different meanings.

Vessel Tonnage is of Three Kinds: displacement, gross register, and net register. The displacement tonnage of a vessel is its weight, and is equal to the weight of water displaced by the ship when floating. The gross register tonnage is obtained by dividing the number of cubic feet in the capacity of the ship by 100. A vessel has one "gross" ton for each 100 cubic feet of capacity. The net register tonnage is obtained by dividing by 100 the capacity in cubic feet of the space available for cargo and passengers. From the entire capacity of the ship are deducted the spaces occupied by machinery, crew accommodations, and certain other housings, carefully designated by law; and then the number of cubic feet in the remaining capacity is divided by 100 to obtain the net register.

In the shipping statistics of all countries a ton gross register means 100 cubic feet of ship capacity; but as the rules applied in measuring the capacity are not identical in all countries, vessels of the same size under different flags may vary slightly as to gross tonnage. In the determination of the figures for net registry the laws of different countries vary more than they do in regard to gross registry; nevertheless, with the exception of the '' Danube '' measurement, which is applied to all vessels passing the Suez Canal, the British practice as regards the measurement of gross and net tonnage is followed with minor variations by all commercial countries.

The rules of the Danube measurement were adopted at Constantinople in 1873 for the Suez Canal by the International Tonnage Commission. The net register tonnage of vessels when measured by the Danube rules will average fully one fifth more than when measured in accordance with British or American laws. The canal tolls are levied on net tonnage.

The Cargo Ton is of Two Classes, Weight and Measurement.—The weight ton is of three kinds. It may be the '' short '' ton of 2,000 pounds, the '' long '' ton of 2,240 pounds, or the metric ton of 2,204.62 pounds. The traffic of American railroads and waterways (with the exception of anthracite coal, which is handled by the long ton in the Eastern States—not in the Western) is measured by the short ton, and this ton is the one generally used within the United States. In ocean commerce the weight ton is the long ton of 2,240 pounds, except in the trade of those countries that use the metric system and employ the metric ton of 2,204.62 pounds.

A large share of the cargo of ocean traffic is not shipped by weight, but by the measurement ton of 40 cubic feet. Grain and minerals move by weight; but manufactures, general merchandise, and even lumber, are regularly handled by the measurement ton. The adoption of 40 cubic feet for a measurement ton is said to be due to the fact that a long ton of wheat occupies 40 cubic feet in the hold or berth of the ship. In the Government statistics of the cargo tonnage of ocean commerce, both the long ton and the measurement ton are included, and it is not possible to ascertain from published statistics the actual weight of the traffic of ocean commerce. Indeed, this can be determined only by an investigation of the relation of the value of actual shipments to their tonnage.

The ratio of net register to the gross register tonnage and cargo tonnage of a modern vessel loaded with general cargo is as 1 to $1\frac{1}{2}$ and to $2\frac{1}{4}$. The net register is about two thirds the gross, and the cargo tonnage averages about $2\frac{1}{4}$ times the net register. For example, a cargo steamer of 6,000 tons gross register will measure 4,000 tons net register, and she will carry about 9,000 tons of cargo. In the large modern sailing vessel the net register is about seven eighths of the gross, and the cargo tonnage of the loaded vessel will average about $1\frac{2}{3}$ times the net register. The ratio of net register, gross register, and cargo tonnage being 7 to 8 to about 12 for the sailing vessel. Thus a sailing vessel of 2,100 tons net register will measure 2,400 tons gross, and have a cargo capacity of about 3,500 tons.

American Shipping includes Both Documented and Undocumented Craft.—Barges, lighters, floats, and other craft that are towed are not documented; but sailing vessels and steamers of all description flying the American flag are listed and documented by the United States Government.

Before a vessel can be put into service its machinery must be inspected by the United States Steamboat Inspection Service, and the ship must be measured by officials connected with the Bureau of Navigation in the Department of Commerce and Labor. The vessels engaged in foreign commerce are " registered," and those employed in our inland and coastwise commerce are " enrolled." All vessels of less than 20 tons measurement are "licensed." It is customary to use the term "registered" tonnage when speaking of our shipping engaged in foreign trade, and of "enrolled" tonnage when referring to our domestic fleet. The documented vessels comprise somewhat over half the total tonnage of American shipping of all kinds.

In all the statistics of shipping, only the tonnage of documented vessels is included. This misleads nearly every person, it being generally supposed that the figures comprise all kinds of craft. The tonnage of the merchant marine of the United States, for example, is ordinarily said to have been 7,300,000 tons gross register in 1908. That, however, was the tonnage of only our registered, enrolled, and licensed vessels—the documented tonnage. In addition to that, there were between 6,000,000 and 7,000,000 tons of undocumented craft—consisting mainly of barges, lighters, floats, and other craft not moved by their own power. The total merchant marine of the United States at the close of 1909 has an aggregate gross tonnage of nearly 14,000,000.

CHAPTER XXIV

THE SAILING VESSEL

The Three Classes of Ocean Craft are sailing vessels, steamers, and barges. In each class there are many different kinds, and this is especially true of steamers which include all types from the mammoth ocean liner down to harbor tugs and small yachts. Both sailing vessels and steamers have required many improvements to reach their present size and efficiency. Mechanical genius has, from the beginning of ship building to the present, sought constantly to adapt the ship more perfectly to its work of transporting passengers and freight. The larger size, and the greater speed and reliability of ocean vessels have made possible the present-day organization of coastwise and foreign trade. It is, however, equally true that the development of trade has given shipbuilders and shipowners their main incentive to construct and operate larger and better vessels.

Types of Sailing Vessels.—The names given to different kinds of sailing vessels are determined by the number of masts and the rig of the sails. The " square-rigged " vessel has sails attached to yards or beams so suspended from the mast as to cross the mast and extend equal distances on each side. The " schooner-rigged " vessel has sails with yardarms that do not cross the mast, but extend outward from one side of the mast.

A " ship " is a full-rigged sailing vessel having three or

201

more masts with the sails all square-rigged. A three-masted vessel with its two forward masts—the fore- and mainmasts —square-rigged and its after or mizzenmast fore-and-aft rigged, is a bark. When the foremast only is square rigged, and the main- and mizzenmast are rigged fore and aft, the vessel is a barkentine. A brig has two masts, both square-rigged; while a brigantine has the aftermast fore-and-aft rigged.

The sloop and the schooner have fore-and-aft rig, the sloop being a vessel of but one mast, the schooner with two

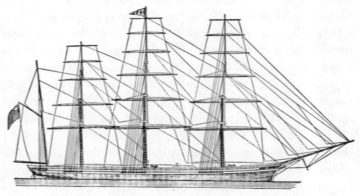

THE SQUARE-RIGGED SHIP "THE GREAT REPUBLIC."

or more. The construction of the first schooner is credited to Captain Andrew Robinson, of Gloucester, Mass., who is said to have launched a two-masted schooner in 1713 or 1714. Because it took place at Gloucester, the vessel has often been called the Gloucester schooner. The schooner was given sharper lines than the old square-rigged vessels had, and could sail faster and closer to the wind. Its sails could be managed more easily than the square sails could, and a smaller crew of men was required. The schooner was especially useful in the Atlantic coasting trade where it was necessary for vessels to sail close to the wind in beating up and down the coast.

Growth in Size of Sailing Vessels.—The far-reaching and relatively large ocean commerce of the American colonies was carried on in ships which to-day would seem tiny. Near the end of the eighteenth century, the standard size of the transatlantic sailing ship was about 200 tons gross register. The coasting trade and much of the oversea traffic was handled in brigs, schooners, and sloops having a register of 50 to 100 tons. During the nineteenth century, and particularly after the War of 1812–15, the size of sailing vessels rapidly increased. At the opening of the century, 300 tons register was considered large even for a full-rigged ship. Before 1820, vessels of 400 to 500 tons gross register were in use, and before 1840 double-decked ships of 1,000 tons had appeared. The first three-deck sailing ship, the *Guy Mannering*, was built in 1849. It had a gross register tonnage of 1,419. Others equally large were soon in service, the demand for large sailing vessels being especially urgent in the United States from 1850 to 1860. Until after the Civil War the largest sailing vessels were square-rigged ships, but since 1885 practically all new vessels have been schooner-rigged. The largest sailing vessel built in America was the *Thomas W. Lawson*, launched in 1899; it had seven masts, and was 5,218 tons gross register. It could carry from 7,000 to 8,000 tons of cargo. This vessel was never especially successful and its career was ended in 1907, when it capsized off the English coast. Several sailing vessels under the German flag are nearly as large as the *Lawson* was, and they have been operated with profit to their owners.

The Packet Lines.—After the close of the War of 1812–

1815, the commerce of the United States with Europe had become regular enough to warrant the operation of vessels as lines with regular schedules of sailing. The Black Ball Line was the first of the packet lines; it started running in 1815. The term packet was applied to the line ships because they carried the mails, i. e., the packages of mail. The American packet lines rapidly multiplied, they were operated with great success, and gave the United States

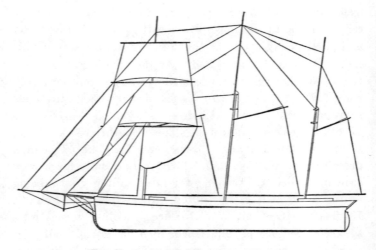

THE THREE-MASTED SCHOONER "HALL."

an envious place in the ocean-carrying trade during the first half of the nineteenth century.

The Clipper Ship.—The fastest and most celebrated ship was the clipper ship, a square-rigged vessel, the first of which was constructed in Baltimore in 1845. The ship derived its name from its sharp lines and its long overhanging prow. It was not so economical a freight carrier as the ordinary square-rigged packet ship was, because it had to sacrifice cargo capacity to secure the sharp lines necessary to secure maximum speed. Two causes brought about the construction of the clipper ship: one was the introduction of the steamer in 1840 in the transatlantic carrying trade. The British steamship lines immediately threatened to take the passenger and express business away from the American sailing vessels, hence American builders sought to perfect the sailing vessel to enable it to compete more successfully with the steamer. A demand for fast sailing vessels also arose in 1849–50, when there was a great rush from the eastern part of the United States to the California gold fields.

The Golden Age of the Sailing Vessel.—The greatest period of prosperity in the business of building and operating American sailing vessels came in the decade from 1850 to 1860. At that time he American oversea commerce was still handled mainly by sailing vessels. Moreover, the large passenger and freight traffic between our eastern and western seaports created an active demand for sailing vessels; and when, in 1854, the California gold fever began to abate, the Crimean War broke out, and both France and the United Kingdom purchased a large number of American sailing vessels for use as transports. In 1855 there were 583,450 gross tons of vessels launched in American yards—a greater tonnage than was constructed during any other year of the nineteenth century.

Decline in the Tonnage of Sailing Vessels.—The tonnage of sailing vessels under the American flag reached the highest point in 1861, upon the opening of the Civil War, when it amounted to 4,662,609. After that year there was an almost uninterrupted decline. In twenty-five years the figures had fallen to 2,608,152, and the total to-day is practically the same as it was in 1885 and 1886. Our steam tonnage, on the other hand, has increased more rapidly than the sailing vessels have fallen off. In 1861 our documented steamers had a gross tonnage of 877,204. At the present time we have nearly 5,000,000 tons of documented steamships, and they comprise about sixty-five per cent of our registered, enrolled, and licensed shipping.

The steamship has taken the place of the sailing vessel, because it is more efficient and economical. Domestic and international commerce is now so organized as to cause traders to put a higher value than they formerly did upon promptness and certainty of delivery of commodities; moreover, the marine engine has been so improved as to reduce the fuel cost to such a low point as to deprive the sailing vessel of most of the advantage it formerly had from the fact that the wind which supplied the motor power cost nothing. A modern freight steamer requires only one tenth of a ton of coal, costing thirty or thirty-five cents, to transport a ton of cargo 5,000 miles.

The Future of the Sailing Vessel.—It is not to be inferred that the sailing vessel is to cease to be used in American coastwise and oversea commerce. Schooners can be put into service for a small investment of capital, and will continue for some time to be useful in transporting relatively small cargoes of commodities that are shipped in bulk. The schooner is especially serviceable in the coastwise lumber trade, and can also be employed to advantage in international trade with those sections where commercial exchanges are small or variable in volume. The sailing vessel will not disappear, but its rôle is to be one of decreasing importance.

CHAPTER XXV

THE STEAMSHIP

Invention and Introduction of the Ocean Steamship.—Although Robert Fulton was not the first man to propel boats by steam power, the success of the *Clermont,* which he fitted with engines and ran from New York to Albany in 1807, entitled him to the credit of having demonstrated the commercial practicability of the steamship. The use of the steamboats upon the rivers and bays became general within a few years after 1807; it was, however, about thirty years before it was possible to drive a vessel across the ocean by steam power.

The first vessel to cross the ocean without using sails was the *Royal William,* which made the run from Quebec via Nova Scotia and the Isle of Wight to London in 1833. Five years later the *Great Western* and three other steamers made such successful runs between England and New York as to cause their owners to establish regular transatlantic steam services. The present great Cunard Company was the third British transatlantic company. Its first steamers, ordered in 1839, were put in operation in 1840, from which year we may say that the permanent transatlantic steamship service dates.

Comparison of Earliest and Latest Steamers.—The progress that has been made in ocean transportation is strikingly shown by comparing the steamers which the Cunard Company put into service in 1840 with their latest creations, the *Mauretania* and *Lusitania*, which began running in 1908. The Cunarders of 1840 were of 1,140 tons gross register; they were a little over 200 feet long, and of 35 feet beam. Their speed was from eight to ten knots per hour; and, under exceptionally favorable conditions, they made the passage in two weeks—often three weeks were required, especially for the trip westward against winds and currents. Their engines had 740 horse power. The *Mauretania* and *Lusitania* have a gross register tonnage of 32,500, 28 times that of their early ancestors; their length

THE "LUSITANIA" OF THE CUNARD LINE. Largest ship afloat in 1909. Length, 790 feet. Breadth, 88 feet. Gross register, 32,500 tons. Engines, 68,000 horse-power.

is 790 feet, and they are 88 feet in breadth. They have a speed of over 25 knots an hour. Their engines, which are turbines, develop 68,000 horse power, 92 times the power of the first Cunarder.

The Three General Problems of Steamship Improvement.— To develop the ocean steamship of to-day out of the first crude steamships required the solution of three general mechanical problems: (*a*) The efficient application of power, first by means of paddle wheels, later by means of screw propellers; (*b*) the mechanical generation of power in the marine engine; and (*c*) the design and construction of the ship so as to give it larger size and greater buoyancy and to increase its speed. It will be well to refer briefly to each of these general mechanical problems.

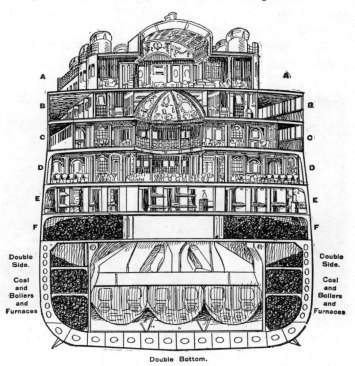

Double Bottom.

CROSS-SECTION OF THE "LUSITANIA."

From Paddle Wheels to Propellers.—The first steamships were constructed of wood, and were driven by paddle wheels; it was not until after 1850 that the screw propeller came to be generally adopted in place of the side wheels. The credit for the invention of the screw propeller belongs equally to John Ericsson (who later achieved great fame as the architect of the first *Monitor*) and Francis P. Smith, an English farmer. These men, each working in his own way, propelled a ship successfully with screws in 1836. Smith's ship, the *Archimedes*, built in 1839, was so successful as to convince builders of the practicability of the use of the screw for the ocean service.

The screw did not quickly displace the paddle wheel, because it was some years before the efficiency of the screw

The "Scotia" of the Cunard Line, 1862.   The last of the transatlantic paddle-wheel steamers.   Length, 379 feet.   Gross register, 3,871 tons.

was as great as that of the side wheels. There were two reasons for this: The early screws were not so well designed as those now in use, and the early marine engines had a slow piston stroke that was more effective in driving large paddle wheels than in driving small screws. By 1850, these difficulties had been sufficiently overcome to cause the Inman Line to adopt the screw for its fast ships; other British companies soon took similar action. Unfortunately, American builders continued to construct side-wheel steamers for some time after 1850.

Up to 1880 the ocean vessels were too small to have more than one set of engines and thus to have more than one propeller; but after 1880 the use of twin screws became increasingly common, first experimentally, but soon with

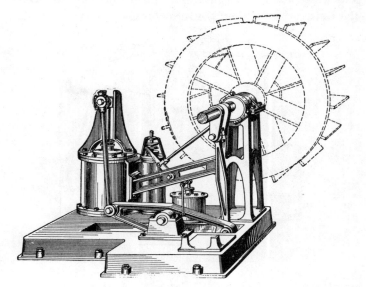

SIDE LEVER TYPE OF MARINE ENGINE.

all ocean liners. Double screws were used on war vessels before they were on merchantmen.

The Development of the Marine Engine.—The marine engines now in use are of two general types: the reciprocating and the turbine. The reciprocating, which is still the more usual form of engine, is one which drives a piston back and forth; whereas the turbine engine drives or revolves a drum or shaft in one direction. The reciprocating

engine has had an interesting technical evolution. Only a
few of its main types will be referred to here.

The first Cunarders and the other early ocean steamships had what were called *side-lever engines,* which were
like the walking-beam engines, still seen on ferry boats,
except that the beam was not placed above the cylinder
and wheel shaft, but below and at the side, as is shown in
the illustration. When the screw propellers came into use,

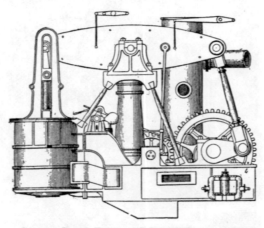

GEARED BEAM ENGINE, CONSTRUCTED IN 1855.

it was necessary to increase the speed of the revolution
of the shaft, and to accomplish this the geared engine was
introduced, i. e., an engine which drove a large cog wheel
that geared into a smaller wheel that revolved the propeller shaft. The general arrangement of the *geared-beam
engine* is shown in the illustration. Another geared engine
frequently used was the one with *oscillating cylinders.*
The piston in this engine was connected directly with
the crank shaft and as the crank revolved the entire
cylinder oscillated upon its central axis of support. The

general design of such an engine is indicated by the illustration.

The gearing of the engine caused loss of power; and from the time the screw propeller was introduced, efforts were made to perfect a *direct-acting engine.* It was difficult at first to do this, because the vessels were not wide enough to permit the engine to be placed at a right angle to the shaft between the propeller shaft and the side of the vessel. In course of time this problem was solved by placing the cylinders of the engine in an inverted position

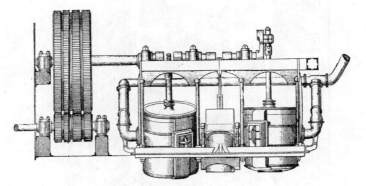

THE OSCILLATING GEARED ENGINE.

directly above the propeller shaft. Thus, about 1870, originated the *inverted direct-acting marine engine.*

The early engines, as will be explained presently, had a very low pressure of steam in the boilers; but, after 1870, boilers were built that could stand a pressure of sixty pounds or more to the square inch. It was then possible to introduce the *compound engine* in which the steam was used successively in two cylinders. In 1881 a *triple-expansion engine* was put into service; and, in 1894, the first *quadruple-expansion engine* made its appearance. Since then practically all marine engines installed have been *quadruple-expansion inverted direct-acting engines*. The arrangement of one of these is shown in the illustration.

The Turbine Engine, now used upon some ocean steamships, was invented in 1884 by C. A. Parsons, of Sweden,

THE QUADRUPLE-EXPANSION INVERTED DIRECT-ACTING MARINE ENGINE.

who applied to the steam engine the principle that had long been used in constructing water wheels. The following brief description of Parsons's turbine is given in the volume published by the United States Census of 1902 (vol. x, Part 4, page 397):

"The Parsons's type of turbine has a series of disks
mounted upon a common shaft, and alternating with parallel blades fixed within the casing of the shaft. There are
buckets or cups, upon both the revolving disks and the
fixed blades, the fixed buckets being reversed in relation
to the moving cups. The steam, admitted first through a

ONE OF THE TURBINES OF THE "GOVERNOR COBB." The low-pressure and
astern rotor in place in the stator. The upper half of the stator is
suspended to show the arrangement of the blades upon rotor and
stator.

set of stationary blades or buckets, impinges at an angle
upon the first rotating disk and imparts motion, passing
thence through another set of fixed blades to the second
disk upon the main shaft, and thus through the entire
series of alternately fixed and rotating buckets. The area
of the passages increases progressively to correspond with

the expansion of the steam as it is used on the successive disks.''

By studying the illustration it will be seen that the propeller shaft is encircled by a series of closely placed rims on the edge of each of which are small disks or blades, against which the steam expands under high pressure, thus causing the shaft to revolve. The pressure of steam in

TURBINES IN THE "GOVERNOR COBB" LOOKING FORWARD IN THE ENGINE ROOM.

passing the length of the engine, and from one row of disks to the next, is maintained by the cylindrical casing or stator that surrounds the revolving shaft. The inner surface of the stator is covered with a series of rows of disks, which are so placed as to face the disks on the interior revolving shaft.

The Boiler and the Furnace.—The engine applies the

power, the boiler generates it; and it is the boiler that determines the efficiency of the engine. The first boilers were flat-sided and box-shaped, and the pressure of the steam within them was as low as 10 or 12 pounds per square inch. It was not possible to raise the pressure above 40 or 50 pounds to the square inch until after 1868, when cylindrical boilers with internal furnaces were first constructed; after this had been done, the improvement

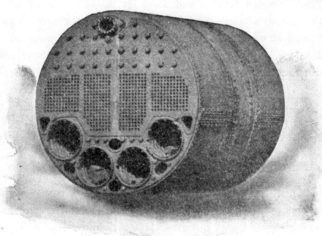

THE MARINE BOILER.

of the boiler was merely a matter of detail. The most important step made since 1868 has been the adoption of corrugated cylindrical furnaces. The marine boiler now almost universally used is one with internal corrugated furnaces, and with return horizontal tubes. In these boilers the fire passes from the furnace through the tubes, and thus up the stack. This is the fire-tube boiler.

Some use is made of water-tube boilers. In these boilers the water is in the tubes and the fire passes around the tubes instead of through them. Such boilers have greater heating efficiency, but the tubes must be constructed of copper which is more expensive than steel. These boilers also cost more to maintain. Their use for this reason has been confined mainly to naval vessels, where expense is a secondary consideration. The experience of the navy with water-tube boilers has not been very satisfactory, and their future use is not probable.

From Wooden to Iron and Steel Hulls.—The use of wood in the construction of vessels was universal until after 1840, and it was not until about 1850 that iron came to be used on a large scale in vessel construction. In Great Britain comparatively few wooden vessels were built after 1850; in the United States, on the contrary, where wood was cheap and iron expensive, shipbuilders continued to use wood until 1870; and even at the present time a relatively large percentage of our marine consists of ships of wooden construction.

The second change in material came about 1880, when British builders began to use steel instead of iron. After a few years steel was more largely used than iron, and at the present time it has practically displaced iron in the shipyards of all countries. The iron hull had greater buoyancy, strength, and durability than wooden hulls had; and, similarly, steel is superior to iron in all these three particulars.

Future Possibilities.—The ocean steamship has been improved with such marvelous rapidity during recent years that it is interesting to conjecture what the future possibilities may be. Engineers seem to be of the opinion that the maximum speed has been nearly attained, and it would seem that the ability to maintain a speed of nearly 26 knots an hour (over 30 statute miles) for the entire distance across the Atlantic, leaves little more to be desired as regards rate of ocean travel. The ocean vessel, although now of huge proportions, unquestionably will be still larger in the future. Indeed, it is probable that ships of 1,000 feet in length will be launched within a few years. As regards the marine engine, the next advance will probably be in the improvement and more general use of the turbine, either instead of, or, what is more likely, in connection with the reciprocating engines. The use of both seems to give better results than the use of either one solely. There are some prophets who are bold enough to predict that the much more efficient internal combustion engine, such as is used in automobiles and in gas engines and upon small vessels, will ultimately be applicable to the heaviest work, even that of propelling ships. Should this prove possible, it will mean a revolution in the ocean steamship service.

CHAPTER XXVI

OCEAN HIGHWAYS AND SEABOARD TERMINALS

Factors Controlling Routes of Steamers and Sailing Vessels.—The routes taken by vessels in steaming or sailing from one seaport to another are influenced by numerous factors. The shortest route between any two places upon the surface of the earth is the arc of a great circle passing through those two points and the center of the earth. By taking a piece of paper or a flexible metal ruler, and bending it over the surface of a globe so that one edge of the piece of paper, or of the flexible ruler, touches two points, like San Francisco and Yokohama, it will be seen that the edge of the paper or ruler marks a course which passes far to the north of the east and west parallel of latitude joining the two cities. It will also be observed that the edge of the paper or ruler is much shorter than the length of the parallel of latitude connecting San Francisco with Yokohama, and that the short route between the two cities is one which skirts the Aleutian Islands.

Except when diverted therefrom to seek traffic or to avoid obstacles, steamers endeavor to follow the great circle route between two ports. Sailing vessels, however, are obliged to shape their course with reference to the location and direction of ocean currents and prevailing winds. Sailing routes are usually longer than those which steamers can follow.

This is well illustrated by the course sailing vessels take

in making the passage from New York to Australia. Starting out from New York in the region of prevailing westerly winds, the vessel's course is nearly east for about 2,000 miles until it is two thirds of the way across the Atlantic, when it swings south into the belt of northern trades which blow from the northeast. The vessel keeps on a course to

THE KIEL OR KAISER WILHELM CANAL.

the south, passes the equator and crosses the belt of southern trade winds which blow from the southeast, and does not swing to the east across the South Atlantic until it reaches a latitude as far south as the Cape of Good Hope, where catching the winds from the west the vessel turns to the east across the Atlantic and sails on past Africa to Australia. The steamer, on the other hand, proceeds by

a direct great circle route from New York to the Cape
Verde Islands and thence to Capetown and on to Australia.
By studying a globe upon which the direction of the prevailing winds in different latitudes is shown, the student
will be able to understand why there is such difference
between sailing and steam routes upon the ocean.

The Seven Most Traveled Ocean Routes.—While there
are innumerable courses taken by vessels in sailing the
"trackless sea," the ocean highways crossing and recross-
ing each other at many points, there are seven main traveled ocean routes:

1. The first and most important of these is the line
across the North Atlantic. At the eastern end of this route
is the English Channel, from which vessels proceed to the
main ports of Europe. At the western end are New York
and the other North Atlantic seaboard cities of the United
States. More than half of the entire shipping of the world
is required to handle the traffic over the North Atlantic
route.

2. Next in importance comes the route connecting the
great seaports of both sides of the North Atlantic with
India, the East Indies and the Orient via the Mediterranean Sea, the Suez Canal and the Red Sea. The use of this
great ocean highway was made possible by the opening of
the Suez Canal in 1869, and as sailing vessels cannot
navigate the canal and the Red Sea, this route is used ex-
clusively by steamers.

3. The next important route is the one around South
Africa connecting both European and American ports on
the North Atlantic with South America and with Australia
and New Zealand. All freight steamers from Europe and
the United States to Australia pass around the Cape of
Good Hope instead of going through the Suez Canal when

on the way to Australia. Ships from European ports might save about 1,000 miles by using the canal route, but the tolls charged for passing through the canal are so high as to make it cheaper for the freight vessels to take the somewhat longer cape route. Passenger and mail steamers take the Suez route.

4. Corresponding with the South African-Australian

TIDAL LOCK AND POWER HOUSE NEAR ENTRANCE TO KAISER WILHELM CANAL FROM KIEL BAY.

route, just described, is the one around South America, connecting the Atlantic ports of America and Europe with the west coast of the three Americas. This route is used much more by the ships from Europe than by those from the United States. the larger part of the traffic between the two seaboards of the United States being handled by the Isthmuses of Panama and Tehuantepec.

5. In-the Gulf of Mexico and Caribbean Sea, which are sometimes called the "American Mediterranean," are numerous routes connecting the adjacent cities. These routes within the Gulf and Caribbean connect, through the Straits of Florida and Windward Passage, with the highways to and from our Atlantic seaboard, and, by way of these Straits and the Mona Passage, with the ocean route to and from Europe.

6. Of the two lines across the Pacific the one most traveled is the great circle route across the North Pacific connecting San Francisco, Portland and Puget Sound ports with Yokohama, Shanghai, Hong Kong, and Manila. This route from San Francisco to Yokohama is nearly 1,000 miles shorter than the course via the Hawaiian Islands.

7. The other ocean highway of major importance is the one connecting the Pacific coast of North America with New Zealand and Australia. Ordinarily vessels on this route call at Hawaii and New Zealand ports. In some cases, however, the course is by way of Tahiti in the Society Islands instead of via Honolulu.

Every student of ocean routes should not only locate the foregoing seven highways upon a map or globe, but should also work out and locate upon a map the probable routes which steamers and sailing vessels would take from the leading ports of the United States to different parts of the world.

Ocean Ship Canals.—To shorten ocean routes, three important ocean ship canals—the Suez, the Kaiser Wilhelm and the Corinth—have been constructed, and a fourth one of still greater consequence will be opened at Panama within a few years. The Suez Canal was constructed between

1859 and 1869 by a French company headed by Ferdinand de Lesseps. The distance from Port Said, on the Mediterranean, to Suez on the Red Sea is eighty-eight nautical, or one hundred statute, miles; twenty-seven miles of

LOCK IN THE MANCHESTER CANAL, NEAR CITY OF MANCHESTER.

this distance is taken up by four lakes created by the canal which filled up depressions or basins between the two seas. The Suez Canal has a depth of thirty-one feet at low water, but will soon be deepened to thirty-six feet. In 1875, the British Government purchased all the shares of canal stock owned by the Khedive of Egypt and thus secured a large measure of control over this waterway. This was done in order to safeguard the commercial and political interests of Great Britain in Egypt and in India. The vast commerce between Europe and India and the Orient passes through the Suez Canal. In 1907 the net tonnage of vessels, commercial and naval, that used the Suez Canal was 14,-728,434. The revenues from tolls are large, and the canal stock yields its owners fifteen per cent per annum.

The Baltic was connected with the North Sea in 1895 by the Kaiser Wilhelm Canal, extending from Kiel Bay to Brunsbüttel at the mouth of the Elbe River. This waterway is located on German soil and was constructed by the German Government for naval and commercial reasons. It shortens the route between the two separated German seaboards by from 300 to 400 miles. The canal has a length of 61 miles; and its present dimensions are $29\frac{1}{2}$ feet depth, 72 feet bottom width, and 190 feet surface breadth. The growth of the traffic of the waterway, which now annually passes vessels with a gross tonnage of about 6,000,000 tons, makes the early enlargement of the canal a necessity.

The Corinth Canal is a short waterway four miles in length connecting the Gulf of Corinth with the Gulf of Ægina. This waterway proved very difficult and expensive to construct and cost $13,750,000. Since it was opened in 1893 its traffic has grown slowly and the receipts from tolls have not been sufficient to meet operating expenses and interest charges. The light traffic is due in part to the small dimensions of the canal, the bottom width being only 69 feet and the depth 26 feet $\frac{1}{4}$ inch. The air and tidal currents through the canal have made navigation somewhat difficult particularly through the part of the canal where there is a deep rock cut, consequently most vessels plying between the ports of the Black and Ægean seas and those of the Adriatic and the Western Mediterranean prefer to keep to the longer open sea route around Morea.

Some years ago the city of Amsterdam found that the Zuider Zee had become too shallow to accommodate ocean vessels, and the city was threatened with the loss of its ocean commerce. The situation was met by the construc-

SHIPS LYING AT ANCHOR IN THE ARTIFICIAL PORT OF MANCHESTER.   View toward Manchester from the first canal lock below the city.

tion of a canal from Ymuiden on the North Sea, a distance of 15½ miles. This waterway is 32 feet deep and 165 feet wide at the bottom. The net tonnage of the vessels passing the tidal lock at Ymuiden is about 5,000,000. This waterway has assured Amsterdam continued growth and prosperity.

Manchester, the greatest textile manufacturing center of the world, was made a seaport in 1894 by the construc-

tion of the Manchester Ship Canal. This waterway is 35½
miles long and has four locks, by means of which vessels
are elevated 60 feet above the sea. The canal is 28 feet
deep, and has a bottom width of 120 feet. At Manchester,
extensive dock areas have been excavated and what was
formerly an inland city has become a seaport, visited annually by 5,000 to 6,000 seagoing vessels aggregating
between 3,000,000 and 4,000,000 tons gross register. The
traffic carried by these ships is approaching 5,000,000 cargo
tons annually.

The Seaport, its Parts and Types.—The seaboard terminal of the ocean route consists of three distinct parts:
the channel to and from the sea, the harbor proper, and
the piers, docks, warehouses and other facilities for receiving and forwarding traffic. All three of these parts are
more or less artificial, there being few large seaports whose
channels and harbors have not required more or less dredg-
ing to make them deep and wide enough to accommodate
modern shipping. Some of the largest seaports in the
world—Hamburg, Bremen, Rotterdam and others—are almost entirely artificial.

Seaports are of four types. Some cities like Boulogne,
France, and others are situated directly on the shore of the
sea, and have no natural harbor or channel of approach;
ships must ride at anchor in the open roadstead. Such
ports are of the roadstead type. The second type of port
is that located on a bay, as are San Francisco and Pensa-
cola. The river ports, such as Philadelphia and New Orleans, represent a third class; while some ports like that
of New York and Mobile are located both at the head of a
bay and at the mouth of a navigable river. Ports of this
fourth class are the most favorably situated of all. The
most rapidly growing seaports of the world are those which

are situated at or near the mouth of a large navigable river. Hamburg on the river Elbe has made the most phenomenal progress of any port in the world.   The advances of Rotterdam, near the mouth of the Rhine, and of New York, with the valley of the Hudson and the Great Lakes for its background, have been hardly less rapid.

Ports are Public, Semipublic, and Private.—Some ports, as, for instance, Hamburg, Rotterdam, and Antwerp, are constructed and managed by the city government, aided

SANDON HALF-TIDE DOCK AT LIVERPOOL.   The gates from the dock into the harbor are open for about two hours at a time each mean tide; i. e. twice daily.

more or less by the State.   Other ports, like Liverpool and London, have been improved and are administered by public "trusts," which are corporations controlled jointly by the public and by the commercial interests of the port. The third class of ports, of which there is a large and increasing number, is typified by Southampton, England, which was constructed and is now controlled by a railroad company.   It is thus seen that the great ports of the world may be divided into three classes according to the authority which controls them—public, semipublic, and private.

American System of Port Improvement and Control.—In the United States the improvement and administration of the seaports are shared jointly by the Federal, State and Local Governments. The United States dredges, buoys, and lights the channel and the harbor, and establishes pier-head lines, i. e., the lines to which piers may extend from the shore into the channel. From the pier-head line to the shore the State Government has authority. It may exer-

ONE OF THE BASINS AT THE PORT OF ANTWERP.

cise this authority directly, as is done in California and a few other States, or it may authorize the city government to regulate and develop the terminal facilities as has been done at New York City and Philadelphia. Whether the port is controlled by State authority or the city government, the piers and other transfer facilities and the ground along the harbor front may be reserved as public property, or may be sold to individuals or corporations. Until recent years, the practice of most American cities has been to permit the private ownership of harbor frontage; the time however, has now come when the commercial necessities of our largest seaports make it desirable for the public to secure possession of the harbor facilities and develop them systematically with reference to the commerce and industry of the port as a whole. The tendency in the United States is now away from the private and toward the public port.

CHAPTER XXVII

THE PANAMA CANAL

Choice of the Canal Route.—The interest of the American people in a canal to be constructed either through Central America or across the Isthmus of Panama dates from the beginning of gold mining in California in 1848–50, and the exodus at that time of large numbers of people to the Pacific coast. Lines of vessels were put into service from New York and other Atlantic ports to the Caribbean shore of the Isthmus of Panama and also between the bay of Panama and California, passengers and freight being transferred across the Isthmus by small boats up the Chagres River and by pack trains over the divide separating the Chagres Valley from the bay of Panama. This route was soon improved by the construction of a railroad, which was opened in 1855.

Another Isthmian route much used was across Nicaragua via the San Juan River and Lake Nicaragua, from which there was a portage of thirteen miles to San Juan del Sur on the Pacific Ocean. This route was developed by Commodore Vanderbilt who ran a line of steamers between New York and Greytown, and between San Juan del Sur and California ports and transferred passengers across Nicaragua by steamboats and stages.

In 1850 and for some years thereafter, it was supposed that the best route for a canal across the Isthmus was one via the San Juan River and Lake Nicaragua, because it

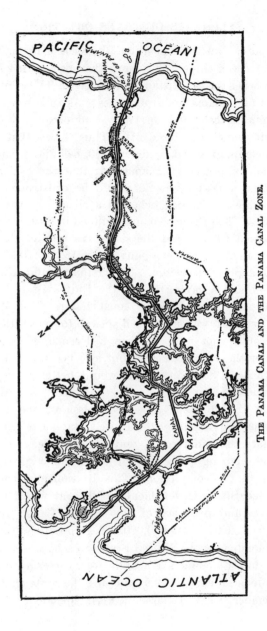

THE PANAMA CANAL AND THE PANAMA CANAL ZONE.

was thought that the San Juan River could be made navigable for ocean ships. This route, however, is 184 miles in length; whereas the distance from ocean to ocean at the Isthmus of Panama is but 41 miles. As time went on, the San Juan River silted up badly and ocean vessels were built with much greater draft. Thus it was that when a French company decided, about 1880, to build a canal they chose the route across Panama. At that time, it was supposed that a sea-level canal would be constructed. This was possible at Panama, whereas a Nicaragua canal must have locks. The French company failed in its effort to build the Panama Canal; and the same was true of the efforts made by an American company, from 1885 to 1893, to put a canal across Nicaragua. The Panama and Nicaragua canal companies having failed, the United States Government began to consider the construction of an isthmian waterway; and was at first disposed to select the Nicaragua route; not only because a French company had control of the Panama route; but also because it was supposed that a Nicaragua canal would better serve American commerce.

From 1895 to 1899, three commissions, one after another, were appointed by the United States Government to investigate the canal route, and the final decision was in favor of securing possession of the Panama project and carrying that to completion. This decision was reached by the United States Government in 1902, at which time the concession and property of the French Canal Company were purchased for $40,000,000. Negotiations were opened with Colombia by the United States to secure a canal concession, but Colombia's demands were so exorbitant that negotiations failed. At this juncture, the State of Panama, in November, 1903, declared itself independent of Colom-

bia, established a republic and, for a payment of $10,000,-
000, granted the United States a concession to build a canal
from Colon to Panama. The United States began construction in a preliminary way in 1904.

The Canal Concession.—The treaty concluded between
the United States and Panama on February 23, 1904, gave
the United States control over a strip of territory ten miles
wide—five miles on each side of the center line of the canal
—extending from Colon to Panama. The United States
has the right to construct, maintain, and operate the canal
and to govern the country within the Canal Zone, exceptions being made of the small town of Colon and of the city
of Panama, which have their own municipal government
subject to the laws of Panama. The United States, however, was given the right to put these two cities in sanitary
condition by providing them with sewers, paving their
streets, and furnishing them, at reasonable rates, with a
supply of pure water. As stated above, the United States
paid ten million dollars for this concession; it also agreed
to pay the republic of Panama $250,000 a year, beginning
nine years after the date of the ratification of the treaty—
a sum which Colombia was receiving from the Panama
Railroad Company, the ownership of whose lines was secured by the United States when it bought out the French
company. The United States Government owns and gov-
erns the Canal Zone, but the political sovereignty over this
territory remains with the republic of Panama which is
technically not dispossessed of any of its territory.

The Three Preliminary Problems.—Before the actual
work of constructing the canal could be begun, or rather
before the work could be carried far, three preliminary
problems had to be solved:

First of all it was necessary to put the Canal Zone and

the cities of Colon and Panama in a thoroughly sanitary condition. Like most Spanish-American cities, they were quite otherwise when the United States took possession of the Canal Zone. At the present time, due to the admirable work of Colonel William C. Gorgas, a member of the Isthmian Canal Commission, and head of the department of sanitation on the Isthmus, the health conditions are everything that could be desired. It took about two years to put the Canal Zone in order from a health point of view, and since then the death rate has been surprisingly low.

Another preliminary problem of great importance was that of deciding whether the work of excavation and construction should be done directly by the United States Government or whether the work should be let out to one or more contractors. Knowing that it would take some time to secure the detailed and exact information which contractors would need to have in order to make intelligent bids, the Government early set at work a small force to determine unit costs for doing the work. It was ultimately found impossible to secure satisfactory bids from contractors, and the United States at the end of two years, decided to proceed with the execution of the work itself.

The third and largest preliminary question to be settled was what the type of canal shouldbe—whether it should be a sea-level waterway, or one with locks. The majority of American engineers have always favored a lock project. In order to secure the fullest possible information on this most important question, President Roosevelt referred the matter to a board of consulting engineers of thirteen members, five of whom were foreigners. The report of this board did not make the settlement of the question much easier; because the majority of the board, including the five foreign members and three of the Americans, reported in favor of a sea-level canal. However, the lock project was favored by a majority of the American engineers on the consulting board and by a majority of the engineers on the board that had been appointed to construct the canal. President Roosevelt referred the matter to Congress which wisely decided in favor of a canal with locks.

The Canal Route and Project.—The canal now being constructed extends from Limon Bay on the Caribbean shore,

PEDRO MIGUEL LOCK SITE.   June, 1908.

near Colon, to the bay of Panama which it enters a short distance from the city of Panama. The length of the canal will be 50 miles, 4½ miles consist of a submerged channel through Limon Bay, and at the Panama Bay end another dredged channel of about the same length is necessary in order to reach 40 feet of water in that bay. For nearly three fifths of the length, the canal route is in the valley of the Chagres River, a typical torrential stream which enters the Caribbean near, but not through, Limon Bay. The part of the Chagres River valley used by the canal will be converted into a lake, which is shown on the accompanying map representing the Isthmus of Panama as it will appear after the canal is completed.

The route may be described as follows: Starting from the Caribbean, there is a dredged channel through the shallow Limon Bay for a distance of 4½ miles to the shore line. The channel is continued through the swampy region inland for 3½ miles to a point where the Chagres River has made a wide opening in the Gatun hills—a low range extending nearly parallel with the coast. At this point a huge dam, 7,700 feet in length, rising 60 feet above mean tide will close the opening in the Gatun hills and convert a large part of the Chagres River valley into a lake, the surface area of which will be 171 square miles. The level of this lake will be from 85 to 87 feet above the sea. To overcome this difference in level, there are three locks at Gatun each one having a lift of 29 feet. There will be a double flight of locks, i. e., twin locks on each level. The locks will have a length of 1,000 feet, a width of 110 feet, and a depth of 40 feet. From the Gatun locks, the canal route will be in the lake for 22 miles to Gamboa where, at a sharp bend in the Chagres valley, the canal route leaves the river valley and crosses the divide between the two oceans. Here in the divide is where the deep canal cut is being dug. The length of the cut will be between 7 and 8 miles, the deepest portion of which will be through the Culebra hill. At Pedro Miguel, 6½ miles from the shore line of the bay of Panama, the canal passes out of the deep cut; and, at this point, a lock with a lift of 30 feet lowers the canal to an elevation of 55 feet above the level of the Pacific at mean tide. Between Pedro Miguel and Miraflores, there will be a small lake about 1½ miles in length; and at Miraflores two locks will overcome the difference in level between the lake and that of the bay of Panama. The locks at Pedro Miguel and Miraflores have the same dimensions as those at Gatun, and are also constructed in pairs. From the Miraflores locks, the canal extends across the swampy country to La Boca— the mouth of the Rio Grande—and on, as a submerged channel 4½ miles, into the bay of Panama.

The depth of the canal in the earth sections and submarine portions will be 41 feet; through the deep cut, 45 feet. The width of the canal will vary with different sections.

PEDRO MIGUEL LOCK SITE, LOOKING SOUTH, DOWN TO GRADE. June, 1908.

The sea-level channels at each end will have a width of 500 feet. In the lake, the breadth of the channel will vary from 1,000 to 500 feet, and in the deep cut the bottom width will be 300 feet. The dimensions of this canal will far exceed those of any other canal in the world. The construction will reach the highest attainable standards, and the construction of all locks in pairs will be a guarantee against interruption in the use of the canal, and will enable the waterway to accommodate all or more than all the commerce that may seek to pass from sea to sea.

The Control of the Chagres River.—The one great prob-

lem connected with the successful construction and maintenance of the Panama Canal is the control of the Chagres
River.   This stream rises in the hills forming the divide
between the two oceans, flows to the Northwest for half
of its course, then turns nearly at a right angle and flows
north into the Atlantic Ocean.   It will be remembered
that the trend of the Isthmus in the neighborhood of the
canal is not north and south, but southwest and northeast.
This accounts for the fact that the town of Colon is 20 miles
west of the city of Panama, and that the general direction
of the canal is from northwest to southeast.   In its upper
and middle courses the Chagres River flows through a well-
defined valley bounded by comparatively high hills.   In
the neighborhood of Bohio, about 15 miles from the
mouth of the river, the stream leaves the high country and
meanders across a swampy district, passes through an opening in the Gatun hills and reënters the swampy district
from which it flows into the sea.   At low water there is
only about one foot of fall from Bohio to the sea.   During
the rainy season the Chagres River is subject to extreme
floods, the river having been known to rise nearly 40 feet
in twenty-four hours.

It was necessary to locate the canal in the valley of the
torrential Chagres River and to make provision either to
take the waters of the river into the canal, or to keep them
safely away from the proposed waterway.   The project
above described provides for the creation of a large lake
occupying nearly half of the valley of the river, and this
body of water will be large enough to take care of the
Chagres floods.   In order to form this lake, however, the
construction of the Gatun dam is necessary ; thus the whole
canal project hinges upon the successful construction of
this dam.   Fortunately, the engineers have solved this

question beyond any reasonable doubt. "The Gatun dam is to consist of two piles of rock 1,200 feet apart and carried up to 60 feet above mean tide. The space between them and up to the required height is to be filled by selected material deposited in place by the hydraulic process." This great structure will be 7,700 feet in length and will rise well above the level of the lake. The dam thus constructed of earth and rock will form a huge dike a half mile or more in width. It is believed that this plan of construction will make the dam unquestionably able to stand any strain that may be put upon it by floods in the Chagres River.

LOOKING SOUTH THROUGH CULEBRA CUT, PANAMA CANAL, 1908.

If a tide-level canal were to be constructed, the solution of the Chagres River problem would be much more difficult. It would then be necessary to keep the water of the Chagres River out of the canal, and in order to do so it would be

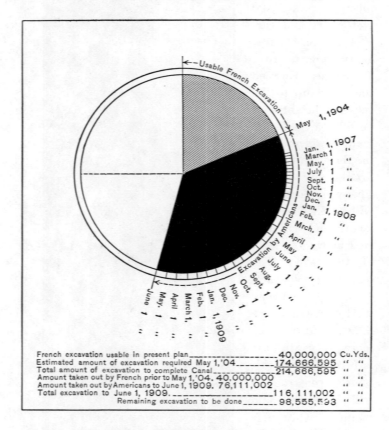

French excavation usable in present plan_____40,000,000 Cu.Yds.
Estimated amount of excavation required May 1,'04._____174,666,595 " "
Total amount of excavation to complete Canal_____214,666,595 " "
Amount taken out by French prior to May 1,'04. 40,000,000
Amount taken out byAmericans to June 1, 1909. 76,111,002   " "
Total excavation to June 1, 1909. _____116,111,002 " "
                Remaining excavation to be done_____98,555,593 " "

necessary to provide an artificial channel to the Caribbean on each side of the canal to carry off the Chagres water. The natural channel would not suffice. To maintain these channels in time of flood and to keep the water from

breaking into the intermediate and lower-lying canal
trench would be extremely difficult, in view of the fact
that there is practically no descent in the general level of
the country from Bohio to the Atlantic Ocean. The flood
waters of the Chagres River would have to be held back
by damming not only the upper portions of the Chagres
River, but also the important tributaries which enter the
Chagres in its lower course. In a word, the technical problems connected with the construction of a tide-level canal
would be more serious than those to be solved in building
a lock canal, and it is believed that such a waterway when
constructed would be less serviceable to commerce than the
lock canal will be with the large Gatun Lake.

Work Accomplished and Rate of Progress.—The construction of the Panama Canal requires the handling of no less
than 214,666,595 cubic yards of earth and rock. In the
accompanying diagram the area of the entire circle represents the total amount of material to be moved. The diagram shows how much of the work was done by the French
Company before the United States began operations, and
it also indicates what has been done month by month since
January 1, 1907. Up to 1907, excavations proceeded
slowly because the work was then being organized; during
the year 1907, the progress was also relatively slow; but
since January 1, 1908, the material has been handled with
unexpected rapidity. At the present time nearly 3,000,000
cubic yards of material are being excavated each month.
At this rate, the excavation work can be completed by the
end of 1912.

There are three big tasks to perform at Panama: One
is the excavation work on the canal trench, in the deep cut
and for the foundations for the locks. Another task is the
construction of the great dam at Gatun; and the third is

the masonry work for the locks. It is now evident that it will take longer to complete the locks than to do the other parts of the work. It is fully expected that the canal will be open for use in 1915.

The Canal and the Navy.—The canal is being constructed by the United States for three reasons: to make its navy more efficient, to serve the needs of commerce, and to enable the industries of the country to develop more rapidly. At present, the two seaboards of the United States are separated by a water route 13,000 to 15,000 miles in length; it thus becomes necessary to maintain strong naval fleets on both oceans. With an Isthmian canal, our seaboards will be brought within 4,000 to 5,000 miles of each other and it will be possible to transfer fleets and squadrons from one ocean to the other quickly and economically; and thus the ability of our navy to protect our seaboards will be practically doubled.

The necessity for this waterway from a naval point of view was brought strongly to the attention of the American people by the celebrated trip of the *Oregon* from our Pacific coast to the West Indies at the opening of the war with Spain in 1898. Fortunately, the *Oregon* arrived at the West Indies in good condition and in time to be of service; but the length of her trip and the risks she ran in making the journey showed how ineffective a fleet on one ocean would be to strike a blow against an enemy upon the other ocean. Again, in 1908, the possible importance of an Isthmian canal to our navy was illustrated by the cruise of the American fleet of battleships around the world. We then realized how long it takes for a naval fleet to pass from one sea to another and what risks are incurred in navigating the Strait of Magellan.

The Canal and Commerce.—The Panama Canal will

benefit American commerce (1) by providing a short route between our Atlantic and Pacific seaboards; (2) by shortening the distance from our Atlantic and Gulf ports to western, central, and south America, Australasia, China, and Japan; and (3) by reducing the distance from our western coasts to Europe by nearly one half. The following table gives the distances via existing routes and by way of the Panama Canal between our two seaboards and between each of our coasts and typical ports in different parts of the world.

Table of Distances via the Panama Canal and via Existing Routes.

	San Francisco.	Yokohama.	Shanghai.	Sydney.	Iquique.
New York via present route.	I. II. 13,714	III. 13,564	III. 12,514	VI. 13,658	I. 9,221
Panama Canal........	5,299	IV. 9,835	V. 10,885	VII. 9,814	4,021
Saving by canal.......	8,415	3,729	1,629	3,844	5,200
New Orleans via present route..............	I. II. 14,114	III. ·14,929	III. 13,879	VI. 14,625	I. 9,621
Panamá Canal.........	4,698	IV. 9,234	V. 10,284	VII. 9,213	3,420
Saving by canal.......	9,416	5,695	3,595	5,412	6,201
Liverpool via present route..	I. II. 14,084	III. 11,640	III. 10,580	VIII. 12,234	I. 9,591
Panama Canal........	8,038	IV. 12,574	V. 13,624	12,553	6,760
Saving by canal.......	6,046	−934	−3,044	−319	2,831

I.   Via Strait of Magellan.
II.   Via Pernambuco and Callao.
III. Via Suez Canal.
IV.   Via San Francisco.
V.   Via San Francisco and Yokohama.
VI.   Via St. Vincent, Cape of Good Hope, Adelaide, and Melbourne.
VII. Via Wellington.
VIII. Suez Canal, Colombo, King George, George Sound, and Adelaide.

While the main service of the canal will be to shorten ocean routes, it will also serve commerce by reducing the risks connected with passing the Strait of Magellan; and

it will also make the mercantile marine of the United
States and other countries more effective in the performance of their transportation services. The shorter and
safer routes via the canal will reduce the expenses of international commerce and will increase the volume of trade.

The Canal and Industrial Progress.—In considering the
influence of the Panama Canal the fact should be kept in
mind that commerce is but incidental to industry. The
great service of the canal will be that of assisting in the
development of the industries of the Pacific coast States, of
the middle, western, and southern sections of the country, and of the manufacturing New England and middle
Atlantic States. While the canal will be used by ocean carriers, its main benefits will accrue to the farmers, manufacturers, lumbermen, and miners in different parts of our
richly endowed country.

CHAPTER XXVIII

THE OCEAN FREIGHT SERVICE

Volume and Value of Ocean Freight Traffic.—The total value of the foreign trade of the United States, import and export, now exceeds $3,000,000,000 annually; the imports comprise about two fifths of the total value, and the exports the other three fifths. The number of tons of cargo handled in the foreign trade cannot be precisely determined, but a careful estimate for 1908 makes the total of our imports to be 19,000,000 tons and that of our exports to be 51,688,148 tons. The total cargo tonnage of the imports and exports was approximately 70,688,000 in 1908. To handle this traffic, vessels aggregating 38,539,195 tons, gross register, entered our seaports from foreign countries, and ships with a gross tonnage of 38,281,696 cleared from our ports to foreign destinations. Not all of these vessels were fully loaded; some of them had part cargoes and others, amounting to twenty-two per cent of the total, entered and cleared in ballast.

These vessels were employed solely in the foreign trade. In addition to them, the coastwise commerce of the United States required the use of a fleet of vessels having a gross tonnage of 3,500,000. The total of entrances and clearances for the coastwise commerce is not known, but it of course amounted to several times the tonnage of the vessels. It is probable that the total tonnage of the entrances and clearances of the vessels engaged in the maritime foreign

and coastwise commerce of the United States amounts
annually to 100,000,000 tons gross register.

**Causes Accounting for the Growth of the Ocean Freight
Traffic.**—The foreign trade of the United States has risen
fast in volume and value since 1895, and its continued
growth is certain.   The rapid development of the industries and internal commerce of the United States gives
rise to a corresponding expansion of international trade.
The large increase in the ocean freight business has been
the result, first of all, of a cheapening in the cost of
transportation that has permitted the shipment of coal
and other minerals, fertilizers, and various other bulky
products across wide oceans.   It has been only since 1870
that it was possible to handle large quantities of low grade
freight over the longer ocean routes.   Another class of
traffic that has latterly entered largely into ocean commerce has consisted of fruits, meats, and other perishable
commodities requiring refrigeration, special warehousing
facilities, speedy transportation, and prompt delivery.

The law of the development of ocean freight traffic may
be stated as follows: *the transportation service upon the
ocean has become cheaper for all classes of traffic; faster
for such articles as require rapid transit, more reliable with
the substitution of steam for sails, and more specialized
with reference to the service to be performed.*   The fruit
steamer, the tank steamer and the ore vessel are instances
of the specialization of the vessel with reference to the
work which it performs.

The Three Parts of the Ocean Freight Service.—The exchange of commodities between the shippers of one country
and the consignees in another country requires three transportation services: (1) the vessel services or the carriage of
commodities from port to port; (2) the traffic services con-

nected with the forwarding of and accounting for freight; and (3) the transfer and other terminal services. It will be well to consider briefly each of these three parts of the ocean freight service.

The transportation or carriage of ocean freight is performed in part by vessels operated as ocean lines and in part by individual ships managed by those who own them or lease them. When the traffic over any given route is of large volume and of relatively constant quantity, companies will establish lines of vessels and provide for fixed sailings from the ports at each end of the route. The number of vessels employed and the frequency of the sailings will depend upon the volume of traffic and its fluctuations from year to year or from one season to another.

Line traffic is of three general kinds: (1) Lines consisting of the largest and fastest ships—the express steamers—which carry only passengers and the mails and parcels; (2) those lines using steamers of moderate speed operated both for the passenger traffic and for the transportation of freight; and (3) freight lines employing vessels that carry no passengers whatever. With the rapid growth of ocean commerce there has been a great increase in the number of lines that carry freight only.

A surprisingly large share of the heavy freight traffic of the ocean is handled by vessels operated as single units. As most of the vessels thus operated are chartered by those who use them, this traffic is called charter traffic. An individual or company desiring to ship a full cargo of coal, of lumber, of structural iron, locomotives, wheat, corn, or cotton, charters a vessel to perform the service, or pays some other person who has chartered a vessel an agreed rate of freight to transport the full cargo to its destination. It is possible, by applying to a shipbroker, for any manufacturer or exporter to secure a vessel to take his cargo from a port in any country to practically any port of the world. A chartered vessel is not limited to any particular route, as a line vessel is; nor is it required to sail upon any fixed date.

Traffic Services of the Shipbroker and Freight Forwarder. —By means of the telegraph and the ocean cable, shipbrokers in every seaport in the world keep informed in regard to the movements of vessels that may be chartered at any particular time for handling different kinds of cargo. They secure vessels for those who wish to use them in much the same way that the real estate agent secures a house for the man who wishes to rent one.

Traffic services of quite as great importance are performed by the freight forwarder who solicits shipments both from seaboard and interior points to foreign destination; likewise in the same manner, he solicits import traffic. It is the business of a freight forwarder to take charge of the goods from the time they leave the shipper until they are received by the consignee. If the goods originate inland, they are transported by a railroad company to the seaboard and thence are reshipped by the freight forwarder, either upon his vessels or upon those owned by somebody else, to the most convenient foreign port, where the goods are taken in charge by the freight forwarder's agent who sends the articles on to their ultimate destination. When the goods leave the shipper at the inland point, they are usually billed through to ultimate destination via the city in which the freight forwarder's main offices are located, and also via the ocean ship line which he employs or controls.

After the goods leave the shipper, he is relieved from all further care as to their transportation and delivery.

THE COSMOPOLITAN SHIPPING COMPANY

COSMOPOLITAN LINE

PHILADELPHIA AND LEITH
(DUNDEE, ABERDEEN, ETC.)

PETER WRIGHT & SONS, General Agents   PHILADELPHIA   NEW YORK

JOHN E. EARLE & CO., General Western Agents   CHICAGO

HUDIG & PIETERS, European Agents   ROTTERDAM AND AMSTERDAM

HENDERSON & McINTOSH, Agents   LEITH

Received, in apparent good order and condition by **The Cosmopolitan Shipping Company**, from...to be transported by the Steamship....................................... to sail from the Port of **PHILADELPHIA**, and bound for **LEITH, SCOTLAND**, (or as near thereto as she can safely get), with liberty to call at any port or ports in or out of the customary route, or failing shipment by said steamer, in or upon a following steamer..

SHIPPER'S MARKS:

SAID TO WEIGH.........................LBS.

being marked and numbered as per margin shippers weight (quality, quantity, gauge, contents, weight and value unknown), and to be delivered in like good order and condition at the port of **LEITH**...unto ....or to his or their assigns, he or they paying freight, primage and charges in cash, immediately on discharge of the Goods, without any allowance of credit or discount, at the rate of ....

ATTENTION OF SHIPPERS IS CALLED TO THE ACT OF CONGRESS OF 1851

Any person or persons shipping Oil of Vitriol, unslaked Lime, Inflammable Matches or Gunpowder, in a ship or vessel taking cargo for Divers persons on freight, without delivering **AT THE TIME OF SHIPMENT** a note in writing expressing the nature and character of such merchandise, to the Master, Mate or Officer, or person in charge of the loading of the ship or vessel, shall forfeit to the United States "ONE THOUSAND DOLLARS."

.... Bushels at .... per			*lbs.,*
.... Ft...... in. at .... per cu. ft.			
.... at .... per.			*lbs.*
.... at .... per			
	5 per cent. Primage,		....
	Charges,		....
	Total,		....

IT IS MUTUALLY AGREED that the Steamer shall have liberty to sail with or without pilots; that the carrier shall have liberty to convey goods in craft and/or lighters to and from the steamer at the risk of the owners of the goods; and, in case the steamer shall put into a port of refuge, or be prevented from any cause from proceeding in the ordinary course of her voyage, to trans-ship the goods to their destination by any other steamer; that the Carrier shall not be liable for loss or damage occasioned by perils of the sea, or other waters, by fire from any cause or whensoever occurring; by barratry of the master or crew; by enemies, pirates or robbers; by arrest and restraint of princes, rulers or people, riots, strikes or stoppage of labor; by explosion, bursting of boilers, breakage of shafts, or any latent defect in hull, machinery or appurtenances, or unseaworthiness of the steamer, whether existing at time of shipment, or at the beginning of the voyage, provided the owners have exercised due diligence to make the steamer seaworthy; by heating, frost, decay, putrefaction, rust, sweat, change of character, drainage, leakage, breakage, vermin, or by explosion of any of the goods, whether shipped with or without disclosure of their nature, or any loss or damage arising from the nature of the goods or the insufficiency of packages; nor for land damage; nor for the obliteration, errors, insufficiency or absence of marks, numbers, address or description; nor for risk of craft, hulk or trans-shipment; nor for any loss or damage caused by the prolongation of the voyage, and that the carrier shall not be concluded as to correctness of statements herein of quality, quantity, gauge, contents, weight and value. General Average payable according to York—Antwerp Rules. If the owner of the steamer shall have exercised due diligence to make said steamer in all respects seaworthy and properly manned, equipped and supplied, it is hereby agreed that in case of danger, damage or disaster resulting from fault or negligence of the master or crew in the navigation or management of the steamer, or from latent or other defects or unseaworthiness of the steamer, whether existing at time of shipment, or at the beginning of the voyage, but not discoverable by due diligence, the consignees or owners of the cargo shall not be exempted from liability for contribution in General Average, but, with the shipowner, shall contribute in General Average as if such danger, damage or disaster had not resulted from such fault, negligence, latent or other defects or unseaworthiness.

IT IS ALSO MUTUALLY AGREED, that this shipment is subject to all the terms and provisions of, and all the exemptions from liability contained in the Act of Congress of the United States, approved on the 13th day of February, 1893, and entitled "An Act relating to the Navigation of Vessels, etc."

1.—IT IS ALSO MUTUALLY AGREED that the value of each package receipted for as above does not exceed the sum of one hundred dollars unless otherwise stated herein, on which basis the rate of freight is adjusted.

2.—ALSO, that the Carrier shall not be liable for articles specified in Section 4281 of the Revised Statutes of the United States, unless written notice of the true character and value thereof is given at the time of lading and entered in the bill of lading.

3.—ALSO, that Shippers shall be liable for any loss or damage to Steamer or Cargo caused by inflammable, explosive or dangerous goods, shipped without full disclosure of their nature, whether such Shipper be Principal or Agent; and such Goods may be thrown overboard or destroyed at any time without compensation.

4.—ALSO, that the Carrier shall have a lien on the goods for all freights, primages and charges, and also for all fines or damages which the Steamer or Cargo may incur or suffer by reason of the incorrect or insufficient marking, numbering or addressing of packages or description of their contents.

5.—ALSO, that in case the Steamer shall be prevented from reaching her destination by Quarantine, the Carrier may discharge the goods into any Depot or Lazaretto, and such discharge shall be deemed a final delivery under this contract, and all the expenses thereby incurred on the goods shall be a lien thereon.

6.—ALSO, that the Steamer may commence discharging immediately on arrival and discharge continuously, any custom of the port to the contrary notwithstanding, the Collector of the port being hereby authorized to grant a general order for discharge immediately on arrival, and if the goods be not taken

Cargo may be discharged into transit sheds or otherwise, immediately after the arrival of the ship, tonnage and shed dues payable by the Consignee of goods. The goods to be taken from alongside by the Consignee, immediately the vessel is ready, and at such risk and expense as customarily discharge; or otherwise they may be landed, weighed, put into crafts or warehoused at his risk and expense. The Steamer having a lien on the goods for all the expense so incurred. Should the Steamer be unable to enter the dock through bad tides, Consignees to provide crafts and take delivery in the river. The Collector of the port is hereby authorized to grant a general order for discharge, immediately after the entry of the ship. The lading and delivery of the cargo to be done by the Consignees of the ship, and the expense thereof to be paid by the Receivers of cargo. In order to facilitate the discharge, the Consignees of the vessel to have power to do the quay porterage, the charges for weighing, etc., to be paid by the Consignee.

from the Steamer by the Consignee directly they come to hand in discharging the Steamer the Master or Steamer's Agent to be at liberty to enter and land the goods, or put them into craft or store at the owner's risk and expense, when the goods shall be deemed delivered and Steamer's responsibility ended, but the Steamer and carrier to have a lien on such goods, until the payment of all costs and charges so incurred.

7.—ALSO, that if on a sale of the goods at destination, for freight and charges, the proceeds fail to cover said freight and charges, the Carrier shall be entitled to recover the difference from the shipper.

8.—ALSO, that freight is payable on damaged or unsound goods; but no freight is due on any increase in bulk or weight caused by the absorption of water during the voyage.

9.—ALSO, that in the event of claims for short delivery when the Steamer reaches her destination, the price shall be the market price at the port of destination on the day of the Steamer's entry at the Custom House, less all charges saved.

10.—ALSO, that merchandise on wharf awaiting shipment or delivery be at shipper's risk of loss or damage not happening through the fault or negligence of the Owner, Master, Agent or Manager of the Steamer, any custom of the port to the contrary notwithstanding.

11.—ALSO, that this bill of lading, duly endorsed, be given up to the Steamer's Consignee in exchange for delivery order.

12.—ALSO, that freight prepaid, will not be returned, goods lost or not lost.

13.—ALSO, that parcels for different consignees collected or made up in single packages addressed to one consignee, pay full freight on each parcel.

All risk of Fire or Flood while Goods are on the Dock, while awaiting shipment, to be borne by Shippers.

AND FINALLY, in accepting this Bill of Lading, the Shipper, Owner and Consignee of the goods, and the Holder of the Bill of Lading agree to be bound by all of its stipulations, exceptions and conditions, whether written or printed, as fully as if they were all signed by such Shipper, Owner, Consignee or Holder.

IN WITNESS WHEREOF, the Master or Agent of the said Steamship bath affirmed to..........................Bills of Lading, besides Captains' copy, all of this tenor and date, one of which being accomplished, the others to stand void.

THE COSMOPOLITAN SHIPPING COMPANY,

PETER WRIGHT & SONS,

GENERAL AGENTS.

Dated in PHILADELPHIA,...................................190

Per.................................

OCEAN BILL OF LADING.

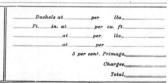

His through bill of lading gives him a receipt for the value of the goods that he has turned over to the railroad company, the initial carrier.

Before the goods start on their way, they are insured. The shipper draws upon the consignee or purchaser of the goods to the amount of their value, attaches to this draft the through bill of lading and the insurance policy, takes the documents to his bank and receives from the bank the value of the goods less the ordinary business discount. Thus the shipper is immediately able to use his capital in further production. This economical and safe organization of international trade and ocean transportation has been made possible by the freight forwarder.

Ocean Shipping Papers.—In the shipping of ocean freight and the operation of vessels to carry that freight, nine important papers are required:

(1) A *receipt* for freight is received by the shipper upon delivery of each dray load or lighter load of freight to the ocean carrier. This paper is also spoken of as a wharf receipt.

(2) The receipts for freight are exchanged for a *bill of lading* giving the names of the consignor and the consignee, describing the goods, stating their weight or tonnage, their destination, and the rate of freight. The bill of lading is usually made out in triplicate, the original being retained by the shipper, one being kept by the captain, while the third is sent to the consignee. Bills of lading are negotiable.

(3) An *invoice* of the goods must be prepared by the exporter, describing the several articles of freight, stating the prices paid, or the value of the commodities. The correctness of this invoice must be certified to by the resident Consul from the country to which the freight is being

shipped. This invoice is sent with the bill of lading to the foreign consignee who must present both papers to the customs officers in order to secure possession of the goods.

(4) A *manifest* is made out containing a list and description of all the goods carried on each ship. The ship's manifest contains "the name or names of the places, where the goods on board have been laden, and the place or

DUPLICATE FOR WHARF OF RECEIPT FOR OCEAN SHIPMENT.

places to which they are respectively destined; a particular account and description of all the packages on board with the marks and numbers thereon, the goods contained in such packages, the names of the respective shippers and consignees, as far as such particulars are known to the master of the ship."

(5) A *clearance* must be secured from the collector of the port before the vessel can start on its journey. In

DUPLICATE FOR WHARF.

Rec...

MA...

THIS RECEIPT MUST BE RETURNED IMMEDIATELY TO THE OFFICE AND EXCHANGED FOR BILL OF LADING.

CL

THE COSMOPOLITAN SHIPPING COMPANY,

COSMOPOLITAN LINE.

For Bills of Lading Apply at Office, 305 and 307 Walnut Street.   PETER WRIGHT & SONS, General Agents.

Philadelphia, _____ 190___

Per Steamer _____

Received, in apparent good order, for shipment by THE COSMOPOLITAN SHIPPING COMPANY,

of _____

THE FOLLOWING PACKAGES TO BE FORWARDED SUBJECT TO THE CONDITIONS IN THE BILLS OF LADING.

CONDITIONS.—Notice of the terms of the Bill of Lading is hereby submitted, and this Property is received subject to all the provisions therein contained.
It is hereby stipulated and agreed, that in case the whole or any part of the goods specified herein is prevented by any cause, from going in the steamship for which they are received, the Agents are only bound to forward them by succeeding Steamship of this Line, or by any other Line or Steamer due notice of which is to be given to shipper.

Merchandise on wharf awaiting shipment is at shipper's risk of loss or damage by fire and/or flood.

This receipt MUST BE EXCHANGED for the usual Bill of Lading of the Line before the sailing of the Steamer by which the Goods are to be shipped.

FULL NAME OF CONSIGNEE MUST BE GIVEN ON THIS RECEIPT.

MARKED:

Gross Weight, _____ *lbs.*

Value of Shipment, _ _ _ $ _____

_____ *Receiving Clerk.*

RECEIPT FOR FREIGHT FOR OCEAN SHIPMENT.

INVOICE OF_____ 16,000 Bus. 2 Red W. Wheat

SHIPPED BY **GRAFTON & CO.,** PHILADELPHIA, U. S. A

GRAIN
Receivers, Shippers and Exporters
The Bourse

*Shipped per S/S*_____ Laurentian _____*for*_____ Glasgow

*For Account and risk of*_____ New

*Freight*_____ 2½ d. per 60 lbs & 5% _____ *Insured*_____ Ins. Co. of North America

_____*Sale*_____ October 9th, 1905 _____*Contract No.*_____

16,000 Bus. @ 90c.		$14,400
Freight £166.13.4		
5% 8. 6.8		
£175. 0.0 @ 4.83		845
		$13,554

Documents with Drafts
- Bills Lading   2 Setts 8,000 Bus. dated 10/25
- Insurance   2 " $69.80 Ctfs. Nos. 136630-31
- Ctfs. Weights & Inspection 2 "

E. & O. E.

Philadelphia,_____ October 25th, 1905 _____

INVOICE OF AN OCEAN SHIPMENT.

THE ATLANTIC SHIPPING COMPANY.

ATLANTIC LINE. { New York—Liverpool / New York—Havre / New York—Cherbourg

PETER JAMES & SONS, GENERAL AGENTS
NEW YORK-PHILADELPHIA

Manifest of part of Cargo shipped by **THE ATLANTIC SHIPPING CO., Peter James & Sons, General Agents,** on board the ———— whereof ———— is master, for ———— 190

MARKS	NUMBERS	PACKAGES AND CONTENTS	QUANTITIES Lbs. Gallons, etc.	No. 1 Value of DOMESTIC Merchandise	No. 2 Value of Foreign Merchandise FREE	No. 3 Value of Foreign Merchandise FROM BONDED WAREHOUSE	No. 4 Value of Foreign Merchandise not FROM BONDED WAREHOUSE which has paid duties	No. 5 Value of Foreign Merchandise on THE PASSAGE (IN TRANSITU) from one foreign country to another	TO BE LANDED AT

MANIFEST OF AN OCEAN SHIPMENT.

Art. 135, Customs Regs., 1899
Sec. 4201, Rev. Stats.
(Ed. 12-16-04—15,000)

DEPARTMENT OF COMMERCE AND LABOR
BUREAU OF NAVIGATION

Cat. No. 1378

The United States of America.

CLEARANCE OF VESSEL TO A FOREIGN PORT.

District of _____

Port of _____

These are to certify all whom it doth concern:

That _____

Master or Commander of the _____

burden _____ Tons, or thereabouts, mounted with _____

Guns, navigated with _____ Men, _____

_____ built, and bound for _____

_____

having on board _____

_____

_____

_____

_____

hath here entered and cleared his said vessel, according to law.

Given under our hands and seals, at the Custom House of _____

_____, this _____ day of _____

one thousand nine hundred _____, and in the _____

year of the Independence of the United States of America.

_____   _____

Deputy Naval Officer.   Deputy Collector.

CLEARANCE OF A VESSEL TO A FOREIGN PORT.

Cat. No. 1380
Art. 132, Customs Regulations of 1899
COMMERCE AND LABOR CIRCULAR NO. 1

THE UNITED STATES OF AMERICA.
BILL OF HEALTH.

————

Custom House, Port of————

To all to whom these Presents shall come:

Whereas, *the*————

of————, *of which*————

is Master, is now ready to depart from the Port of

————*for*————, *and other*

places beyond the sea, with————

persons, including the Master of the said vessel:

We, therefore, *by these presents, do make known*

and Certify that no plague, nor any other dangerous or

contagious disease in an epidemic form, at present

exists in the said Port.

GIVEN under our hands and seals of office, this————

day of————, *190*——.

————
Collector of Customs.

————
Naval Officer.

BILL OF HEALTH.

order to secure the clearance, the master of the ship must file a copy of the manifest of the vessel's cargo, and he must also have complied with all conditions required by the Government.

(6) Before sailing, the master of the ship secures a *bill of health* from the collector of the port, stating what are the general health conditions of the port. If there are no dangerous or contagious diseases prevalent, a clean bill of health is issued.

(7) Every master of a vessel possesses a document called the *ship's articles* containing the names of all the members of the crew and the title of the position each man fills.

(8) The master must also possess the *ship's register*, a document issued by the Government of the country under whose flag the vessel sails. The register states the name of the vessel, dimensions, tonnage, etc.

(9) Lastly, before sailing, the master of the vessel applies to the resident consul of the country in which the ship's destination is located to secure the consular *visé* of the ship's manifest, clearance, and other documents. The consul issues a certificate as to the accuracy of the documents, especially of the correctness of the statements, made in the ship's bill of health.

When a vessel enters a port, the master must file the ship's manifest with the customs officials, and he must deposit the articles and register with the consul of the country under whose flag the ship sails. When the master is ready to sail, these documents are returned to him after he has fulfilled the conditions above described.

Transfer and Terminal Services.—Economy and dispatch in the handling of ocean freight depend largely upon the facilities for storing and transferring freight at terminals.

In the best organized ports of the world, the warehouse and transfer facilities are controlled and managed by the authority which has control of the port. If it is a municipal port the administration is by the authority of the city government; if a semipublic port, by a harbor "trust"; if a private port, probably by a railroad corporation. In most American cities, however, each railroad or general carrier provides such facilities as may be necessary to its particular business.

The administration of the terminal facilities by a single authority, as at Antwerp and Hamburg, has many advantages. The quays in those and other ports similarly managed are equipped with capstans, cranes and derricks, operated from a power plant, usually hydraulic; special machinery for handling ore, coal, and grain are provided; facilities are provided in one section of the port for handling certain kinds of cargo and in other sections for different classes of commodities; storage or warehouse accommodations are provided in each section of the port according to its needs. In this way, terminal expenses can be reduced to a minimum; and this is the type of port organization that should be adopted wherever political and other conditions are favorable.

CHAPTER XXIX

THE OCEAN PASSENGER, MAIL, AND EXPRESS SERVICES

I. *The Passenger Service*

Luxury and Safety of Ocean Travel.—In the transportation of freight, every effort is made to reduce cost; but, in the passenger service, speed and safety rather than economy are the objects sought. Year by year, the luxury and safety of ocean travel become greater and, to secure these better services, travelers are willing to pay higher rates. In the early days of ocean travel it was customary for all people religiously inclined to request prayers for a safe journey; now few people regard the risk of ocean travel as being any greater than the dangers of a railroad journey—as a matter of fact, the risks are less on the sea than on the railways. With ocean steamships from 500 to 800 feet in length, from 65 to 90 feet in breadth, built with numerous watertight bulkheads, with double steel bottom, and provided with twin screws, the dangers of ocean travel have been reduced to a minimum; and the comforts to be secured on the steamship are quite equal to those to be obtained at a first-class hotel in a large city. It is, of course, still possible for ships to strike hidden rocks and to collide with each other; but accidents are seldom serious when they occur near shore or even when some distance out at sea; because the vessels can make their condition and wants known by wireless communication with the shore or with passing ships.

Volume of Cabin and Steerage Traffic.—The passenger traffic on the ocean has increased with surprising rapidity. In 1898 the total number of passengers arriving at American ports from other countries was 343,963. In 1907 the figures were 1,630,266. The larger part of this great increase was the result of the growth in the third-class traffic. The immigrants entering the United States rose from 229,-299 in 1898 to 1,285,349 in 1907. The high tide of immigrant traffic was reached in 1907, there having been a temporary falling off in 1908 due to the financial depression prevailing in the United States during that year. With the slowly returning prosperity in 1909 immigrant travel began to rise, and the figures for 1910 and subsequent years will doubtless exceed those of any previous year.

Cabin passenger traffic is of about equal volume, outbound and inbound; but ordinarily the arrivals of steerage passengers in the United States greatly exceed the departures. In 1908, however, when large numbers of laborers were out of employment, the departures of third-class passengers were nearly equal to the arrivals. This indicates greater prosperity and greater mobility on the part of the foreign-born population in the United States than it was supposed to have.

The Third-class and Immigrant Traffic has been more profitable to ocean carriers than has the transportation of cabin passengers. A large passenger steamer can carry four or five third-class passengers for each person in the first and second cabin; expenses are very much less for the steerage passengers; and, when the steerage is full the steamer's voyage is highly profitable. This accounts for the systematic efforts made by all the passenger lines running vessels from Europe to America to organize and develop the emigration from Europe to the United States. Low fares, comfortable accommodations on the ocean, and a well-organized system of caring for the immigrant from the time he leaves his home in central Europe until he reaches his friend or destination in America have brought about the very rapid increase in the steerage traffic.

One of the latest developments in the handling of the steerage business has been to separate the steerage passengers into third-class and immigrants. A large number of foreigners who are not immigrants travel back and forth across the North Atlantic, and they are willing to pay a somewhat higher rate for more space and greater comfort. When the third-class passengers are separated from the immigrants, they may engage reserved berths in state rooms, their accommodations have baths, and they have a dining room separate from the immigrants.

When the passenger steamer reaches its dock at New York, where most of the immigrants enter the United States, the cabin passengers are landed on the company's pier, while the immigrants are transferred by tender from the steamship to the immigrant station at Ellis Island. Each applicant for admission to the United States is examined by the immigration officers and by physicians of the Public Health and Marine Hospital Service. After having satisfactorily passed the inspection, the immigrants are transported by special trains to their destination in different parts of the United States. The handling of this immigrant traffic is well organized by the railroad companies, which have divided it up among each other equitably.

Development of Ocean Travel.—Reference has just been made to the systematic and successful efforts of the carriers to organize and increase third-class or steerage traffic.

Numerous agencies have also been created to stimulate and facilitate cabin-passenger travel. The steamship companies themselves spend large sums annually in advertising and in soliciting business. Many private tourist agencies relieve the traveler of business details, secure him hotel accommodations, provide him with banking facilities, and supply him with such guides, couriers, and interpreters

"Titanic," White Star Line. Largest steamship being constructed in 1909. Length, 860 feet. Breadth, 92 feet. Gross register, 45,000 tons. Displacement, 60,000 tons.

as he may desire while traveling in different countries. During recent years university bureaus of travel have made their appearance to supply tourist parties with educated conductors to lecture on the art and history of the countries and cities visited. The result of all this is that a very large share of the people who travel now do so for its educational value. Formerly, men traveled mainly for business reasons, and, to some extent, because of their love of adventure; at the present time, however, it is the desire to see other countries, and learn something of their art and culture, that causes most people to cross the sea.

II. *The Ocean Mail Service*

Volume and Growth of Ocean Mails.—It is estimated by the Post-office Department that during the year ending June 30, 1908, there were 308,001,320 pieces of mail sent by sea from the United States to foreign countries. The weight of this mail matter was 14,697,759 pounds; the mail received from foreign countries was somewhat less, there being 259,122,981 pieces brought to our ports from abroad. The rapidity with which the ocean mails are growing is indicated by the fact that the number of pieces of ocean mail, outbound and inbound, for the year 1908 (558,124,-301) exceeded the number handled in 1905 by 116,349,807, the gain in three years having been twenty-six per cent. The total amount of postage received by the United States from the foreign mails was $8,585,564.

The aggregate cost to the United States for the transportation of foreign mails was $3,072,623; and, after making a liberal allowance for the cost of transporting the mail between the seaboard and the interior points within the country, the United States Government made a handsome net profit from the international mails.

Payment for Carrying Ocean Mails.—The Post-office Department makes two kinds of payments for the transportation of ocean mails—contract and noncontract payments. By act of Congress, passed March 3, 1891, the Postmaster General was authorized to contract with American steamship companies for periods of five to ten years for the transportation of mails over routes specified by the Post-office Department. The rate of payment varies with the size and speed of the ship used in carrying the mail. The principal contract is with the American Line of the International Mercantile Marine Company which operates four express steamers between New York and Southampton. Seven other contracts are in force with steamship lines over various routes.

Under the noncontract system, steamers are paid in accordance with the amount of mail dispatched. If the mail is sent under the noncontract system by a steamer flying the American flag, the United States Government pays the steamship company the rate of the international postage which with most countries is five cents an ounce for letters, i. e., the steamship company obtains $1,600 a ton for letters and post cards and $160 per ton for other articles. If the steamer is under a foreign flag, the receipts are 4 francs per kilogram (about 35 cents per pound and $700 per ton) for letters and post cards, and 50 centimes per kilogram (about $4\frac{1}{2}$ cents a pound and $90 per ton) for other classes of mail.

Sea Post Offices and Terminal Dispatch of the Ocean Mails. —In order to expedite the dispatch of mails to destination upon the arrival of the steamship, the United States Government maintains sea post offices upon steamers of four of the fastest steamship lines on the North Atlantic. When the ship reaches our ports, the mail has been sorted and sacked with reference to destination; and as soon as the vessel reaches quarantine at New York it is met by a special mail boat to which the mail is transferred. '' Mails for New York City are immediately sent to the New York Post Office, and those for other places are forwarded to destination at the earliest opportunity practicable '' without passing through the New York Post Office.

The International Parcels Post.—Although the United States has not yet established a parcels post in connection with its domestic mail service, it now accepts parcels for transportation to most countries and receives packages from them for delivery in the United States. The international parcels post is arranged for by special agreements between the United States and each foreign country. The rate per pound upon parcels is twelve cents, and in most cases parcels weighing as much as eleven pounds may be dispatched. The number of parcels sent and received through our international parcels post for the year ending June 30, 1908, was 551,000, and the growth from year to year is rapid. As the Assistant Postmaster General states: '' Its extension to all countries with which we have direct mail communication is desirable ''; and it may be added incidentally that it would be well to establish a similar service in connection with our domestic mails.

The Universal Postal Union.—In 1874 the leading nations of the world signed the Universal Postal Convention regulating the international postal services. In accordance with the provisions of this treaty of 1874, the several countries formed the Universal Postal Union which meets once in five years in the Universal Postal Congress, composed of delegates from all the governments belonging to the Union. The last Universal Postal Congress met in 1906 at Rome, Italy. This is the legislative body; the administrative body is called the International Bureau, the offices of which are in Bern, Switzerland. This bureau is in charge of a director, and is under the supervision of the post-office department of Switzerland.

READ THE CONDITIONS OF THIS RECEIPT. (212—Jan., 1905.)

COLUMBIAN EXPRESS COMPANY.

72 Broadway, New York,

190

NEW YORK CITY OFFICES:
Gen'l Office, 72 Broadway, nr. Wall St.

PRINCIPAL BRANCH OFFICES:

49 West Broadway.
32 Canal Street.
5 West 14th Street.
434 Broadway.
21 Columbus Avenue.
275 West 12th Street.

Received of _____

_____ *given as* ____ NOT NEGOTIABLE.

Value asked and _____ *said to contain* _____ Dollars,
————————— 100

Marked _____

Which this Company undertakes to forward to the nearest point to destination reached by it, subject to the following conditions, and which conditions are agreed to by shipper or owner in accepting this receipt.

4. This Company is not to be held liable for any loss or damage, except **as forwarders** only, nor for any loss, damage, or delay, by the dangers of navigation, by the act of God or the public enemies of the Government, by the restraints of Government, strikes, mobs, riots, insurrections, piracies, or from any of the hazards or dangers incident to a state of war.

2. Nor shall this Company be liable for any default or negligence of any person, corporation or association to whom the said property shall or may be delivered by this Company, for the performance of any act or duty in respect thereto, at any place or point off the established route or lines run by this Company; and any such person, corporation, or association, is not to be regarded, deemed or taken to be the agent of this Company for any such purpose, but, on the contrary, such person, corporation or association shall be deemed and taken to be the agent of the person, corporation or association from whom this Company received the said property. If being understood that this Company relies upon the various Railroad and Steamboat lines of the country for its means of forwarding property delivered to it to be forwarded, it is agreed that it shall not be liable for any loss or damage caused by the detention of any train of cars or of any steamboat or other vehicle upon which said property shall be placed for transportation, nor by the neglect or refusal of any Railroad Company, Steamboat or other transportation line to receive and forward the said property. Nor shall this Company be liable for any losses or damages caused by detention of said property due to Customs Regulations.

3. It is further agreed that all property covered by this receipt and passing over ocean routes in transit subject to the Conditions expressed in the Bills of Lading of Ocean Steamship Companies accepted for the shipment.

4. It is further agreed that this Company is not to be held liable or responsible for any loss or damage by any part thereof, from any cause whatever, unless in every case the said loss or damage be proved to have occurred from the fraud or gross

negligence of said Company or its servants; nor in any event shall this Company be held liable or responsible, nor shall any demand be made upon it beyond the sum of **Fifty Dollars,** unless the just and true value thereof is stated herein, and an **extra charge** is paid or agreed to be paid therefor, **and the said property packed and secured for transportation** nor upon any **fragile fabrics, or any fabric consisting of, or contained in, glass,** nor upon **any thing unless properly packed and secured for transportation**, nor upon any thing unless its just and true value is stated herein; nor unless the charges on said property, and the same be not paid, or if in any case the consignee on delivery of the said property, and the same be not paid, or if in any case the consignee cannot be found or refuses to receive such property, or for any other reason it cannot be delivered, the shipper agrees that this Company may return said property to him subject to the conditions of this receipt, and that he will pay all charges for transportation, and that the liability of this Company for such property while in its possession for the purpose of making such collection, shall be that of Warehousemen only.

6. In no event shall this Company be liable for any loss, damage or delay, unless the claim therefor shall be presented to it in writing to this office within ninety days after date of shipment, in a statement to which this receipt shall be annexed.

7. It is further agreed that any carrier or party liable on account of loss or damage to any of the said property, shall have the full benefit of any insurance that may have been effected upon or on account of said property.

8. And it is also understood that the stipulations contained herein shall extend and inure to the benefit of each and every company or person to whom, through this Company, the said property may be entrusted or delivered for transportation.

9. Deliveries at destination are only to be made within the delivery limits established at such points as this Company may have the delivery limits established at such points as this Company may, and prepayment in such cases shall only cover places within such delivery limits.

For the Company,

_____

_____ **Agent.**

The Liability of this Company is limited to $50, unless the just and true value is stated in this receipt and an extra charge is paid or agreed to be paid therefor, upon such higher value; and such liability ceases on delivery by the Company of property at nearest point to destination it can carry same. Fragile fabrics and fabrics consisting of, or contained in glass, at owner's risk.

EXPRESS RECEIPT.

III. *The International Express Service*

The International Express Traffic includes parcels, papers and documents too heavy for the mails, currency, coin, and various articles requiring prompter delivery than can be secured by the ocean freight service. The companies engaged in the foreign express business also do international banking to the extent of providing travelers with checks that can be cashed in any one of the leading cities in Europe.

American Companies Engaged in Foreign Express.—Three of the express companies doing business in the United States have organized an international service. The American Express Company and the United States Express Company handle traffic to and from Europe and other countries reached from our Atlantic seaboard. The express traffic handled from our Pacific coast is carried on mainly by Wells, Fargo & Company.

The Organization of the International Express Service.— The amount of business which these express companies have in foreign countries is not great enough to require them to maintain offices and agencies in many foreign cities. Each company enters into an exclusive agreement with some foreign agent, and the company consigns all of its foreign express matter to its forwarding agent, who in turn sends the traffic he may receive to the United States in care of the express company with which he has made a contract.

The Papers Employed in the Foreign Express Service are similar to those used in the exportation and importation of freight. The shipper receives from the express company a *receipt*, such as he would obtain were he sending express matter to some place in the United States. If the shipment is large the express company issues to the shipper an *export bill of lading* describing the goods, giving the name of the shipper and the consignee, the destination of the goods, weight and description of the articles, and the rate and amount of agreed through charges. As is the case with a freight bill of lading, this paper is made out in triplicate, one copy being given to the shipper, one kept by the express company, and the third forwarded to the express company's foreign agent. The bill of lading sent to the foreign agent must be accompanied by the shipper's invoice or *manifest*, stating the value of the goods, in order that the foreign agent may enter the commodities at the customs house. When the express company turns over to the carrier the commodities which it has received from numerous shippers, it makes out a *waybill*, just as the railroad company does in the shipment of freight. This is the express company's own record, and it describes the articles, states the origin and destination of the goods, gives the weight, freight charges, total, prepaid, and to be collected. Lastly, the express company receives from the steamship company the *steamship bill of lading*, describing the goods shipped and the rates to be paid thereon. As this indicates, the express company is a shipper as well as a forwarder for individual shippers.

The Business Relations of the Express Company and the Ocean Carrier.—The express company does not enter into any special or exclusive contracts with steamship companies; its relation to the ocean carrier is the same as that of other shippers. The express company, like other shippers, pays the regular freight rates on all articles dispatched. In this particular the international express differs from that carried on within the United States. In the domestic express business, each railroad company gives some one

FREIGHT EXPORT BILL OF LADING.

COLUMBIAN EXPRESS COMPANY.

NEW YORK, 72 Broadway.   ST. LOUIS, 17 North Fourth St.
CHICAGO, 65 Monroe St.   BOSTON, 431 Franklin St.

(B/L No.—————   **Contract No.**—————)

Received at————————————————————————

From ———, ——————————————————————

the following property, in apparent good order, except as noted (contents and condition of contents of packages unknown), marked, consigned and destined as indicated below, to be carried to the Port of NEW YORK / BOSTON and thence by———————————

———[Scheduled to sail———sailed———] or the next available steamer (or line) and to be delivered in like order and condition to Port of———————

unto ———————————————————————————

at————————————————————or his or their assigns :

(ARTICLES) ——————————————————————

MARKS, NUMBERS OR ADDRESS ON GOODS	SUBJECT TO CORRECTION			VALUE
	WEIGHT	CUBICAL MEAS'T		
		FEET	INCHES	

APPLY for delivery to————————————————————

The Agent or Correspondent of **COLUMBIAN EXPRESS CO.**, named above will NOTIFY————————————————————————————

where and through whom final delivery of goods will be made.

CHARGES - - { Prepaid by Shipper as Below. { Collect of Consignee as Below.

FOR	FROM	TO	@	PER	AMOUNT
CARRIAGE					
CARRIAGE					

Marine Insurance
for sum of———————————————————— { Prepaid. { Collect.

In Witness Whereof, The Agent of the said **COLUMBIAN EXPRESS CO.**, hath affirmed to———Bills of Lading, all of this tenor and date, one of which being accomplished the others stand void.

Dated at————————this————————day of————————190

————————————————————————Agent.

EXPRESS COMPANY'S EXPORT BILL OF LADING.

Owner's or Agent's Manifest of Articles exported by Railway. (Col. Ex. Co. 365 April, 1905.)

List or manifest of articles of domestic production or manufacture, and of foreign articles free of duty, or duty paid, delivered by _____ (Name of Owner or Agent.)

to Columbian Express Co. at _____ State of _____ Agent _____ (Name of Ex. Agent.)

For Exportation to M _____ (Name of Consignee.)

At _____ (Name of place of intended Destination in Foreign Country.)

via _____ (Name of last port in United States whence articles pass into the Foreign Country.)

Marks and Numbers of Packages.	Description of Articles.	(1) Domestic Articles.		(2) Foreign Articles Free of duty, or duty paid.	
		Quantities.	Values.	Quantities.	Values.
			Dollars.		Dollars.

I, _____ (Name of Owner or Agent.) hereby certify that the above is a full and true statement of the kinds, quantities and values, and destination of all the articles delivered by me for exportation as aforesaid.

Residence, _____

Date, _____ 190 ___ _____ [Signature of Owner or Agent.]

Any owner or agent may include in a single manifest all articles exported by him on one train.

SHIPPERS INVOICE OR MANIFEST OF GOODS EXPORTED BY EXPRESS.

From **COLUMBIAN EXPRESS CO.,** *72 Broadway, New York, per S. S.* _____ *To* _____ *W/B No.* _____

MARKS ON GOODS Articles—Contents—Value	FROM	CONSIGNEE AND DESTINATION	Weight	Advanced Charges	Our Charges	Total To Collect	PREPAID	REMARKS
								1
								2
								3
								4
								5
								6
								7
								8
								9
								10
								11
								12
								13
								14
								15
								16

EXPRESS COMPANY'S WAY BILL.

express company an exclusive monopoly of its parcels traffic.

The competition of the international express and the parcels post has greatly increased during recent years. At the present time it is possible for the people of the United States to send by mail packages weighing as much as eleven pounds to thirty-six countries and colonies. The rate of twelve cents per pound by parcels post is lower than the international express rates, and the services within the United States and in foreign countries are more extensive and are prompter. The exchange of traffic between different countries has been greatly facilitated by the general adoption of the international parcels post.

CHAPTER XXX

THE ORGANIZATION OF OCEAN TRANSPORTATION

A High Degree of Organization Necessary.—To perform the many and complicated services described in the two preceding chapters, it is necessary for the ocean-transportation business to be highly organized. As has been pointed out, the ocean carrier is, for a large part of the traffic, but one link in a chain which connects shippers in the interior part of one country with the consignees in many parts of other countries. Thus the carriers on the high seas must coöperate not only with each other but with inland transportation agencies. The ideal sought to be reached in the development of transportation organization is to secure economy, speed, safety, and regularity in handling the tens of millions of tons of freight and hundreds of thousands of persons that are annually carried over the sea.

Stages in the Development of the Organization of Ocean Transportation.—Transportation on the high seas has been performed in various ways at different times in the history of the world. The present state of efficiency is the result of a long evolution, the principal stages of which have been as follows:

1. When commerce revived after the disintegration of the Roman Empire and merchants began to send their ships on long voyages, they united their vessels into a merchant fleet which was accompanied by naval convoys.

The Venetian fleet had its regular sailings to different parts of the commercial world of its time. The ships in the fleet were owned by Venetian merchants and the vessels were sent out in fleets in order that the government might protect them against pirates and enemies upon the land.

2. A second stage in the evolution of commerce and ocean transportation was the union of commercial cities into a league such as the Hanseatic League of the northern German cities. From 1300 to 1600 the international trade of northern Europe was controlled mainly by the powerful Hanseatic League, which secured, and maintained by force of arms, almost complete monopoly of the commerce about the Baltic and North seas.

3. As the nations of Europe developed, and their governments became stronger in the latter part of the Middle Ages, numerous trading companies came into existence. The Venetian trading fleets and the Hanseatic League were supplanted by trading companies chartered by England and France, each company being given the monopoly of the trade between its country and some section of the world, or a monopoly of the trade in some staples with certain parts of the world. The trading companies were in part protected by their governments, but were also given large political authority in India, Africa, America, and the other frontier regions where new commerce was being built up.

The trading companies had two general types of organization. In part they were associations of individuals, each trading with his own capital and ships according to the rules of the company with which he was associated; the other form of organization was the stock company, trade being carried on by the company with joint stock. Some of the large trading companies combined both forms of organization. As examples of the great trading companies, the British East India Company, the Dutch West India Company, and the Muscovy Company may be cited.

America was settled by four trading companies—the London, Plymouth, Dutch West India, and the Canada companies. Each of these companies, at the outset, was given the monopoly of the trade with a part of America, and was given the authority to govern the region covered by its grant of territory. These companies failed as commercial organizations within a comparatively short time after the settlement of America, but they were serviceable in starting the colonization of the new continent.

4. When, in the second quarter of the seventeenth century, the London, Plymouth, and Dutch West India companies lost their monopoly of American commerce, trade with the New World was taken up and carried on by individual merchants, each trader operating as many ships as his business required. To some extent the people of the New World exported their products in their own ships, the vessels being owned by the southern planters and the New England fishermen, lumbermen, and farmers. With the growth of the trade, American merchants and traders came to share with the British traders the commerce between the Old World and the New; and, before the end of the eighteenth century, large merchant traders like Derby, cf Salem, Peabody, of Boston, and Girard, of Philadelphia, had come to be relatively numerous. The seventeenth and eighteenth centuries were the period of the merchant trader.

5. Since the beginning of the nineteenth century ocean transportation has been carried on mainly by common carriers and not by merchants. In England the merchants began to employ common carriers about the beginning of the century; in America little is heard of the common car-

rier as distinct from the merchant until the close of the War of 1812–15. While international trade was relatively small and irregular in volume, exchanges were made by merchants using their own vessels; but, when the flow of commerce became large and regular, the work of the merchant carrier was divided and the transportation services on the ocean, as had long since been the case with transportation on the land, were taken over by common carriers. At the beginning, as at the present time, common carriers might own the ships they used or might charter them; moreover, they might operate vessels as units or unite several vessels into a line and establish schedule sailings.

6. The first ocean lines were the packet lines of sailing vessels, the pioneer in the United States being the Black Ball Line, which began running between New York and Liverpool in 1816. Until after the Civil War most of the commerce between the United States and Europe was handled by these packet ships. Lines of steamships were put into operation by British companies in 1840; after that date they increased rapidly, and soon secured most of the mail, express, and passenger business. Only a few transatlantic steamship lines were started by Americans before the Civil War.

7. Although a large part of the commerce of the world throughout the nineteenth century was handled by vessels operated as single units, the greater portion of the traffic from 1820 to about 1870 was carried by the sailing packet and steamship lines; but about 1870 a large development of charter traffic began. This is due to the fact that the marine engine had become efficient enough by that time to make it profitable to use steamers in handling bulk cargoes. A large tonnage of chartered steamers was put into serv-

ice during the last third of the century; and at the present time it is probable that more than half of the tonnage of ocean traffic is handled by chartered vessels. During recent years, however, international commerce is becoming so large and so regular as to lead to the establishment of many strictly freight lines; and much traffic that formerly was handled by chartered vessels is now handled by steamships operated as lines with sailings almost as regular as prevail in the passenger service. It seems probable that charter traffic will tend to decline with the future progress of ocean commerce.

8. During recent years there have been three striking tendencies manifest in the development of ocean transportation: One has been the rise of the mammoth steamship company. The largest of these companies, the Hamburg-American, had a fleet of less than 200,000 tons of vessels in 1890; at the present time its tonnage is nearly 1,000,000. The North German Lloyd Company is two thirds as large as the Hamburg-American. Each of several British companies has between 250,000 and 500,000 tons of ships. The organization of ocean transportation, as well as that of industry, has brought about the establishment of the giant corporation.

9. Another recent tendency in the development of transportation organization is the federation of large steamship companies. This is typified by the International Mercantile Marine Company, which in 1902 brought under one management five transatlantic lines whose aggregate fleet of 136 vessels had a tonnage of 1,034,884. The success of the International Mercantile Marine Company has been but moderate, and has not encouraged the formation of other similar federations. From time to time rumors are heard of the consolidation of the two great German com-

panies, and their union in the not distant future is more than probable.

10. Another marked phase of commercial organization is the union of ocean transportation with production. The Standard Oil Company, for instance, operates a large number of vessels on the ocean; the United States Steel Corporation has a fleet of ore vessels on the lakes, and many coal and lumber companies have their own coastwise fleets of vessels and barges. This is, in part, a return to the ocean transportation methods that prevailed in the days of the merchant carrier, and it is probable that the progressive integration of industry and trade may cause more large producers to take over the transportation services.

CHAPTER XXXI

COMPETITIONS, CONFERENCES AND CONSOLIDATIONS OF OCEAN CARRIERS

Competition on the Ocean is Widespread and Keen.—Upon all the main-traveled ocean routes there are several lines, each seeking to obtain as much traffic as possible; while everywhere and at all times vessels may be chartered to handle cargoes in bulk, if shippers feel that the rates and facilities offered by the line vessels are inadequate or unreasonable. Ocean carriers compete with each other much more actively than do railway companies, and there are four causes that account for this:

1. The ocean is a free highway, which any man who owns or charters a ship may use. Every port of the world is open to the ships of all countries, and it matters little whether the terminal facilities of a seaport are owned and managed by public authority, or are the property of individuals and corporations; whatever the ownership of the facilities may be, their use is public.

2. The ocean is a universal highway connecting each seaport with every other ocean port in the world. A man may ship goods without break of bulk from practically every seaport to every country on the globe. He is not dependent upon line vessels which operate over fixed routes, but he may secure the services of the chartered vessel; thus the competition on the seas, like the tides, reaches every shore.

279

3. It is easy to engage in the ocean transportation business. A limited amount of capital will purchase a ship, but even that is unnecessary because vessels may be chartered, just as houses may be leased. The exporter of cotton, lumber, grain, coal, iron, or any other commodity moved in large quantities may always secure the services of chartered vessels at competitive rates.

4. It is as easy to retire from the business of ocean transportation as it is to enter it; for this reason men do not hesitate to charter vessels nor to invest money in them. Although the shipowner may find his capital idle during periods of depression, trade is sure to revive; and it then is possible for him to use his vessel profitably or to sell it to advantage. When a railroad is constructed the capital becomes fixed; but when a ship is built, it represents a more mobile form of investment.

Restraint of Ocean Competition a Necessity.—The competitive forces in ocean transportation are so powerful that it is necessary to regulate them. If this cannot be done, the rivalries of carriers tend to become destructive, and thus to endanger both the property of the owners of the vessels and the welfare of the public they serve. It is practically impossible to restrain, to any great extent, the competition of chartered vessels with each other for bulk traffic. As long as there are vessels to be leased, this competition will continue; but the situation is somewhat different as regards the rivalry of ocean lines. The competition among the great steamship companies is local, but inevitably intense. Each corporation has a heavy investment at stake, and the prize to be gained by successful competition is large. The line that is most successful in securing the cabin and steerage traffic across the North Atlantic or North Pacific, and in getting the best mail contracts, or is most successful in obtaining the remunerative package and commodity freight over these routes, secures a profitable business of large volume and of certain growth. The struggles of ocean giants for prizes so great are apt to be destructive of both combatants. As with rival railroads, so with competing steamship companies, coöperation to regulate competition is necessary.

The Ocean Carriers Restrain Competition by " Conferences."—The associations which ocean carriers have established to regulate competition are called " conferences." It is the practice for the lines from Europe or from the United States to each important section of the world to unite in a conference, such as the South African Conference, the China Conference, and the Australian Conference of the European lines. In some instances the steamship lines from the United States are members of the conference to which European lines belong; and sometimes American lines have their own separate associations.

Types of Conferences.—Conferences of ocean carriers are established for various purposes and have different forms of organization. The following are the leading types:

1. The informal association which brings together for conference the representatives of steamship lines operating from any port. At these informal conferences, consideration will be given to the dates of sailing, the frequency of the service, classification of traffic and rates, and other matters of mutual interest. The purpose of these conferences is to come to a mutual understanding; and, if possible, to get common action without formal agreement.

2. Formal conferences in which the members unite in an association with a chairman, secretary, and other offi-

cers. The North Atlantic Steam Traffic Conference, which
has been in existence for many years, is a good example
of this type. This organization has done much to harmonize the conflicting interests of its members; but it has only
partially, and then for a short time, succeeded in regulating competitive freight rates.

3. An association of the owners of sailing vessels to fix
minimum freight rates is another form of conference. This
is exemplified by the Sailing Ship Owners' International
Union, which was organized in 1903 for the object of fixing
minimum rates of freight for the principal voyages in
which sailing vessels are engaged in bringing freight to
European ports from countries outside of that Continent.
The difficulties of enforcing agreements as to sailing-vessel
rates are so great that the permanent success of this form
of organization is doubtful.

4. The Chamber of Shipping of the United Kingdom is
a general organization in which the leading British ocean
carriers have membership. The association is similar to a
chamber of commerce. It is concerned with general questions of shipping policy, and does not attempt to regulate
competition, rates, or services of rival carriers.

Activities of Ocean Conferences.—The conferences of
ocean carriers are established to deal with one or more of
the following questions:

(*a*) The formal and informal agreements of the members of the conference to fix or regulate the rates on competitive traffic; indeed, the primary purpose of the conference is to limit the effect of competition upon ocean rates.
Enforcement of rate agreements is difficult, frequent
changes in rates are inevitable, and experience shows that
competition even among conference lines can be only very
partially controlled. Where pooling of rates from competi-

tive traffic is possible, competition can be successfully regulated; but pooling is practicable only to a very limited extent.

(b) Another question that is dealt with by conference is the classification of ocean freight. While most of the traffic carried on the ocean is handled at commodity rates, it has been found possible to group package and general cargo freight handled over some routes into five to seven classes. The commodities exported from the United States are mostly of a bulky character, and classification is not general; but those from Europe to different parts of the world consisting, as they do, largely of manufactures, have been successfully classified, and rates are largely by classes instead of by commodities.

(c) Another function of the conference is to assist in the enforcement of the policy of granting a rebate to shippers who patronize only vessels belonging to conference lines. In order to induce shippers not to seek lower rates by giving their traffic to outside and rival lines, it is customary, particularly in Great Britain, for the steamship companies who are members of a conference to grant to their shippers a rebate of ten per cent from the freight rates in case the shippers have not sent any traffic by non-conference lines. Rebates are calculated each year, six months after the close of the rebate period.

There has been some controversy as to the justice of the rebate policy, but it does not seem that the practice has been to the disadvantage of the shippers. By being freed from the interference of dangerous rivals, the companies operating the conference lines can furnish shippers with regular sailings and with an adequate supply of tonnage; and can guarantee that all shippers shall be charged equal rates for equal services. This enables manufacturers and merchants to develop their business under most satisfactory conditions.

(d) Conference agreements sometimes provide for the territorial division of business among its members. There are a few instances of the division of the traffic to and from certain ports among several lines doing business at those ports.

(e) There are, lastly, conference agreements providing for the pooling of profits on competitive business. The maintenance of such pools is very difficult, because of the highly competitive character of ocean transportation; and the result has been that profit pools have been few in number and of relatively short duration.

Instability of Ocean Conferences.—It is not to be inferred from the foregoing discussion of ocean conferences that their membership includes all ocean carriers, or that the conferences are permanent organizations. When times are prosperous and all ships are employed, it is relatively easy to enforce conference agreements; but when business is scare and ships are idle, the temptation to violate the terms of the agreement is too strong to withstand.

The inability of rival carriers to control competition adequately by means of the conference has led to the absorption of weaker lines by strong ones, and the consolidation of some of the largest ocean carriers in order thereby to control more successfully competitive rates and services. The tendency of ocean carriers to consolidate is also strengthened by the fact that it is more expensive to maintain and operate several rival lines than one consolidated or federated line. As in railway transportation and in manufacturing, the economy of large scale organizations has been a strong incentive to the consolidation of competing concerns.

Coöperation of Ocean and Rail Carriers.—Commerce is now organized with a view to the prompt and economical shipments of commodities from any point of production directly to all places of consumption, and to make this possible a high degree of coöperation between rail and ocean carriers is necessary. When the railways are entirely distinct from the ocean lines they have their through traffic arrangements, which are operated sometimes with and sometimes without the assistance of the freight forwarder. The Hamburg-American Packet Company, for instance, has its own soliciting agents in the principal inland cities of the United States as well as of Europe; so that shipments, whether eastbound or westbound, are handled from shipper to consignee on through bills of lading.

Combination of Ocean and Rail Transportation.—The railroads leading to the North Atlantic seaports of the United States were constructed after the ocean transportation business was well developed; but the railroads to the Pacific ports were not thus served by ocean lines; consequently the leading steamship lines from the Pacific ports of the United States have been established and are now operated by the transcontinental railway companies. By doing this, our railways to the Pacific have made it possible for the people in the Central West and the eastern portions of the United States to exchange commodities directly with the people of the Orient, and facilities for through shipment without rebilling have been provided. Naturally, the principal object the railroad company has sought to accomplish in operating steamship lines has been to increase its railway traffic. Most of the transcontinental roads have lines 2,000 miles in length, which as yet have relatively light traffic. All of the freight, export and import, handled by steamships is also rail tonnage, which adds to the company's net revenues. It is commonly stated that the railroad steamship lines of the Pacific have generally not been profitable as ocean carriers; but they have been more than justified by the increased revenues they have brought to the railroad.

There are a few railway lines on the Atlantic, for instance, the one from Newport News to Liverpool and London, controlled by the Chesapeake & Ohio Railway, and the Philadelphia Transatlantic Line to London and Avonmouth, much of the capital for which was supplied by the Philadelphia & Reading Railway. The Canadian Pacific also has a transatlantic line. Several of the strong coastwise lines, as, for instance, those of the Old Colony Steamboat Company and the Morgan Line, are controlled by the railroads. In general, however, ocean transportation to and from our Atlantic and Gulf ports is carried on by carriers not controlled by the railway companies.

CHAPTER XXXII

OCEAN FARES AND RATES

Cabin and Steerage Fares.—The competition of the principal steerage lines for the passenger traffic is constant and active, their rivalry to secure the steerage business being especially keen. Ordinarily, however, it is possible for the relatively small number of companies engaged in the ocean passenger traffic to regulate their competition by agreements as to routes, rates, sailings, and accommodations. The fares charged passengers in the first and second cabins are decided upon year by year without serious difficulty, and the agreements are not often broken. In the steerage business, rate wars occur more frequently, because of the fluctuation in the volume of steerage traffic, and because of the large profits that can be obtained by any line that is able to keep its steerage accommodations fully occupied.

The competition for the cabin-passenger business has brought about frequent improvements in speed and comfort. The tendency of the steamship companies has been to offer cabin passengers a luxurious service and to charge higher rates year by year. There seems to be an unquestioned demand for this on the part of travelers, due doubtless to the fact that those who take trips abroad are able to pay high rates. In the immigrant services there has also been a great increase in comfort; and the third- and fourth-class passengers have the same advantages in speed that the cabin passengers have. The rates charged for the steerage, however, have been kept down by competition. The growth of the steerage traffic has been so rapid that the steamship companies have been able to provide better services at constant or declining fares, this is one explanation for the rapid growth in the volume of steerage traffic.

The Ocean Freight Services may be Grouped under Three Headings.—(a) The transportation of commodities as full cargoes, usually in chartered vessels; (b) the carriage of freight as berth and supplemental cargo, usually by line ships, but sometimes in chartered vessels; and (c) the handling of package freight and general cargo, in part at regular rates, and also to some extent at rates fixed by bargaining between the shipper and carrier. Each class of service has its own peculiar rates.

Trip and Time Charters.—Persons wishing to secure the use of a vessel which they do not own may charter it. If the vessel is desired merely to carry a single cargo across the sea, it is chartered for the trip; if, however, the shipper or freight forwarder wishes to use the vessel for a period of time, six months or a year, he charters it for a certain length of time; thus there are trip charters and time charters. When the shipper secures a vessel for a single trip, the ship is operated by the owner who pays all expenses including the terminal charges. The only payment made by the shipper or charterer to the owner or operator of the vessel is an agreed rate per ton on the cargo; or, in the case of grain, a certain rate per bushel or quarter.

The contract between the owner and charterer of a vessel is different in the case of a time charter. In this instance, the man who owns the vessel operates it, provides and feeds the crew, and keeps the ship in repair; while the charterer furnishes the fuel and pays all port and terminal charges. The payment for vessels secured upon time charters is an agreed amount per month per net register ton of the vessel. Ordinarily the time charter rates will be equal to about one dollar per ton of the ship's cargo capacity; i. e., a vessel of 7,000 tons dead weight capacity will charter for $7,000 per month. Charter rates, both trip and time, are highly competitive and fluctuate with every change in the relation of traffic to available shipping.

How Vessels are Chartered.—The owners of vessels charter them to shippers and freight forwarders through the agency of the shipbrokers, and in every large seaport there are numerous shipbrokers' offices. Trip charters are much more numerous than time charters. As soon as a vessel leaves a port in any part of the world with a cargo that has been shipped under a trip charter, its owners notify the shipbroking firm with which they do business that they have a vessel that will reach a certain port of the world at a specified date, and that the vessel will then be available for chartering. The owners describe the character of the vessel in so far as that may be necessary, and state the kind of services for which the vessel is best adapted. If freight is moving in large quantities, this firm of shipbrokers will probably be able to secure a cargo for the vessel as soon as the ship is available. If, however, the volume of freight moving is relatively light, the shipbrokers will probably not be able to find a cargo; and, if such be the case, they will communicate by wire with the shipbrokers in other parts of their own country, and very probably with brokers in other countries. If there is no available outbound cargo to be gotten at the ports of the country where the ship discharges its inbound cargo, the vessel will be sent in ballast to the nearest point at which

PETER JAMES & SONS,

35-37 Walnut Street, Philadelphia

Morris Building, Broad and Beaver Sts., New York.

Cable Address: { James, Philadelphia.
                 { James, New York.

Freighting Department

Represented in the United Kingdom by

JOHNS & TOWNSEND,

18, 19 and 20 Great St. Helens, London, E.C.

Cable Address, Albana, London.

STEAM. PHILADELPHIA—GRAIN—BERTH TERMS.

Philadelphia, _____

It is this day Mutually Agreed, *BETWEEN* { PETER JAMES & SONS, by Cable
                                               { authority of _____

Owners of the _____ Steamship _____

of _____, built _____, at _____ of _____

net tons register, or thereabouts, and guaranteed _____ Qrs. of 480 lbs. of heavy Grain, _____ per cent. more or less

capacity and _____ Qrs. of 320 lbs. of Oats, 10 per cent. more or less capacity, classed _____ in

or _____ now _____ and _____

Parties in interest and Description of Vessel.

Loading Ports.

2. That the said Steamship being tight, staunch and strong, and in every way fitted for the voyage, with liberty
to take outward cargo to _____ for owners' benefit, shall with all convenient speed sail and proceed
to _____ and there load, always afloat, from said charterers, or their agents, a

Description of Cargo.

full and complete cargo, subject to limits above guaranteed of WHEAT, INDIAN CORN, RYE and OATS.
or

Orders for Loading Port.

3. Orders as to loading port to be given within 24 hours after receipt of notice of arrival at port of call in the
United States, if in ballast; or before 12 o'clock noon on the day of completion of discharge at a port in the United
States, if with cargo, except on Saturdays, when orders shall be given before 11 o'clock A.M. If not discharged on
the day on which demand for loading port is made, vessel to ask again for orders.

Loading Under Inspection.

4. Vessel to load under inspection of Underwriters' Agents, at her expense and to comply with their rules, not exceeding what she can reasonably stow and carry over and above her Cabin, Tackle, Apparel, Provisions, Fuel and Furniture; and being so loaded shall therewith proceed to LONDON, LEITH, TYNE, LIVERPOOL, GLASGOW, HULL, PLYMOUTH, SOUTHAMPTON, AVONMOUTH, BELFAST, DUBLIN, ANTWERP, ROTTERDAM or AMSTERDAM,_____

Discharging Ports.

one Port only, as ordered on signing Bills of Lading, and deliver the same, agreeable to Bills of Lading, on being paid freight, in British Sterling or its equivalent, as follows: (but free of extra freight in Bills of Lading if ordered to London).

Rate of Freight.

_____ shillings and _____ pence ( ) Per quarter of 480 lbs. of Heavy Grain.
_____ shillings and _____ pence ( ) Per quarter of 320 lbs. of Oats.
all English weights delivered.

Additional Discharging Ports.

5. Charterers having the privilege of ordering vessel to _____
_____ pence per quarter more than the above rate.
in which case rate of freight shall be _____

Liability of Steamer Under Charter.

6. It is also mutually agreed that the Carrier shall not be liable for loss or damage occasioned by causes beyond his control, by the perils of the seas or other waters, by fire from any cause or wheresoever occurring, by barratry of the master or crew, by enemies, pirates or robbers, by arrest and restraint of Princes, rulers or people, by explosion, bursting of boilers, breakage of shafts or any latent defect in hull, machinery or appurtenances, by collisions, stranding or other accidents of navigation of whatsoever kind (even when occasioned by the negligence, default or error in judgment of the pilot, master, mariners or other servants of the ship owner, not resulting, however, in any case, from want of due diligence by the owners of the ship or any of them, or by the Ship's Husband or Manager.)

Harter Act.

7. It is also mutually agreed that this contract is subject to all the terms and provisions of, and all the exemptions from liability contained in the Act of Congress of the United States, approved on the 13th day of February, 1893, and entitled "An Act Relating to Navigation of Vessels, etc."

Signing Bills of Lading.

8. Captain to call at Brokers' Office, as requested, and sign Bills of Lading, as presented, without prejudice to this Charter Party, any deficiency to be paid at Port of Loading in cash, less insurance, and any surplus over and above

Difference in Freight.

estimated freight to be settled there before the Vessel clears at the Custom House, by Captain's draft, in Charterers' favor, upon Consignee, payable five days after arrival at Port of Discharge.

Stevedore.

9. Stevedore employed by Vessel to be approved by Charterers,

Lay-days and Demur-rage.

10. Steamer to be loaded according to berth terms, with customary berth despatch, and if detained longer than five days, Sundays and holidays excepted, Charterers to pay demurrage at the rate of four pence (4 d.) British Sterling or its equivalent per net register ton per day, payable day by day, provided such detention shall occur by default of Charterers or their agents.

Date of Commencement of Charter, Cancellation of Charter.

11. Time for loading, if required by Charterers, not to commence before the _____ day of _____

12. Should the Steamer not be passed by Board of Underwriters' surveyor as ready for cargo at her loading port before 12 o'clock noon on the _____ day of _____ followed by the presentation of said surveyor's pass to the Charterers or their agents at their office before said hour, the Charterers or their agents shall at said hour and at any time after, not later than presentation of the surveyor's pass at said office, have the option of cancelling this Charter Party.

Bills of Lading and Discharging.

13. It is also mutually agreed that this contract shall be completed and be superseded by the signing of Bills of Lading on the same form as in use by regular line steamers from loading port to port of destination; or, if port of destination be one to which there is no regular line of steamers from loading port, this contract shall be superseded by the signing of Bills of Lading in the form customary for such voyages for grain cargoes, which Bills of Lading shall however contain a clause providing for discharging as fast as vessel can deliver during ordinary working hours, any custom of the port to the contrary notwithstanding.

Discharging at Night.

14. Receivers of the cargo are in no case obliged to take delivery at night without their consent, and in any event the steamer must bear all extra expenses incurred by working at night. This clause to be expressly stipulated in all Bills of Lading.

Dead Freight, Demur-rage.

15. Charterers' liability under this Charter to cease on cargo being shipped, but the Vessel to have a lien thereon for all freight, dead freight, demurrage or average.

General Average. Disbursements.

16. General Average, if any, according to York-Antwerp Rules, 1890.

17. Cash for vessel's ordinary disbursements at Port of Loading to be advanced by Charterers, if required by Master, at current rate of exchange, subject to insurance and two and a half per cent. commission.

Commission, Freight Brokerage, Agency.

18. A commission of five per cent. and the customary Freight Brokerage is due by the Vessel on signing of this Charter Party to **Peter James & Sons,** Vessel lost or not lost, whose agents at Port of Loading are to attend to ship's business on customary terms.

_____ Witness to the signature of

_____ Witness to the signature of

_____ By cable authority of

_____ Agents for Owners.

WE HEREBY CERTIFY That this is a true and correct copy of the original stamped Charter Party on file in our office.

_____ BROKERS.

desirable traffic can be obtained. This may be across the English Channel or the North Sea or across the Atlantic or the Pacific Ocean; and in some instances it may be half the way around the world. It is the shipbroker that makes possible the economical employment of vessels, and thus enables shippers to secure prompt transportation at low rates for any and all classes of traffic.

Berth and Supplemental Cargo Rates.—Both line vessels and chartered ships often have unoccupied space in their holds in addition to that required by the general cargo or bulk traffic which the vessel has contracted to carry. This space, or "berth," will gladly be sold to a shipper of grain or other bulk traffic at less than the regular rates in order that the master may load his vessel as nearly as possible to its full capacity. At a large port like New York there are hundreds of line vessels having regular sailings, and all of the grain and much other traffic is handled at berth rates; while, from a smaller port with fewer lines of vessels, most of the grain and nearly all of the other bulk traffic is handled as full cargoes by chartered vessels.

Oftentimes grain, steel, or some other heavy commodity is desired as supplemental cargo for vessels that are loaded with bulky and relatively light package freight. On the contrary, ships loading with steel rails or grain usually desire to secure light bulky freight as supplemental cargo. By combining both light and heavy commodities in the same lading, the tonnage of the ship's cargo, and hence its earnings, will be greater than would be possible by carrying only one of the two kinds of freight.

Rates on Package Freight and General Cargo.—Export shipments of most manufacturers, and the import and export trade of merchants consist mainly of package freight and miscellaneous cargo. This traffic is handled chiefly by line vessels, to some extent at fluctuating competitive rates, and in part at regular and fairly permanent tariff charges. Wherever the general cargo shipments are irregular in volume, they are handled at rates agreed upon by special contract between the shipper and carrier; they are often sent as berth or supplemental cargo.

On the other hand, when manufactured goods are shipped in large quantities in a fairly constant volume, as from the leading European ports of the North Atlantic, they are carried at regular tariff rates. Under these conditions it has been found possible to classify the package and general cargo freight handled by ocean lines. The classification of ocean freight, however, is not general; most of it is handled at commodity rates, and the charges fluctuate in accordance with the extent of competition. None of the vast export traffic from the United States is classifi d.

With the development of freight lines, there has been an increasing volume of freight handled at rates fixed by time contract between large shippers and the carriers. The manager of a line of freight vessels is ordinarily glad to contract ahead for freight, because this guarantees him a steady volume of traffic and enables him to operate his vessels upon a fixed schedule, with fewer risks of dispatching vessels with only partial cargoes. The manufacturer, likewise, finds it to his advantage to know in advance what space he can have upon line vessels from any port week by week and month by month, and what his freight rates are to be. This knowledge enables the manufacturer or exporter to decide at the opening of his business season what prices he can quote; he can also guarantee to deliver to his foreign patrons such quantities as they may desire to buy week by week or month by month; and he can prob-

ably inform them exactly what the goods will cost for a
definite period of time.

Through Rates.—A large part of the international trade
of the world is now handled on through bills of lading
from the inland point of origin to the interior cities of ultimate destination. These through rates are made by bargaining between freight forwarders and shippers—they are
competitive and fluctuating. Formerly, the through rate
was divided on a percentage basis between the ocean and
rail carriers. At the present time, however, the railroads
in the United States are obliged by law to publish and file
with the Interstate Commerce Commission all their rates;
and ordinarily their charges may not be changed except
upon thirty days' notice to the commission and the filing of
another schedule of charges. The variation in the through
rail and ocean rates is now entirely in the ocean carriers'
portion of the through rate.

There has been no serious objection to this as far as
the traffic between the United States and Europe is concerned; but the transcontinental railroads, most of which
have steamship lines of their own on the Pacific, have ob-
jected strongly to the necessity of separating the through
rate to and from the Orient into rail and water portions,
and of maintaining the rail portion of the rate without
change except upon notice to the Interstate Commerce Commission. The commission, however, has, and probably with
wisdom, insisted upon enforcing the law; but, instead of
requiring the rail carriers to give thirty days' notice of a
change in the rail rates on export and import traffic, the
commission has reduced the period to ten days.

CHAPTER XXXIII

GOVERNMENT AID AND REGULATION OF OCEAN TRANSPORTATION

I. *Federal Aid and Regulation*

The Purposes of the Government Regulation of ocean transportation are rather to foster than to restrain—to secure more and better services rather than to interfere with charges. Thus far rates and fares on the ocean have been controlled by competition with results that have in the main been satisfactory. Besides promoting the business of ocean transportation, it is the duty of the Government also to protect the lives and property of passengers and shippers, to enforce such quarantine regulations as the public health may require, to safeguard the welfare of seamen, and to insure the use of channels, harbors, and port facilities by all shippers and carriers without unjust discrimination.

Forms of Government Aid.—The United States Government gives assistance to ocean transportation in four ways: (1) It provides the seaports with channels and harbors of such depth and area as shipping and trade may require; (2) it makes charts of the seacoasts, it buoys and lights channels, maintains lighthouses and a life-saving service, all for the purpose of facilitating navigation and increasing its safety; (3) it pays ships under the American flag liberal sums for carrying our foreign mails, and it reserves the vast coastwise and inland water commerce to American ships; (4) it aids the ship-building industry in several ways, and goes so far as to admit to American registry only such ships as are built within the United States. The details of Government aid to shipping and ocean navigation will be presented in the following chapter.

Agencies of Federal Aid and Regulation.—The promotion of ocean transportation and commerce, and their regulation in the public interest have brought about the establishment of numerous bureaus and services in the executive departments of the United States Government. Most of the activity of the Department of Commerce and Labor has to do with maritime commerce, there being eleven bureaus and services in that department that have been created because of the Government's interest in maritime industries. Among these bureaus and services are the Light-House Board which constructs and operates the light-houses; the Coast and Geodetic Survey which surveys and charts the coasts; the Steamboat Inspection Service, whose name designates the duties it has to perform; the Bureau of Navigation which measures and documents all ships and enforces the laws regarding seamen; the Bureau of Manufactures which edits and publishes the consular reports; and the Bureau of Immigration which inspects immigrants and administers the laws for the exclusion of undesirable persons.

The great work of improving the lakes, rivers, and harbors, and of constructing canals is intrusted to the Corps of Engineers of the United States Army, which is, of course, attached to the Department of War. There are four important services in the Treasury Department having to do with international commerce and ocean transportation—the Customs Service which supervises the collection of import duties; the Revenue Cutter Service which seeks to prevent the violation of our revenue laws; the Life-Saving Service and the Public Health and Marine Hospital Service. In the Department of Agriculture is the United States Weather Bureau which has become of incalculable value to ocean shipping. Connected with the Navy Department is the Hydrographic Office which makes charts of the ocean. Under the State Department is the United States Consular Service which is maintained both to promote our foreign trade and to protect American seamen and other citizens of the United States when they are in foreign countries. The Post-Office Department pays steamship companies, by contract or otherwise, for carrying the ocean mails; and the Department of Justice takes such action as may be necessary to enforce the navigation laws. Indeed, the Secretary of the Interior is, apparently, the only member of the President's Cabinet that is not concerned with the regulation or promotion of ocean commerce and transportation.

II. *Joint State and Federal Regulation*

Commercial Powers of the States under the Constitution. — The Constitution of the United States gives the Federal Government the power to regulate commerce with foreign nations and among the States, and it also provides that "no State shall, without the consent of the Congress, lay any imposts or duties on imports or exports, except what may be absolutely necessary for executing its inspection laws," and also that "no State shall, without the consent of Congress, lay any duty on tonnage."

These provisions of the Constitution have been interpreted by numerous decisions of the United States Supreme Court and the boundary between the authority of the nation and the States is now clearly defined. Congress has exclusive power to regulate interstate and foreign commerce, including the vessels employed in that trade. Vessels enrolled or registered by the United States for the coastwise and foreign trade cannot be burdened by State laws imposing conditions upon shipping in addition to those laid down by the United States; nor may the States tax the use of vessels employed in coastwise and international commerce. The property which men have in ships may be taxed by State laws as may other forms of property, but no State license fees and tonnage taxes are constitutional.

Control of Pilots and Pilotage.—The regulation of pilots and pilotage is exercised both by the States and the Federal Government, although the States exercise their authority by permission of the United States. Before the adoption of the Constitution, each State had detailed pilotage laws; and Congress, in 1789, confirmed those laws by providing that, "until further provision is made by Congress all pilots in bays, inlets, rivers, harbors, and ports shall continue to be regulated by the laws of the States wherein such pilots may be, or with such laws as the States may respectively enact for the purpose."

In general, the States regulate pilots, but the Congress requires that the captain and mates of all steamers enrolled for the coastwise service shall qualify as pilots and be licensed by the United States; and the States are prohibited from requiring these Federal pilots on steam vessels to secure a State license in addition to the one granted them by the United States. A coastwise steamer may thus enter a port without taking a pilot. Sailing vessels cannot do this, nor can steamers to and from foreign countries.

Health and Quarantine Regulations.—Both the State and Federal governments have the power to enforce such health and quarantine regulations as the public welfare may require. The States derive their authority in this regard from their general police power, whereas the Congress of the United States derives its authority from its power to regulate interstate and foreign commerce. It is thus necessary for the States and the nation either to coöperate in the enforcement of health regulations, or for one of thcm to delegate to the other the exercise of its authority. At New York, the largest of all American ports, the Federal Government leaves to the State of New York the administration of quarantine regulations, with the exception that the health officers of the United States also inspect all immigrants applying for admission to the country. It is necessary on the Delaware River, on the contrary, for the Federal Government to maintain a quarantine service because this stream lies on the boundary of three States. The State of Pennsylvania also maintains quarantine services on the Delaware, while New Jersey and Delaware do not deem it necessary to do so.

Regulation of Harbors and of Port Facilities.—The United States has authority over navigable channels from the ocean to the harbor, and also over the harbor area to what is called the pier-head line, i. e., the line fixed by the United States Government as the extreme limit to which piers may extend from the shore into the harbor or channel. From the pier-head line to the shore the States have authority, and they may also determine whether the property along the harbor front shall be retained by the public or shall be sold to individuals and corporations. Thus the States may decide whether the port and terminal facilities shall be constructed and administered by public authority or by individuals and by corporations. Some States have followed one policy and some the other. At the port of New York, the State has reserved to the municipality the ownership of the harbor frontage and the right to construct such piers and other facilities for handling traffic as the commerce may require. In times past, the principle of the municipal port has not been closely adhered to by the city of New York, which made long-term leases of portions of the harbor frontage. That policy has been abandoned, and the city is now gradually regaining control of all the port terminal facilities.

The policy of the public port prevails in most of the great seaports of Europe; but, in our country, the majority of the States have permitted corporations to secure the ownership of most of the harbor frontage and have allowed the owners to construct such piers and other facilities as they may think needful. This policy is open to serious objections; it permits corporations to secure a monopoly of the best harbor frontage, and makes it difficult for the State or municipality to provide public facilities for the general use of shippers and carriers who do not have terminals of their own.

The Taxation of Shipping.— Having power to regulate interstate and foreign commerce and the instrumentalities thereof, the United States Government can levy tonnage duties or taxes upon ocean ships. Since 1886, vessels entering any port of the United States from any foreign port or place in North America, Central America, the West India Islands, the Bahama Islands, or the coast of South America bordering on the Caribbean Sea, have been required to pay a duty of three cents per ton net register with a maximum of fifteen cents per ton upon any one ship within a year. Vessels entering from all other foreign ports pay six cents per ton at each entry with a maximum of thirty cents per ton per annum. The Federal tonnage taxes, which amount to over $1,000,000 annually, are devoted to the maintenance of the United States Marine Hospital Service.

Every State has the power to tax the property of its citizens, including that which they have in the form of ships. These taxes must be based upon the value of the ship and not upon tonnage; and may not be in the nature of a license fee. The right to use a ship in interstate and foreign commerce is secured from the Federal Government, and that right may in no wise be interfered with by State tax laws; hence those laws must be limited to assessments upon property valuation. The majority of the States tax shipping, but some of the States wisely exempt that form of property from their tax levies in order not to place any hindrances in the way of the development of their shipping and commercial interests.

Port and Terminal Charges.—Although every great port in the world is open without discrimination to ships of all nations, the heavy expenses incurred in developing and maintaining the ports, and particularly the terminal facilities for the transfer and storage of cargo, make it necessary for the authority having control of the port to place certain charges upon the vessels that make use of the port. These charges, however, are kept as low as possible; and, with the exception of tonnage taxes, they include comparatively little except fees for the services which a vessel requires in making a port, discharging and loading cargo and in clearing the port on its outward voyage. The number of these fees, however, is comparatively large.

The following table states the expenses actually incurred by a vessel of about 4,000 tons net register in entering the port of Philadelphia with a cargo of sugar and clearing outward in ballast. It will be seen that two thirds of the total expense was for discharging the cargo of nearly 8,000 tons. Had the vessel taken on an equal tonnage of freight its terminal charges would have been much greater. The expenses incurred by this vessel in entering the port and discharging its cargo amounted to forty cents per freight ton. It will thus be seen that out of a freight rate of two or three dollars per ton for carrying cargo across the ocean a considerable share must be paid for terminal expenses.

Port and Terminal Charges Incurred by a Steamer Inbound at Philadelphia from Java, with 7,962 Tons Sugar, and Outward in Ballast, 3,923 Tons Net Register, 6,057 Tons Gross Register.

Tonnage tax, 3,923 tons, at 6 cents	$235.38
Entrance surveys	5.50
Health fees	10.00
Noting protest	1.50
Custom-house brokerage	2.50
Inward pilotage, 26 feet, at $5	130.00
Tug boats for inward docking	30.00
Boatman running lines	6.00
Survey on hatches and cargo	13.00
Copy surveyor's report	1.75
Custom-house permit, certificate of weights, etc.	1.00
Wharfage, 10 days, at $31.92	319.20
Cooperage, 7,962 tons, at 2 cents	159.24
Stevedore, discharging, 7,962 tons, at 28 cents	2,229.36
Tally clerks, 11½ days, at $3	34.50
Custom-house clearance	2.95
Custom-house brokerage	2.50
Consul fees	4.25
Attendance fee	51.14
Towage to stream	30.00
Outward pilotage, 16½ feet, at $5	82.50
Total	$3,352.27

CHAPTER XXXIV

THE MARITIME POLICY OF THE UNITED STATES

Our Maritime Policy in General has been liberal in many respects toward both the building and the navigation or operation of ships. As far as the use of our ships in domestic trade is concerned, our maritime policy has been thoroughly successful; in the foreign trade, however, American ships have not been able to compete to much extent with foreign vessels. It will be well to consider what our policy actually has been toward the shipbuilding industry, and to inquire why we have not succeeded in developing a large merchant marine for the transportation of our foreign commerce.

Policy Toward Shipbuilding.—The United States Government has aided the shipbuilding industry in four ways:

(1) With minor exceptions, only vessels built within the United States are admitted to registry under the American flag. We have not permitted our citizens to import ships, and the yards in our country have been given a monopoly of the American market for ships.

(2) Our vast coastwise and inland water commerce is open only to vessels of American build and registry. This has been our policy since 1817, and at the present time there are over 12,000,000 tons of vessels, barges, and lighters used in the coastwise and domestic commerce of the United States. The tonnage of our domestic fleet is

twelve times as great as that of American ships engaged in our foreign trade.

(3) Shipbuilders are permitted to import, free of duty, such material as they may desire to use in constructing or repairing vessels to be sold to foreigners or to be sold to the citizens of the United States for use in the foreign trade or in the commerce between the Atlantic and Pacific ports of the United States.

(4) Since 1885, the United States has been rapidly building up a large and efficient navy. All of the naval vessels are products of American yards; and our shipbuilders have been enabled, by virtue of the Government orders to modernize their plants, and thus to adapt them to the more economical construction of merchant vessels. It 's probable that few of our latest and best shipyards would have been established had it not been for the naval policy of the United States. It has been the reservation of the coastwise and domestic commerce to American ships, and the liberal and wise naval policy of the United States that have kept many of our shipyards from becoming bankrupt, and has made possible the moderate success of our shipbuilding industry, during the past twenty-five years.

Why American Yards Build Few Ships for the Foreign Trade.—In most lines of heavy manufactures, production costs are as low in the United States as in any other country in the world, but in the building of ships we are not able to compete with Great Britain and Germany, from the yards of which countries most of the world's steel merchant shipping now comes. There are three general causes which fully account for the higher cost of building ships in the United States than in Great Britain or Germany: The high prices of materials in the United States, the high labor costs in our shipyards, and the relatively small amount of tonnage now being constructed in the United States. It will be well to consider each of these causes briefly:

(1) Most of the material used in the building of ships is steel; and for many kinds of steel, the prices are as low in the United States as elsewhere; indeed, some manufactures of steel can be made cheaper here than abroad. It is, however, undoubtedly true that the shipbuilders on the Clyde and Tyne can secure plates, boilers, and engines more cheaply than they can be bought under present conditions in the United States. The chief reason for this is that British builders construct several ships of the same design at the same time. Materials and equipment for several vessels are purchased by a single order, and are secured at correspondingly lower rates. Furthermore, the British builder has the advantage of the buyer who can duplicate his orders frequently. It is also maintained that steel prices have in the past fluctuated more in the United States than in Great Britain and Germany, and that shipbuilders have been obliged to bid for work at higher prices in order to protect themselves against loss caused by fluctuations in the prices of materials to be purchased in carrying out their contracts.

(2) The greatest handicap American shipbuilders have in competing with the British and German yards is the higher labor costs in the United States. It is probable that the labor costs per ton in constructing a vessel in the United States are nearly fifty per cent more than they are in Great Britain and Germany. This is due not only to the relatively high wage scale in the United States; but also, and probably more, to the fact that the large tonnage constructed in foreign yards enables those yards to stand-

ardize processes and permits employers to secure a large amount of labor on the piecework system of payment. When several cargo steamers are constructed at the same time in any one yard and the operations are repeated year after year in succession, the shipbuilders owning such a yard can secure both material and labor economically; workmen repeat their tasks and increase their efficiency; the yards standardize their processes; the piecework plan of payment becomes possible and general. This method of doing work has been carried out successfully in the United States in the manufacture of stationary and locomotive engines, machinery and tools, but the conditions prevailing in shipbuilding have not permitted the organization of our shipyards in accordance with this plan.

(3) There are nearly 2,000,000 tons of shipping launched annually from the British yards and over half of the output is sold to foreigners. Practically all of this tonnage consists of steel ships. This is over four times the tonnage of such vessels ever built in American yards in any one year. The largest figures were reached in 1908 when there were 450,000 gross tons of steel ships launched in our yards. By constructing a large tonnage every year, and by having the entire world as a market for their product, the British shipbuilders, and to a less degree the Germans also, are able to make contracts for ships at a much lower figure than American builders can quote.

There is no immediate prospect that American ship-builders will be able to construct ships for sale in competition with British and German builders. Our present disadvantages will naturally grow less year by year with the increase of the annual output of our yards; as time goes on we shall be able to purchase material more economically; and labor costs will be reduced. It is probable that the Government can do but little to change the present conditions of competition between American and foreign shipbuilders, except by adopting a policy that will encourage the larger use of American ships in our foreign trade, and will create a greater annual demand for the output of American yards.

The Policy of the United States Toward Ocean Navigation. —The shipping policy of the United States has already been referred to in various connections. It is necessary here only to summarize the measures that have been adopted by Congress to encourage the ownership and operation of American vessels under the American flag.

(1) The United States has always kept its tonnage taxes light and its tax laws have favored American shippers in two ways: Vessels engaged in our coastwise and domestic commerce are exempted from all tonnage taxes. In fact, over ninety per cent of American vessels are exempted from tonnage taxes. Furthermore, the policy of charging tonnage taxes of only three cents per ton, per entry, and fifteen cents per ton per annum, on vessels between the ports of the United States and those of North America, the West Indies and the Caribbean coast works to the advantage of American shipping, because it is in this near-by international trade that the larger part of the American fleet engaged in the foreign trade is employed.

(2) The United States Government improves, maintains, lights and buoys the harbors and channels of our ports without any cost to shipping. Our tonnage taxes are much less than the "light dues" imposed by Great Britain, or the charges exacted by continental countries. The maintenance of our lighthouses, alone, costs five times as much per year as our tonnage taxes yield.

(3) The United States follows the policy of other

countries in favoring the shipping under its flag in its payments for carrying the ocean mails. The contract service is restricted, by the law of 1891, to American vessels, and, when mails are carried without such a contract, the payments to American ships are larger than those to foreign vessels for the same services.

(4) The laws of the United States as regards tonnage taxes, harbor improvements, and mail payments are intended to give assistance to owners of vessels; but the legislation for the protection of seamen necessarily and wisely imposes greater burdens upon the owners of vessels under the American flag than upon those who operate their vessels under the flag of a foreign nation. The requirements of the United States as regards rations and air space for the crew, and the provisions of our laws concerning the employment and discharge of seamen are said to be more stringent than those of other countries; and it is claimed by reliable authorities that "the general conditions of life in the American Merchant Marine—wages, food, quarters, etc.—are superior to those in foreign countries." Of course, no one would wish to change this. It is better that we should maintain a relatively high standard of life on board our merchant fleet than that we should make more rapid strides in the increase of the tonnage of our registered shipping.

Results of our Maritime Policy.—The foreign commerce of the United States has grown rapidly with the industrial progress of our country; but about nine tenths of this commerce is now carried in vessels under foreign flags. It must be admitted that the policy of the United States regarding its international merchant fleet has been but slightly successful. The causes for this, as has been explained, are chiefly economic, and the future success of our maritime policy must mainly depend upon a change in the economic conditions now prevailing in the United States in the building and operating of ships.

The present situation can hardly be said to be satisfactory. It is unquestionably true that the development of our foreign trade, particularly with South America, has been hampered by the fact that there are so few lines of vessels operated from American ports. The foreign competitor of the American manufacturer has a more frequent, and, in many ways, a better ocean transportation service to many parts of the world. Moreover, our navy could be built up on a surer foundation if there were a larger deep-sea fleet under the American flag. If it were not that the people of the United States have a large tonnage of vessels engaged in coastwise transportation, our small oversea tonnage would be a serious matter from a naval point of view. Whatever brings about the more rapid progress of our maritime fleet, will be to the advantage of our navy.

CHAPTER XXXV

THE MERCHANT MARINE QUESTION; OUR FUTURE ON THE SEA

Decline in our Registered Tonnage.—At the opening of the Civil War, the American people owned 2,500,000 tons of ships engaged in the foreign trade; at the close of that great struggle, our registered shipping had declined 1,000,-000 tons. Although the downward tendency was checked for a while with the revival of business after the war, the decrease began again in 1880 and continued with occasional interruption until 1898, when our vessels in the foreign trade had a total tonnage of less than three quarters of a million. Since then, there has been a gradual gain, but at the present time our deep-sea merchant fleet measures barely a million tons. Fortunately, this represents only a small portion of the total shipping of the United States. Our domestic commerce being open only to American vessels, we have an enrolled and licensed fleet of 6,425,377 tons; and in addition to this there is an equal tonnage of undocumented craft. The total shipping of the United States is large, but in that part of our merchant marine where we come into competition with foreign carriers we have, until recently, steadily lost ground.

Causes of the Decline of our Registered Shipping.—The decrease in the tonnage of our registered fleet has been brought about by several causes, the chief of which are the following:

311

(1) The substitution of steamers for sailing vessels and the use of iron instead of wood in shipbuilding, which became general in the United Kingdom about 1850, soon gave that country an advantage over the United States as a maritime nation. The cost of iron and the rate of wages were so much higher in the United States than they were in Great Britain that we were unable to construct iron vessels, and were obliged to continue to build and use wooden ships. For the same reason, we adhered to sailing vessels instead of changing to steamships. As late as 1870, only three per cent of the tonnage annually constructed in the United States consisted of iron vessels; whereas at that time in England eighty-two per cent of the new vessels were of iron. Moreover, it was not until sometime after 1870 that the substitution of metal for wood became general in American shipyards.

(2) The withdrawal of Government support to American shipping in 1858. While Great Britain was securing the leadership by substituting iron for wood and steam for sails, the United States Government repealed the ship subsidy laws that had been in force since 1847. During the eleven years ending in 1858, the Government mail contracts with various American lines had brought their owners $14,500,000 of Government aid; the withdrawal of this support at this critical period increased the difficulties which the American marine had to contend with in meeting foreign competition.

(3) The effect of the Civil War upon our marine was disastrous. During the five-year period when our fleet should have largely gained in tonnage it lost fully a million tons. Moreover, this severe shock came at a time when our shipping interests were confronted with the necessity of changing from sails to steam and wood to iron.

(4) The taxation of shipping after the Civil War. After the close of the War, Congress gave manufacturers liberal protection by continuing the war tariffs; and it sought to aid shipbuilding by reserving to American shipyards the monopoly of constructing vessels for registry and enrollment under the American flag. Practically nothing, however, was done to aid our shipping to compete with that under foreign flags; indeed, our registered as well as enrolled tonnage was subjected to unnecessary burdens. Congress refused to permit the return to our flag of vessels that had been sold to foreigners during the Civil War; it did not repeal, until 1868, the special taxes that had been placed upon shipping during the war period; and it was not until 1872 that materials might be imported, duty free, for use in constructing and equipping wooden vessels for the foreign trade. The builders of steel vessels were obliged to pay duty on imported materials until 1890.

(5) The neglect of the American navy from 1865 to 1885. Congress lost interest in the navy after the Civil War, and it was not until 1885 that our present policy of building up our naval power was adopted. Had Congress placed liberal orders with American shipbuilders for iron and steel naval vessels immediately after the Civil War, it would have helped our yards to reorganize their plants and to put them in shape for the successful construction of merchant ships.

(6) Ship subsidies and subventions by foreign countries. While the United States was giving little or no aid to the American marine, our leading rivals were giving liberal Government support to their shipping. Whether their policy was altogether wise or not, it certainly had the effect of increasing the difficulties of successful competition on the part of American shipping.

314 ELEMENTS OF TRANSPORTATION

(7) The internal development of the United States required all our available capital and labor. The American people found more was to be gained by devoting themselves to the construction of railroads, to opening up of the West, and to the development of the vast natural resources of the country than to building and operating ships in competition with the people of other countries in which both capital and labor were relatively abundant.

General Bounties and Special Subventions to Shipping.— Government aid to the merchant marine may take one or both of two forms: It may consist of general navigation bounties, such as are granted by France which pays the owners of vessels a certain sum per vessel ton for each day the ship is operated, and also gives the owners a certain amount per ton per annum regardless of the use to which the vessel is put. The other kind of Government support is the special subvention made by the Government to certain lines for the transportation of the mails and for the performance of various services which the owners of the vessels would otherwise not find it profitable to perform. The plan of special subventions is typical of the policy of Germany and Great Britain.

Objection to General Navigation Bounties.—Both forms of Government aid to shipping are open to the objections that may be urged against Government aid to industry. The French policy of general navigation bounties is particularly subject to criticism. When an industry receives aid from the Government, except in payment for the performance of special services, it develops artificially instead of advancing step by step in accordance with economic needs. Industries built up by Government bounties tend to become dependent upon support and not independent of the Government, whereas industries that grow in response to an economic demand rest upon a sure foundation.

Experience as well as theory is against the policy of general navigation bounties. The countries that have granted such bounties, France, Austria–Hungary, and Italy, have had small maritime success in comparison with Great Britain, Germany, and Japan where Government aid has consisted mainly of special subventions. The success of Great Britain and Germany is, of course due mainly to economic conditions and only secondarily to Government assistance; but the presumption is in favor of the form of Government aid prevailing in the countries that have had maritime success.

Another potent reason in support of special subventions as against general navigation bounties is that the policy tends to produce definite and practical results by building up the strongest ocean lines. The general navigation bounties assist, in a small way, both the weak and efficient lines; special subventions granted to the best vessels and the strongest companies put them in a position to compete successfully with foreign rivals. Unquestionably, the way to get results is to strengthen the strong. This policy is, moreover, justified by the fact that the weaker lines and chartered vessels are also benefited indirectly. The existence of profitable lines well supported by the Government strengthens the shipbuilding industry and thus enables builders to construct vessels for all buyers under more favorable conditions.

The Outlook for the Future.—The economic conditions prevailing in the United States as regards the cost of materials and labor are still unfavorable to the building and operation of vessels in competition with the most successful maritime nations of the world. Moreover, as was explained in the previous chapter, these conditions will probably not greatly change in the immediate future. The outlook, however, is not without encouragement to those who earnestly desire the restoration of the United States to a position of leadership among the maritime nations of the world. The geographic conditions in the United States are all favorable to maritime development; our seaboards and Great Lakes are well supplied with harbors; we front both upon the Atlantic and Pacific oceans, and our now separated seaboards are soon to be joined by the Panama Canal; our country of vast continental proportions is well supplied with coal and iron and the other materials required for the construction of ships; and our highly efficient railroads are able to place those materials in our yards at low freight costs. In view of these facts, it seems probable that when the annual output of our yards becomes larger the costs of materials used in our yards will be as low as those prevailing abroad.

Political conditions also favor the development of the American marine. We have acquired the Philippines, Hawaii, and Porto Rico and have assumed serious responsibilities in Cuba and upon the Isthmus of Panama. We have ceased to become merely a continental country. We have urgent political reasons for strengthening our position on the sea. The international relations of the United States in connection with the maintenance of the Monroe Doctrine and with the insistence upon the open-door policy in the East suggest the political and economic necessity of regaining our former leadership in maritime shipping.

It is also clearly evident that the American people will become increasingly interested in maritime affairs. We feel more and more strongly the chagrin of our insignificant position as an ocean carrier. That we have the aptitude and hardihood required for success on the ocean is amply proven by the history of our country for the two hundred and fifty years from the beginning of the seventeenth century to the middle of the nineteenth century; the fundamental traits of the American people certainly have not changed during the past fifty years. If this be so, it is reasonable to expect that, as the economic conditions in the United States become more and more similar, as they must, to those in other countries, the geographic, political and psychologic factors favoring the development of our American marine will become effective in building up the tonnage of our ocean shipping. For the present we must wait; but, for the future, there is hope.

PART IV

*INLAND WATERWAYS; RIVER, LAKE,
AND CANAL TRANSPORTATION*

CHAPTER XXXVI

THE INLAND WATERS IN THE UNITED STATES

Our Extensive System of Waterways.—The inland waterways of our country comprise about 25,000 miles of rivers that are now navigated and an equal mileage of streams that can be made navigable. In addition to these 50,000 miles of rivers, there are five Great Lakes with a combined length of 1,410 miles and various canals which have a total length of 2,120 miles. Along our Atlantic and Gulf seaboards, there are 2,500 miles of sounds, bays, and bayous which can be connected with each other by the construction of canals having a total length of about 1,000 miles. When these canals are constructed, they will add 3,500 miles of safe inner coastal waterways to the general transportation system. The waterways of our country as a whole have an aggregate length of 55,000 or 60,000 miles, about half of which mileage is now in actual use for navigation.

Rivers of the Atlantic.—A detailed knowledge of the numerous rivers and other waterways which make up the 55,000 or 60,000 miles of American inland waterways can be secured only by a careful study of specially prepared maps. Those desiring full knowledge regarding any particular stream should secure the latest annual report of the Chief of Engineers of the United States Army, which can be obtained upon request. An excellent map for the study of our waterways is to be found in the volume containing the Preliminary Report of the Inland Waterways Commission, 1908. References will here be made only to the most important rivers.

In New England, the hilly country comes close to the seashore, and most of the rivers have falls and rapids near their mouths. Thus, with the exception of the Connecticut River there is no stream in New England that is navigated above its tidal sections.

The Hudson River in New York State is used more for navigation than is any other river, except the Ohio, in the United States. The subsidence of the Hudson River valley in a previous geological age changed the river into a tidal stream. The ocean tides extend up the stream 170 miles to the city of Troy. The natural depth of the river to within 28 miles of Troy was 12 feet; from that point to Troy the depth decreased until it had a minimum of 4 feet. However, Congress, in 1899, provided for the construction of a 12-foot channel from Troy to deep water in the stream.

The large rivers south of the Hudson, the Delaware, Susquehanna, Potomac, and James are also navigable only in their tidal portions. The tides extend up these rivers to the "fall line," somewhat over 100 miles from the sea. The Delaware ceases to be navigable just below Trenton; the Susquehanna can be ascended a few miles above Havre-de-Grace; and the falls of the James River are at the city of Richmond. The Chesapeake Bay has numerous arms and tidal affluents which are used by local steamboat lines.

The rivers flowing into the Atlantic between the Chesapeake and central Florida were formerly extensively navigated for a distance of 100 to 200 miles from the sea. Although these streams are now used to some extent, their channels are more choked than they formerly were, and the efficiency of the railroads has made it unnecessary for

commerce to make as much use of the waterways as it formerly did. Savannah is situated a few miles from the sea, and Jacksonville is located 27½ miles upstream. Both of these cities have good channels for ocean shipping.

The River System of Alabama.—The most important, although by no means all of the navigable, rivers entering the Gulf between the mouth of the Mississippi and the peninsula of Florida, converge upon Mobile Bay; and thus lie mainly within the State of Alabama. The short Mobile River is formed by the union of the Alabama and the Tombigbee. The Alabama receives the important Coosa River —a stream that is navigable from northern Georgia through eastern Alabama. An affluent of the Tombigbee River is the Warrior River, the upper reaches of which are called the Black Warrior. Birmingham, the center of the coal and iron district of the South, lies between the Black Warrior and the Coosa rivers. The canalization of the Warrior and Tombigbee rivers, which is being carried out, suggests the desirability of constructing a canal from the Birmingham district to the Warrior River. When this has been done the river system of Alabama will be of much greater service than it now is.

The Mississippi River System has 16,000 miles of navigable rivers and is surpassed only by the Amazon and its tributaries. Up to New Orleans deep-draft vessels may navigate the river; and barges and large river steamboats can make St. Louis without difficulty in ordinary stages of water. The head of navigation of the Mississippi is at the Falls of St. Anthony at Minneapolis. Except during the lowest stages of water, steamboats drawing 6 feet can navigate the channel between St. Paul and St. Louis. The Mississippi River, however, has numerous bars and has great fluctuations in depth of channel; it is, moreover, such

a large river as to be difficult to control, and much has
yet to be accomplished before the river can be made a reliable transportation route at all seasons of the year.

The Ohio River has more traffic than any other portion
of the Mississippi system, more even than the Mississippi
itself. This is due to the fact that a large tonnage of coal
is brought to the Ohio from Pennsylvania and West
Virginia mainly by the Monongahela and Great Kanawha
rivers. A portion of this coal is marketed in Cincinnati,
Louisville, and other cities on the river, and a large part is
taken down the Mississippi as far as New Orleans.

The Missouri River has a much larger flow of water
than does the upper Mississippi. Its depth, however, is
subject to great variations; the stream is apt to change its
bed; and thus the control of the river for navigation is extremely difficult. The river is now used in portions, particularly between Kansas City and St. Louis; and it is the
belief of the people occupying the populous and productive
Missouri valley that the river will, in time, become as important commercially as it was in the anterailroad days.
The Cumberland and Tennessee, particularly the latter,
are navigated and are of greater prospective importance;
the same may be said of several of the other larger affluents
of the great Mississippi River. The river that promises
to be most used in the near future is the Illinois, because
it forms part of the water route between Lake Michigan
and the Mississippi.

The Rivers of the Pacific.—The Coast Ranges skirt the
Pacific shores of the United States so closely as to eliminate
rivers from most of our Pacific seacoast. There are, however, two important systems—the Columbia and the rivers
that converge upon San Francisco Bay. The northern portion of the great California valley is drained by the Sacra-

mento; the southern portion by the San Joaquin River, both of which streams, particularly in their lower stretches, are of service to commerce. The great river of the Pacific coast is the Columbia, which is now navigable, without interruption, for 250 miles from the sea, i. e., to The Dalles where the river breaks through the Cascade Mountains. A portage railroad now transfers cargo around The Dalles; but the United States Government is constructing locks and a short canal by means of which vessels will be able to pass The Dalles without break of cargo. The Columbia River above The Dalles has an available depth of 4 or 5 feet for nearly 200 miles; and the Snake River, which enters the Columbia from the east, has a similar navigable channel for 146 miles. Thus the Columbia and Snake rivers promise to provide the rapidly developing Northwest with a most useful waterway.

A short distance from the Columbia, on the Willamette, is the City of Portland, 110 miles from the ocean, with which it is connected by a channel 25 feet in depth. Above Portland, the Willamette is navigable for light-draft vessels for 150 miles. The State of Oregon has improved this stream.

The Great Lakes and St. Lawrence.—The greatest inland waterway in the world is that made by the five Great Lakes, four of which lie upon our northern boundary. The five lakes have a combined length of 1,410 miles, the length of the four on the boundary being 1,075 miles. Together with the St. Lawrence, these lakes provide a waterway which reaches inland 2,000 miles from the sea. Lakes Superior, Michigan, Huron and Erie, and their connecting channels have a minimum depth of 21 feet and are now regularly used by vessels of 20-feet draft. The Welland Canal from Lake Erie to Lake Ontario is 14 feet in depth, as are also the canalized portions of the St. Lawrence down to Montreal. From Montreal to the sea, deep-draft ocean vessels can be accommodated. The improvement of the St. Lawrence has been made by the Canadian Government, and the river lies mainly in Canadian territory; this, however, does not greatly lessen the importance of the stream for the commerce of the United States.

The Canals in the United States are of two classes: those constructed to improve navigable rivers, and those built to connect separated rivers or lakes. Examples of the first class are the canals around the Des Moines rapids in the Mississippi, around the Ohio rapids at Louisville, and in those portions of the valleys of the Delaware, Schuylkill, Potomac, and other rivers that have been canalized. Instances of the second class are the Erie Canal in New York, those in Ohio, and those across northern Illinois. The most important canal at the present time is the Erie, which was opened in 1825 to connect the Great Lakes with the ocean via the Hudson River. In the future, a canal of equal importance will connect the Great Lakes with the Mississippi River and thus with the Gulf of Mexico.

The New York Canals.—In 1903, the State of New York decided to spend $100,000,000 in enlarging and modernizing the Erie, Oswego, and Champlain canals. At present these canals are 7 feet deep, and can accommodate with difficulty small barges drawing 6 feet of water. When the improvements now in progress have been completed, the canals will have a depth of 12 feet and will be 75 feet wide at the bottom. The locks will be 328 feet in length, 28 feet wide, and will have a minimum depth of 11 feet. It will then be possible to use barges drawing 10 feet of water, carrying 1,000 tons, and propelled by mechanical power at a speed of six or more miles an hour.

The Illinois Canals.—The people of the Central West are
making earnest demands upon Congress to connect the
Great Lakes with the Mississippi River by a channel at
least 14 feet in depth. Chicago and the State of Illinois
have made a beginning with the execution of this project.
Some years ago Chicago constructed a sanitary and ship
canal 20 feet in depth from Lake Michigan across the low
divide to Lockport on the Des Plaines River, a tributary of
the Illinois. This increases the volume of water in the
Des Plaines and Illinois rivers, and makes more prácticable
the maintenance of a 14-foot waterway through the valley
of the Illinois River. Congress has made the surveys for
a channel of this depth from Lake Michigan to St. Louis
and to New Orleans. The engineers who made the survey
for the waterway have also studied the water power which
can be created by carrying out the project. In 1908 the
people of Illinois by a referendum vote authorized the
State to borrow $20,000,000 to use in improving the navi-
gability of the Des Plaines and Illinois rivers, and in creat-
ing water power from which the State is to derive a permanent revenue.

The action of the United States and of the State of
Illinois together with the earnestness of the people of the
Middle West indicate that the lakes to the Gulf waterway
will in time become a reality; but it is not probable that
the construction of a 14-foot waterway below St. Louis will
be undertaken until the traffic demands have become
greater than they now are. The United States engineers
estimate that such a waterway would cost $128,000,000 to
construct, and $6,000,000 a year to maintain.

At the end of 1907, the Hennepin Canal, connecting
the Mississippi River at Rock Island with the Illinois River
at Hennepin by means of a 7-foot waterway was com-

pleted. It is not probable, however, that this canal will be very greatly used; it will certainly not be of much commercial importance until the old Illinois and Michigan Canal, now practically out of service, is replaced by the more efficient waterway which Chicago and the State of Illinois are gradually bringing into existence to connect Chicago with the lower Illinois River and St. Louis.

CHAPTER XXXVII

TRAFFIC ON OUR WATERWAYS

Volume of Traffic.—The traffic upon canals, rivers, and lakes in the United States was carefully investigated for the year 1906 by the Federal Bureau of the Census; and the results of this investigation are presented with appropriate detail in the census volume upon " Transportation by Water," published in 1908. During the year 1906 the total traffic upon the inland waterways of the United States amounted to over 100,000,000 tons, of which 75,610,-000 tons were transported on the Great Lakes and St. Lawrence River; 19,530,000 tons upon the Mississippi River and its tributaries; 6,527,000 tons upon the Hudson River; and 3,717,000 tons upon the other inland waterways of the country. The larger part of the traffic was moved upon three waterways: the Great Lakes, the Hudson, and the Ohio rivers; which together account for 97,364,000 tons, or 92.7 per cent of the total.

Canal Traffic.—The traffic upon the barge canals of the United States is relatively small, and has tended to decline during recent years, as the result of the increasing efficiency and economy of the railroads as carriers of bulky commodities. The canals most used are those in New York State upon which, according to the statistics kept by officials of the State of New York, somewhat over 3,500,000 tons of cargo are annually transported, two thirds of this freight being handled upon the Erie Canal. Upon the barge canals other than those in the State of New York, the annual traffic amounts to less than 1,000,000 tons. The small and declining tonnage of canal-barge traffic indicates clearly that the old type of canals, capable of accommodating barges drawing only 5 or 6 feet of water and carrying from 100 to 250 tons of freight have ceased to be of much service.

The experience of other countries indicates that canals of greater dimensions will be extensively used by shippers, and the State of New York is now spending a large sum of money in making the canals of her State up-to-date waterways. The vigorous and persistent agitation in many parts of the United States, both for the canalization of rivers and for the construction of canals, is evidence that the business interests of the country believe that canals as well as rivers are capable of reducing the cost of transportation.

River Traffic is handled both by steamboats and by barges. Formerly steamboats were used extensively on our important rivers, particularly upon those in the Mississippi Valley, for handling both passengers and general cargo freight. During recent years steamboat traffic has fallen off greatly, and the freight business has become limited mainly to the barge traffic of the Ohio and other rivers so situated as to be able to handle bulk traffic down stream. The Ohio River far exceeds all others in the volume of freight, because of the great quantities of coal barged and floated down the river from Pennsylvania and West Virginia. Of the 15,227,000 tons of Ohio River traffic, nearly 11,000,000 consists of coal, and nearly 2,000,-000 tons of stone and sand; the remaining 3,250,000 tons being made up chiefly of miscellaneous merchandise, grain, lumber, and iron ore.

The great Mississippi River, which was so largely used for freight and passenger traffic before and for some time after the Civil War, has come to have a relatively small tonnage. The freight handled on the Mississippi River above St. Louis, in 1906, amounted to 1,758,000 tons, and that on the stream below St. Louis to 2,546,000 tons. The total

DEPARTURE OF A COAL FLEET FROM PITTSBURG.

for the two portions of the stream being 4,304,000 tons. As late as 1889 Mississippi River traffic totaled 12,492,000 tons; the volume of business done in 1906 was only thirty-four per cent of that handled in 1889.

The Hudson River continues to be used largely for freight and passenger business. In 1906 there were 8,655,-000 tons of cargo handled upon the Hudson River, about one fourth of which consisted of the traffic to and from the

New York canals. When the New York canals have been improved in accordance with the project now being executed, the Hudson River will undoubtedly have a large increase in traffic. Indeed, there is every reason to believe that the importance of this transportation highway will become steadily greater with the industrial development of the State of New York.

Although now having but little traffic, the Columbia River will, when improvements in progress are completed, afford such an excellent waterway that it can hardly fail to be increasingly used as the great Northwest develops in industry and population. At the present time the tributaries of the Columbia are being more and more used for irrigation and water power, and the impetus which this will give industry and settlement will be accented by the transportation services rendered by the Columbia River.

Traffic on the Great Lakes.—Over seven tenths of the traffic handled on the inland waterways of the United States is transported on the Great Lakes, and the rate of increase has been little less than marvelous. At the present time the tonnage is three times what it was in 1890. The tonnage on the Great Lakes is about one tenth as great as the traffic handled on all the railroads of the United States. This comparison, however, does not do full justice to the lakes, because the average distance which a ton moves upon the Great Lakes is three times the average journey of a ton of freight upon the railroads; in other words, the number of tons transported one mile, the ton mileage, on the Great Lakes is three tenths of the ton mileage of the entire railway traffic in the United States.

The vast commerce of the Great Lakes has several well-defined characteristics:

1. The eastbound tonnage, or the traffic down the lakes

is nearly five times the volume of the westbound business—
a fact which is easily accounted for by the heavy shipments
of iron ore from the regions about Lake Superior to be
smelted in Pennsylvania, Ohio, and Illinois. There is also
a relatively large eastbound movement of grain and lumber.

VESSELS ENTERING A LOCK. SOO CANAL, ST. MARY'S RIVER.
AMERICAN SIDE.

The westbound shipments consist chiefly of coal and package freight.

2. The number of commodities transported on the lakes
is relatively small. Iron ore amounts to nearly one half
of the aggregate tonnage; coal comprises about one fifth;
grain and flour, one twelfth, and lumber one twentieth of
the aggregate shipments. These four classes of freight
include about five sixths of the total tonnage. Although

coal makes up the larger volume of the westbound shipments, the package freight is of greater value. There are numerous lines devoted entirely to the handling of this package freight from the manufacturing East to the agricultural and mining West and Northwest. Seven eighths of the total package freight is shipped westward.

3. By far the greater part of the freight on the Great Lakes is shipped the entire length of the lakes, and not from one port to another on the same lake. It is carried nearly 800 miles. This explains why the average distance a ton of freight is moved on the lakes is three times the average haul by rail. It can be easily understood why it is possible for the lake carriers to handle their traffic profitably at the lowest freight rate per ton per mile to be found anywhere in the world except upon the ocean.

4. Although there are about two hundred ports on the Great Lakes, the larger share of the shipments is made between a relatively small number of places. Iron ore, for instance, is nearly all shipped from six Lake Superior ports, and more than half of the total is loaded at two points—Duluth and Two Harbors. Most of the ore is discharged at ten cities, over half being unloaded at Ashtabula, Cleveland, and Conneaut. Nearly nine tenths of the ore is shipped from Lake Superior to Lake Erie. In the case of wheat, the concentration of traffic is almost equally marked. The grain vessels are loaded, for the most part, at Duluth, Superior, Chicago, and Milwaukee, and nearly all of it is unloaded at Buffalo elevators; Erie and Ogdensburg also receive some consignments. The westbound anthracite coal is mostly loaded at Buffalo, and while it is unloaded at numerous places about Lakes Superior and Michigan, most of the traffic is handled through or to Superior, Milwaukee, and Chicago.

5. Another marked characteristic of the traffic on the
Great Lakes, and one which will be discussed in the following chapter, is that it is handled by a relatively small number of carriers.   There is a high degree of consolidation in
the transportation business on the Great Lakes, most of the
carrying being done by vessels owned by railroad compa-

A WHALEBACK PASSING THROUGH THE LOCK AT THE SOO.

nies and by the United States Steel Corporation.   There
are, however, numerous individual carriers which supple-
ment the service of the larger organizations.

Conditions Precedent to Growth of Canal and River Traffic.
—From the facts presented in this chapter, it is evident
that the traffic on canals and rivers in the United States
is decreasing, and that the present decline will probably
continue at least for some years to come.   There are excep-

tions to the general rule. Some rivers are maintaining their traffic, and will probably show increases in the near future. Speaking generally, as regards our rivers and canals as a whole, their traffic can hardly be expected to become larger until many belated improvements have been made. For nearly fifty years our rivers and canals have been neglected in the sense that little effort has been made to keep them technically abreast of the railroads. When our waterways have been as fully improved as have those of Germany, for instance, they will unquestionably be largely used by those sections of the country where population is relatively dense and where manufacturing industries are numerous. The use of waterways becomes greater in every country, and in particular sections of a country with the increase in population and the development and specialization of industry. The significance of this law will be made clearer by the discussion contained in the concluding chapter of this book.

CHAPTER XXXVIII

THE EQUIPMENT AND SERVICES OF INLAND WATERWAYS

Relative Efficiency of Canal, River, and Lake Equipment. —In order to understand fully the traffic and services described in the preceding chapter, it is necessary to know something of the equipment used in performing those services and of the organization that has been developed to conduct and transportation upon our inland waterways. The efficiency of the service upon any transportation route is determined by the equipment used and by the business organization by which the work is carried on.

The equipment used upon our canals is crude, and has been but slightly improved since the early days of canal transportation. While the railways have made one change after another until they have reached their present marvelous degree of efficiency, the canals and their equipment in the United States have received but little attention; much the same is true of the equipment and service on the rivers; although, in the case of the Hudson, Ohio, and our most used navigable streams, equipment and business methods have been at least partly modernized during recent years. On our northern lakes, transportation is as highly developed as anywhere in the world; indeed, the lake carriers have surpassed the railway in the introduction of facilities for the rapid and economical handling of traffic.

Equipment Used on Canals. —On the most used strictly

barge waterway in the United States—the Erie Canal—is still to be found the old type of wooden barges, most of which are moved by animal traction. The draft and capacity of these barges are the same as they were in 1870—6 feet and 240 tons; moreover, the Erie Canal permits the use of larger craft than do those operated in Pennsylvania, Maryland, and Ohio. The enlargement of the Erie Canal now in progress will revolutionize transportation upon that waterway; and if the enlarged canal proves successful it will doubtless do much to bring about the modernization of canals connecting separated natural waterways in other parts of the United States. The Erie Canal will, in the future, be used by barges carrying 1,000 tons; and it is probable that a steam-driven canal boat, itself with a cargo of 500 to 1,000 tons, will tow two barges, each loaded with 1,000 tons. This will place the equipment on the Erie Canal abreast of that used on the best inland waterways of European countries.

Unorganized Character of Canal Services.—Canal transportation has little or no organization. An individual or a small partnership may own and operate one barge or several barges without investing much capital, and this is done upon the New York canals and to some extent upon those in other States. Some of the canals have been purchased by railway companies and others are owned and operated by coal-mining concerns. Such canals are used almost entirely by their owners. The improved Erie Canal and other similar canals that may be built in the future will, of course, be public highways, for the most part; but it will be necessary for the Government to permit or to establish a more highly organized and more economical management of traffic than has characterized canal transportation in the past. This problem of efficient organization of canal

The Ohio River Steamboat "Joseph B. Williams" Pushing a Tow of 58,120 Tons of Coal Down the Mississippi River.

transportation has naturally arisen in Prussia, where the State has expended large sums in the construction of waterways, and the government has found it advisable to provide towage service on some of its waterways.

River Transportation Equipment.—The successful navigation of rivers with channels of various depth and often shallow has necessitated the use of a special type of flat-bottom, stern-wheel steamboat; and, although this vessel has been enlarged and improved in various ways, its general design has not been changed from the days of the early river steamboats. On the Ohio and Mississippi, the large steamboat now used is 200 to 250 feet in length, about 40 feet wide, with a hold 8 to 10 feet in depth. When loaded the vessel will draw from 4 to 6 feet of water, depending upon the amount of cargo, which in turn is determined by the available depth of the river channel. Having a flat bottom and wide hull these river steamers will carry several hundred tons of cargo with a draft of only a few feet.

The other type of river craft, and the one which transports by far the larger share of the tonnage, is the barge, of which there are several species. Wooden barges, so built as to be loaded to a draft of 6 to 9 feet, are used to transport grain, building materials, and, to some extent, other bulky cargo down the Mississippi River as far as New Orleans. Such barges are usually hauled back upstream empty. By far the greater share of the barge traffic on the Ohio and Mississippi consists of coal, and in the transportation of this three types of craft are used:

(1) Coal boats, propelled by their own engines, drawing from 8 to $8\frac{1}{2}$ feet of water and carrying from 1,000 to 1,100 tons; (2) coal barges with a draft of 6 to 7 feet and a burden of 500 tons; and (3) coal floats consisting of cheaply constructed barges of 200 to 300 tons capacity. The coal

barges are constructed mostly of wood, but those made of steel are now used to some extent.   After their cargo has been discharged they are towed upstream for reloading. The coal floats, however, are used for only one trip, at the end of which they are broken up and sold for lumber.

Organization of River Transportation.—Traffic upon the Hudson, Ohio, and Mississippi and other navigated rivers is handled by lines of steamboats, by independent packets and towboats, and by manufacturing and coal-mining com-

THE "J. PIERPONT MORGAN," A TYPICAL LAKE ORE CARRIER.   Length 600 feet, beam 58 feet, gross register 7,161 tons, average carrying capacity 11,128 tons gross.

panies.   The acme of comfort and speed in the passenger traffic upon the rivers is reached in the day- and night-line boats on the Hudson River.   On the Ohio River there are numerous lines, less elegant than those upon the Hudson, plying between Pittsburg and Cincinnati and from Cincinnati to other cities in the valley.   From St. Louis to points north and south on the Mississippi River there are several lines of steamers.   The Ohio and Mississippi steamboats carry both freight and passengers.   The freight service on the rivers is also handled by independent packets not operated as lines; and there are also numerous towboats whose services can be secured by any person desiring to have traffic barged from one point to another.

The transportation of coal down the Ohio River is so organized as to reduce the cost to a minimum. The larger share of this coal originates along the Monongahela River above Pittsburg. It is loaded from the mines into the barges and floats as above described, which are brought in small fleets of about 3,000 tons each by towboats down through the Monongahela locks to the " pool " at Pittsburg. Here the small coal fleets are tied up, if necessary, to await a sufficient rise in the Ohio River. When the channel in the Ohio is 10 feet or more in depth, i. e., sufficient to accommodate barges drawing 8 feet of water, fleets of 10,000 to 15,000 tons each are pushed down the river by stern-wheel steamboats to Cincinnati and Louisville. At Louisville, below the rapids in the Ohio where the river becomes wider and of greater depth, the fleets are united into larger ones of 35,000 to 40,000 tons each, and these fleets are towed, i. e., pushed, down to St. Louis or to New Orleans. A fleet of barges and floats containing 40,000 tons of coal covers about ten acres.

In former years vast quantities of lumber were rafted down the Mississippi River, mainly from the pine forests of Wisconsin and Minnesota; during later years, however, there has been but little lumber rafted, because the supply of timber along the streams of Wisconsin and Minnesota has been exhausted and such lumber as is now cut in this northern pine belt is shipped to market by rail.

Equipment used on the Great Lakes.—The fleet on the Great Lakes has an aggregate gross tonnage of nearly 3,000,000. Taken as a whole, this is the most modern and efficient part of the American merchant marine. Five sixths of the entire tonnage consists of steel steamers, the average gross tonnage of each vessel being over 1,200 tons. This average, however, includes a large number of comparatively small vessels, which will soon cease to be used. The typical lake steamer of to-day is from 5,000 to 8,000 tons gross register. During the year ending June 30, 1908,

THE "DELAWARE." A package freight carrier on the lakes.

16 steel lake steamers of between 4,000 and 5,000 tons gross were launched; and 38 with a gross tonnage of between 5,000 and 8,000. These 54 steel steamers had an aggregate gross tonnage of 314,877, or an average of 5,831 gross tons per vessel. These vessels are built to be loaded to a draft of 20 feet.

There are three types of craft used on the Great Lakes:

1. Vessels of about 5,000 tons cargo capacity, most of which are operated as lines for the handling of package

freight, and, to some extent, for the transportation of passengers. Vessels similar to these are operated by independent carriers chiefly for the transportation of lumber and grain.

2. Barges, which consist in part of small craft used for moving various kinds of bulk traffic from one port to another. Large steel barges also used for carrying ore down the lakes.

3. The bulk cargo carriers used mainly for the transportation of ore. The largest of these bulk carriers can transport from 12,000 to 14,000 tons of ore.

Organization of the Lake Transportation Services.—The transportation business on the Great Lakes includes, in addition to the car ferries, of which there are several, two classes of services: the handling of general cargo or package freight, and the movement of bulk traffic, such as iron ore, grain, and lumber. These two services are performed by three kinds of carriers:

1. The independent carrier. Formerly most of the traffic was handled in small vessels owned by persons and companies whose sole business was that of conducting transportation on the lakes. These independent carriers are still an important factor. They now handle most of the grain and lumber down the lakes, and some of the coal up the lakes.

2. Manufacturers operating their own vessels. At the close of 1907 the Pittsburg Steamship Company, which is controlled by the United States Steel Corporation, had a lake fleet of 101 vessels with a total tonnage of 368,165 gross register, which was about sixteen per cent of the total gross tonnage of all lake vessels at that time. Other steel companies also operate ore vessels on the lakes.

3. The package freight lines owned by railroad compa-

nies. The eastern trunk line railroads are interested in
package freight lines on the lakes, some having lines which
they independently own, and others having a joint interest in lines controlled by two or more steam railroad companies. The largest of these lines are the Western Transit
Company, belonging to the New York Central Railroad,
and the Erie and Western Transportation Company
(Anchor Line), owned by the Pennsylvania Railroad Com-

THE "NORTHWEST" OF THE NORTHERN STEAMSHIP.COMPANY. A
luxurious lake passenger steamer.

pany. The best passenger ships on the lakes are owned by
the Great Northern Railway Company.

Consolidation and Coöperation in Lake Transportation.—
The larger part of the lake transportation business is conducted by a small number of companies. The general cargo
package freight is handled by fourteen lines, most of which
are controlled by the railroads. Most of the ore traffic is
handled by bulk carriers owned and operated by a few
manufacturing concerns. The individual carriers perform
a useful and supplemental service in lake transportation,

but they are not controlling factors. The rates on iron ore, the heaviest single item of traffic, are fixed at the opening of each season by the United States Steel Corporation. Lumber and grain are transported at competitive rates and largely by independent carriers. The package freight lines owned by railroad companies are members of the Association of Lake Lines, an organization which has to do mainly with the regulation of rates and traffic matters. This association has been successful in preventing the rivalries of lake carriers from becoming ruinous. The competition of the package freight carriers is keen, and unless regulated by joint action could hardly avoid becoming disastrous.

The transportation business on the Great Lakes is highly developed, the main carriers coöperate with each other successfully, and the services are performed with an economy and efficiency unexcelled even by our best-managed railroads and the best-organized ocean carriers.

CHAPTER XXXIX

IMPROVEMENT AND EXTENSION OF INLAND WATER-WAYS; THE FUTURE OUTLOOK

Power of the Federal Government over Inland Waterways.—Having been vested by the Constitution with the power to regulate commerce with foreign nations and among the States, the National Government has authority over routes of interstate trade and over the vehicles used in that commerce. Any waterway, natural or artificial, that may be used by interstate commerce is subject to the control of Congress as regards its navigability. Even if the natural waterway lies wholly within a single State it still comes under the jurisdiction of Congress, if it connects with a river that passes a State boundary. When a State constructs a waterway, such as the Erie Canal, which lies entirely within its boundaries, but which connects with a navigable waterway lying in other States, the plans for the canal must be submitted to and approved by the Secretary of War and the Chief of Engineers of the United States Army.

State and National Improvement of Waterways, Past and Present.—Until some time after the Civil War, most of the work for the improvement and extension of waterways was carried on by the several States. Congress made appropriations for harbor improvements, and gave some aid to the betterment of river navigation before 1870; but the amount of money spent was slight in comparison with that appropriated by the several States. New York, Pennsylvania, Maryland, Ohio, Indiana, and Illinois carried on extensive canal construction works, and other States also gave liberally to build or aid in building canals and other work of internal improvement.

After 1850, it became increasingly evident that most of the original canals would not be able to compete with the railways for the transportation even of bulky freight. When this fact became manifest, the States began to give more support to railroad construction than to canal building; and as time went on neglected the canals, so that most of them became of relatively little service. Some of the canals were sold, others were abandoned; and with this ended, for the most part, State aid to the improvement and extension of inland waterways.

The appropriations by the Federal Government for inland waterways have been relatively large only since 1890. Of the total sum appropriated by Congress for rivers and harbors from 1802 to 1907, inclusive—$552,943,025—that voted since 1890 has amounted to $338,903,139; in other words, 61.3 per cent of the appropriations have been made since 1890. During recent years Congress has spent about $25,000,000 annually for the improvement of rivers and harbors.

Federal Method of Making Improvement.—The United States is blessed with so many rivers and with such a great number of inland waterways that appropriations have to be distributed among a large number of works. Some of the streams that receive aid are of minor importance, but most of the money is spent upon the harbors and channels of the Great Lakes, upon the large rivers, like the Mississippi, Missouri, Ohio, Hudson, and Columbia, and upon the chief harbors. The work of carrying out the improvements is in charge of the Corps of Engineers of the United States Army. Under instructions from Congress, the United States engineers make surveys and report to Congress as to the feasibility, cost, and possible results of improving such waterways as Congress deems worthy of consideration. With the reports and recommendations of the engineers in hand, Congress each two years passes a river and harbor bill authorizing a relatively large number of improvements.

The execution of the works thus authorized is supervised by the Corps of Engineers. Since 1890 the work of improving the larger rivers and harbors and the Great Lakes has been made under the " continuing contract system," which enables the Secretary of War to make contracts for the execution and completion of an entire project as authorized, the appropriations for carrying on the work as it progresses being made by the Congress year by year. Before 1890 practically all of our river and harbor improvements were made in accordance with the " driblet " system of appropriations, the plan followed by Congress being that of authorizing the work and of making partial appropriations year by year sufficient only to carry on the work from one grant of funds to the next. The continuing contract system is more economical and more expeditious.

The Present Campaign for More and Better Waterways.— During recent years an active campaign has been carried on in many parts of the country to persuade Congress to enter upon the improvement of a large number of inland waterways. In the case of the Great Lakes and of each of many of our largest streams, a waterway association has been organized to create a sentiment in favor of early and liberal appropriations by Congress. Among the more aggressive of these organizations are the Ohio River Valley Improvement

Association, the Lakes-to-the-Gulf Deep Waterway Association, the Missouri River Improvement Association, the Upper Mississippi River Improvement Association, the Western Waterways Association, the Columbia River Association, and the Lake Carriers Association. Similar to the foregoing in activity and aims are the Atlantic Deeper Waterways Association and the Interstate Inland Waterway Association, which two organizations are endeavoring to hasten the construction of the canals needed to connect the bays and sounds along the Atlantic and Gulf coasts so as to make a safe inner waterway along our Atlantic and Gulf seaboards.

Each year in December, the National Rivers and Harbors Congress meets and brings together in Washington delegates from all over the United States representing influential national organizations.

The movement for the improvement of our inland waterways was given a great impetus by President Roosevelt and his administration. The President established the Inland Waterways Commission in March, 1907, " to prepare and report a comprehensive plan for the improvement and control of the river systems of the United States.'' Under the able leadership of Hon. Theodore E. Burton, for many years chairman of the Rivers and Harbors Committee of the House of Representatives, the Inland Waterways Commission prepared a valuable preliminary report, which was published in 1908. The President further manifested his interest in the improvement of inland waterways by calling a three-days' conference at the White House in May, 1908, of the governors of the States, representatives of national organizations, and experts of recognized standing for the purpose of considering the general question of the conservation of natural resources, including not only our water resources, but also those of our forests, minerals, and lands.   The discussions of this conference attracted wide attention and its influence was enhanced by the subsequent appointment by the President of the National Conservation Commission, which was active during 1908, and which made, for the first time, a census of the natural resources of the United States.   The census thus prepared was submitted to a second conference of the gov-

THE "ROBERT FULTON" OF THE HUDSON RIVER DAY LINE.   "The most magnificent river steamer in the world."

ernors of the States and delegates of national organizations.   This gathering was convened by the National Conservation Commission in December, 1908, and the report of this commission, now being prepared (1909), will, when published, contain a vast amount of information regarding the needs and possibilities of water conservation and improvement.

Reasons why Inland Waterways will be Increasingly used

in the Future.—The vigorous efforts being made to bring about a more rapid development of our inland waterways is the result of the growing conviction on the part of the American people that their natural waterways can be of real service in the economic development of the country. The following facts readily account for the waterways' movement:

1. The internal commerce of the United States is growing rapidly, and is certain to increase with accelerating speed. The demands for transportation facilities are expanding so swiftly as to make it apparent that the products of our farms, mines, forests, and factories cannot secure ready and economical transportation unless at least the larger trunk-line water routes of the country are adapted to the needs of commerce.

2. Waterways are to be regarded not only as competitors, but as feeders and complements of the railroads. The two means of transportation serve commerce in different ways; and while it is true that the competition of efficient waterways often compels railroads to adjust their rates with reference to water competition, the net effect of the use of waterways is to increase the volume and profits of the railroad business. The volume of transportation on the Great Lakes affords a good illustration of the value of waterways as complements to railroads. In no part of the United States is railroad transportation more highly developed than in the region about the Great Lakes. The more tonnage moved on the lakes, the greater is the traffic handled by the railroads serving the adjacent territory.

3. The necessity for the development of our waterways is strengthened by the fact that there is little prospect of any considerable reductions in the cost of rail transportation. Up to the present time the principal aim of the

American railroads has been to transport traffic in the largest possible train loads at the lowest possible ton mile cost. It seems clear, however, that this general method of handling freight traffic will not always be adapted to the transportation work required in the United States. In England, France, and Germany, the organization of the railroad freight services has for a long time been such as to accomplish the quick movement and schedule delivery of parcels, packages, and general commodity freight; and it seems reasonable to expect that the service of American railroads will, in the future, be developed more and more with reference to the handling of commodities expeditiously and in small units. There is no reason to suppose that our practice will permanently differ from that prevailing in other countries. Should this reorganization of the railroad freight business take place, it will necessitate higher freight charges on the part of the railroads, and it will make it increasingly desirable that a larger share of the bulky traffic that does not require rapid transit should be handled by waterways.

4. American waterways will, in the years to come, be utilized more for navigation, because we are certain, sooner or later, to conserve and use the entire water resources of the country simultaneously not only for navigation, but also for irrigation, for water power, and for supplying our urban populations with pure water. Moreover, the growing necessity for controlling our streams so as to make possible the reclamation of our vast areas of reclaimable lands will tend to hasten the time when our principal waterways will be so regulated as to be serviceable for navigation.

5. The significance of the foregoing facts may be stated in the form of the following transportation law:

The economy of employing both railroads and waterways for the performance of the transportation services becomes greater in every country and in particular sections of a country with the increase in population and the development and specialization of industry.

INDEX

Atchison, Topeka and Santa Fé Railroad, 34.

Baggage service, 88.
Baltimore and Ohio Railroad, beginning of, 7.
Basing point system of rates, 120.
Berth and supplemental cargo rates, 293.
Bills of lading, 72, 251, 268.
Bonds, classes of, 57; debentures, 58.
Bounties, marine, 314; navigation, 314; objection to, 314; reasons for special, 315.

Cabin fares, 287.
Canal service, unorganized character of, 338.
Canals, equipment used on, 337; traffic on, 329; in the United States, two classes of, 326; ocean ship, 224.
Capital, railway, 58.
Capitalization, true basis of, 62.
Cargo ton, of two classes, 198.
Charter, railway, 50.
Charters, time and trip, 288; how vessels are chartered, 289.
Classification, freight, 68; classifications in use, 68.
Clipper ship, the, 204.

Coal traffic on the Ohio River, 330, 340, 342.
Combination of ocean and rail transportation, 285.
Commercial powers of the states under Constitution, 298.
Commodity tariffs, 69.
Community of interest among railways, 108.
Competition, railway, agreements to restrain, 103; widespread and keen on ocean, 279; restraint of, necessary, 280.
"Conferences," ocean, 281; types of, 281; activities of, 282; instability of, 284.
Consolidations, railway, 107; early, 11.
Coöperation, of ocean and rail carriers, 285; on Great Lakes, 345.
Corporations, defined and classified, 49; the railway company a quasi-public corporation, 50; railway, size of, 51.
Courts, determine meaning and scope of laws, 146; sources of authority of, 146.

"Danube" measurement, 198.
Demurrage charges, 81.
Development of ocean travel, 262.

355